HISTORICAL ESSAYS

HISTORICAL ESSAYS

BY

JAMES FORD RHODES, LL.D., D.Litt.

AUTHOR OF THE HISTORY OF THE UNITED STATES FROM THE
COMPROMISE OF 1850 TO THE FINAL RESTORATION OF
HOME RULE AT THE SOUTH IN 1877

KENNIKAT PRESS, INC./PORT WASHINGTON, N. Y.

908
R476h

PREFACE

IN offering to the public this volume of Essays, all but two of which have been read at various places on different occasions, I am aware that there is some repetition in ideas and illustrations, but, as the dates of their delivery and previous publication are indicated, I am letting them stand substantially as they were written and delivered.

I am indebted to my son, Daniel P. Rhodes, for a literary revision of these Essays; and I have to thank the editors of the *Atlantic Monthly*, of *Scribner's Magazine*, and of the *Century Magazine* for leave to reprint the articles which have already appeared in their periodicals.

BOSTON, November, 1909.

PREFACE

CONTENTS

HISTORY

President's Inaugural Address, American Historical Association, Boston, December 27, 1899; printed in the *Atlantic Monthly* of February, 1900.

HISTORICAL ESSAYS

HISTORY [1]

MY theme is history. It is an old subject, which has been discoursed about since Herodotus, and I should be vain indeed if I flattered myself that I could say aught new concerning the methods of writing it, when this has for so long a period engaged the minds of so many gifted men. Yet to a sympathetic audience, to people who love history, there is always the chance that a fresh treatment may present the commonplaces in some different combination, and augment for the moment an interest which is perennial.

Holding a brief for history as do I your representative, let me at once concede that it is not the highest form of intellectual endeavor; let us at once agree that it were better that all the histories ever written were burned than for the world to lose Homer and Shakespeare. Yet as it is generally true that an advocate rarely admits anything without qualification, I should not be loyal to my client did I not urge that Shakespeare was historian as well as poet. We all prefer his Antony and Cleopatra and Julius Cæsar to the Lives in North's Plutarch which furnished him his materials. The history is in substance as true as Plutarch, the dramatic force greater; the language is better than that of Sir Thomas North, who himself did a remarkable piece of work when he gave his country a

[1] President's Inaugural Address, American Historical Association, Boston, December 27, 1899; printed in the Atlantic Monthly of February, 1900.

classic by Englishing a French version of the stories of the
Greek. It is true as Macaulay wrote, the historical plays
of Shakespeare have superseded history. When we think
of Henry V. it is of Prince Hal, the boon companion of
Falstaff, who spent his youth in brawl and riot, and then
became a sober and duty-loving king; and our idea of
Richard III. is a deceitful, dissembling, cruel wretch who
knew no touch of pity, a bloody tyrant who knew no law
of God or man.

The Achilles of Homer was a very living personage to
Alexander. How happy he was, said the great general,
when he visited Troy, "in having while he lived so faithful
a friend, and when he was dead so famous a poet to pro-
claim his actions"!   In our century, as more in conso-
nance with society under the régime of contract, when
force has largely given way to craft, we feel in greater
sympathy with Ulysses. "The one person I would like
to have met and talked with," Froude used to say, "was
Ulysses. How interesting it would be to have his opinion
on universal suffrage, and on a House of Parliament where
Thersites is listened to as patiently as the king of men!"

We may also concede that, in the realm of intellectual
endeavor, the natural and physical sciences should have
the precedence of history. The present is more important
than the past, and those sciences which contribute to our
comfort, place within the reach of the laborer and me-
chanic as common necessaries what would have been the
highest luxury to the Roman emperor or to the king of
the Middle Ages, contribute to health and the preservation
of life, and by the development of railroads make possible
such a gathering as this, — these sciences, we cheerfully
admit, outrank our modest enterprise, which, in the words
of Herodotus, is "to preserve from decay the remembrance

of what men have done." It may be true, as a geologist once said, in extolling his study at the expense of the humanities, "Rocks do not lie, although men do;" yet, on the other hand, the historic sense, which during our century has diffused itself widely, has invaded the domain of physical science. If you are unfortunate enough to be ill, and consult a doctor, he expatiates on the history of your disease. It was once my duty to attend the Commencement exercises of a technical school, when one of the graduates had a thesis on bridges. As he began by telling how they were built in Julius Cæsar's time, and tracing at some length the development of the art during the period of the material prosperity of the Roman Empire, he had little time and space left to consider their construction at the present day. One of the most brilliant surgeons I ever knew, the originator of a number of important surgical methods, who, being physician as well, was remarkable in his expedients for saving life when called to counsel in grave and apparently hopeless cases, desired to write a book embodying his discoveries and devices, but said that the feeling was strong within him that he must begin his work with an account of medicine in Egypt, and trace its development down to our own time. As he was a busy man in his profession, he lacked the leisure to make the preliminary historical study, and his book was never written. Men of affairs, who, taking "the present time by the top," are looked upon as devoted to the physical and mechanical sciences, continually pay tribute to our art. President Garfield, on his deathbed, asked one of his most trusted Cabinet advisers, in words that become pathetic as one thinks of the opportunities destroyed by the assassin's bullet, "Shall I live in history?" A clever politician, who knew more of ward meetings, caucuses, and the machinery of conventions than he did of history books, and who was earnest for the renomination of President Arthur in 1884, said to me, in the way of clinching his argument, "That administration will live in history." So it was, according to Amyot, in the olden time. "Whensoever," he wrote, "the right sage and virtuous Emperor of Rome, Alexander Severus, was to consult of any matter of great importance, whether it concerned war or government, he always called such to counsel as were reported to be well seen in histories." "What," demanded Cicero of Atticus, "will history say of me six hundred years hence?"

Proper concessions being made to poetry and the physical sciences, our place in the field remains secure. Moreover, we live in a fortunate age; for was there ever so propitious a time for writing history as in the last forty years? There has been a general acquisition of the historic sense. The methods of teaching history have so improved that they may be called scientific. Even as the chemist and physicist, we talk of practice in the laboratory. Most biologists will accept Haeckel's designation of "the last forty years as the age of Darwin," for the theory of evolution is firmly established. The publication of the Origin of Species, in 1859, converted it from a poet's dream and philosopher's speculation to a well-demonstrated scientific theory. Evolution, heredity, environment, have become household words, and their application to history has influenced every one who has had to trace the development of a people, the growth of an institution, or the establishment of a cause. Other scientific theories and methods have affected physical science as potently, but none has entered so vitally into the study of man. What hitherto the eye of genius alone could perceive may become the common property of every one who cares to read a dozen books. But with all of our advantages,

do we write better history than was written before the year
1859, which we may call the line of demarcation between the
old and the new? If the English, German, and American
historical scholars should vote as to who were the two best
historians, I have little doubt that Thucydides and Tacitus
would have a pretty large majority. If they were asked
to name a third choice, it would undoubtedly lie between
Herodotus and Gibbon. At the meeting of this association
in Cleveland, when methods of historical teaching were under
discussion, Herodotus and Thucydides, but no others, were
mentioned as proper object lessons. What are the merits
of Herodotus? Accuracy in details, as we understand it,
was certainly not one of them. Neither does he sift critically
his facts, but intimates that he will not make a positive
decision in the case of conflicting testimony. "For myself,"
he wrote, "my duty is to report all that is said, but I am not
obliged to believe it all alike, — a remark which may be
understood to apply to my whole history." He had none of
the wholesome skepticism which we deem necessary in the
weighing of historical evidence; on the contrary, he is
frequently accused of credulity. Nevertheless, Percy Gardner calls his narrative nobler than that of Thucydides, and
Mahaffy terms it an "incomparable history." "The truth
is," wrote Macaulay in his diary, when he was forty-nine
years old, "I admire no historians much except Herodotus,
Thucydides, and Tacitus." Sir M. E. Grant Duff devoted
his presidential address of 1895, before the Royal Historical
Society, wholly to Herodotus, ending with the conclusion,
"The fame of Herodotus, which has a little waned, will
surely wax again." Whereupon the London Times devoted
a leader to the subject. "We are concerned," it said, "to
hear, on authority so eminent, that one of the most delightful
writers of antiquity has a little waned of late in favor with the

world. If this indeed be the case, so much the worse for
the world. . . . When Homer and Dante and Shakespeare
are neglected, then will Herodotus cease to be read."

There we have the secret of his hold upon the minds of
men. He knows how to tell a story, said Professor Hart,
in the discussion previously referred to, in Cleveland. He
has "an epic unity of plan," writes Professor Jebb. Herodotus has furnished delight to all generations, while Polybius,
more accurate and painstaking, a learned historian and a
practical statesman, gathers dust on the shelf or is read as a
penance. Nevertheless, it may be demonstrated from the
historical literature of England of our century that literary
style and great power of narration alone will not give a man
a niche in the temple of history. Herodotus showed diligence and honesty, without which his other qualities would
have failed to secure him the place he holds in the estimation
of historical scholars.

From Herodotus we naturally turn to Thucydides, who in
the beginning charms historical students by his impression
of the seriousness and dignity of his business. History, he
writes, will be "found profitable by those who desire an
exact knowledge of the past as a key to the future, which in
all human probability will repeat or resemble the past. My
history is an everlasting possession, not a prize composition
which is heard and forgotten." Diligence, accuracy, love
of truth, and impartiality are merits commonly ascribed to
Thucydides, and the internal evidence of the history bears
out fully the general opinion. But, in my judgment, there
is a tendency to rate, in the comparative estimates, the
Athenian too high, for the possession of these qualities; for
certainly some modern writers have possessed all of these
merits in an eminent degree. When Jowett wrote in the preface to his translation, Thucydides "stands absolutely alone

among the historians, not only of Hellas, but of the world, in
his impartiality and love of truth," he was unaware that a
son of his own university was writing the history of a momentous period of his own country, in a manner to impugn the
correctness of that statement. When the Jowett Thucydides
appeared, Samuel R. Gardiner had published eight volumes
of his history, though he had not reached the great Civil War,
and his reputation, which has since grown with a cumulative
force, was not fully established; but I have now no hesitation
in saying that the internal evidence demonstrates that in
impartiality and love of truth Gardiner is the peer of Thucydides. From the point of view of external evidence, the
case is even stronger for Gardiner; he submits to a harder
test. That he has been able to treat so stormy, so contro-
verted, and so well known a period as the seventeenth
century in England, with hardly a question of his impartiality, is a wonderful tribute. In fact, in an excellent
review of his work I have seen him criticised for being too
impartial. On the other hand, Grote thinks that he has
found Thucydides in error, — in the long dialogue between
the Athenian representatives and the Melians. "This dialogue," Grote writes, "can hardly represent what actually
passed, except as to a few general points which the historian
has followed out into deductions and illustrations, thus
dramatizing the given situation in a powerful and characteristic manner." Those very words might characterize Shakespeare's account of the assassination of Julius Cæsar, and his
reproduction of the speeches of Brutus and Mark Antony.
Compare the relation in Plutarch with the third act of the
tragedy, and see how, in his amplification of the story, Shakespeare has remained true to the essential facts of the time.
Plutarch gives no account of the speeches of Brutus and
Mark Antony, confining himself to an allusion to the one,

and a reference to the other; but Appian of Alexandria, in his history, has reported them. The speeches in Appian lack the force which they have in Shakespeare, nor do they seemingly fit into the situation as well. I have adverted to this criticism of Grote, not that I love Thucydides less, but that I love Shakespeare more. For my part, the historian's candid acknowledgment in the beginning has convinced me of the essential — not the literal — truth of his accounts of speeches and dialogues. "As to the speeches," wrote the Athenian, "which were made either before or during the war, it was hard for me, and for others who reported them to me, to recollect the exact words. I have therefore put into the mouth of each speaker the sentiments proper to the occasion, expressed as I thought he would be likely to express them; while at the same time I endeavored, as nearly as I could, to give the general purport of what was actually said." That is the very essence of candor. But be the historian as chaste as ice, as pure as snow, he shall not escape calumny. Mahaffy declares that, "although all modern historians quote Thucydides with more confidence than they would quote the Gospels," the Athenian has exaggerated; he is one-sided, partial, misleading, dry, and surly. Other critics agree with Mahaffy that he has been unjust to Cleon, and has screened Nicias from blame that was his due for defective generalship.

We approach Tacitus with respect. We rise from reading his Annals, his History, and his Germany with reverence. We know that we have been in the society of a gentleman who had a high standard of morality and honor. We feel that our guide was a serious student, a solid thinker, and a man of the world; that he expressed his opinions and delivered his judgments with a remarkable freedom from prejudice. He draws us to him with sympathy. He sounds the same mournful note which we detect in Thucydides. Tacitus deplores the folly and dissoluteness of the rulers of his nation; he bewails the misfortunes of his country. The merits we ascribe to Thucydides, diligence, accuracy, love of truth, impartiality, are his. The desire to quote from Tacitus is irresistible. "The more I meditate," he writes, "on the events of ancient and modern times, the more I am struck with the capricious uncertainty which mocks the calculations of men in all their transactions." Again: "Possibly there is in all things a kind of cycle, and there may be moral revolutions just as there are changes of seasons." "Commonplaces!" sneer the scientific historians. True enough, but they might not have been commonplaces if Tacitus had not uttered them, and his works had not been read and re-read until they have become a common possession of historical students. From a thinker who deemed the time "out of joint," as Tacitus obviously did, and who, had he not possessed great strength of mind and character, might have lapsed into a gloomy pessimism, what noble words are these: "This I regard as history's highest function: to let no worthy action be uncommemorated, and to hold out the reprobation of posterity as a terror to evil words and deeds." The modesty of the Roman is fascinating. "Much of what I have related," he says, "and shall have to relate, may perhaps, I am aware, seem petty trifles to record. . . . My labors are circumscribed and unproductive of renown to the author." How agreeable to place in contrast with this the prophecy of his friend, the younger Pliny, in a letter to the historian: "I augur — nor does my augury deceive me — that your histories will be immortal: hence all the more do I desire to find a place in them."

To my mind, one of the most charming things in historical literature is the praise which one great historian bestows upon another. Gibbon speaks of "the discerning eye" and "masterly pencil of Tacitus, — the first of historians who applied the science of philosophy to the study of facts," "whose writings will instruct the last generations of mankind." He has produced an immortal work, "every sentence of which is pregnant with the deepest observations and most lively images." I mention Gibbon, for it is more than a strong probability that in diligence, accuracy, and love of truth he is the equal of Tacitus. A common edition of the History of the Decline and Fall of the Roman Empire is that with notes by Dean Milman, Guizot, and Dr. Smith. Niebuhr, Villemain, and Sir James Mackintosh are each drawn upon for criticism. Did ever such a fierce light beat upon a history? With what keen relish do the annotators pounce upon mistakes or inaccuracies, and in that portion of the work which ends with the fall of the Western Empire how few do they find! Would Tacitus stand the supreme test better? There is, so far as I know, only one case in which we may compare his Annals with an original record. On bronze tablets found at Lyons in the sixteenth century is engraved the same speech made by the Emperor Claudius to the Senate that Tacitus reports. "Tacitus and the tablets," writes Professor Jebb, "disagree hopelessly in language and in nearly all the detail, but agree in the general line of argument." Gibbon's work has richly deserved its life of more than one hundred years, a period which I believe no other modern history has endured. Niebuhr, in a course of lectures at Bonn, in 1829, said that Gibbon's "work will never be excelled." At the Gibbon Centenary Commemoration in London, in 1894, many distinguished men, among whom the Church had a distinct representation, gathered together to pay honor to him who, in the words of Frederic Harrison, had written "the most perfect book that Eng-

lish prose (outside its fiction) possesses." Mommsen, prevented by age and work from being present, sent his tribute.
No one, he said, would in the future be able to read the history of the Roman Empire unless he read Edward Gibbon.
The Times, in a leader devoted to the subject, apparently
expressed the general voice: "'Back to Gibbon' is already,
both here and among the scholars of Germany and France,
the watchword of the younger historians."

I have now set forth certain general propositions which,
with time for adducing the evidence in detail, might, I
think, be established: that, in the consensus of learned
people, Thucydides and Tacitus stand at the head of historians; and that it is not alone their accuracy, love of truth,
and impartiality which entitle them to this preëminence
since Gibbon and Gardiner among the moderns possess
equally the same qualities. What is it, then, that makes
these men supreme? In venturing a solution of this question, I confine myself necessarily to the English translations
of the Greek and Latin authors. We have thus a common
denominator of language, and need not take into account
the unrivaled precision and terseness of the Greek and the
force and clearness of the Latin. It seems to me that one
special merit of Thucydides and Tacitus is their compressed
narrative, — that they have related so many events and put
so much meaning in so few words. Our manner of writing
history is really curious. The histories which cover long
periods of time are brief; those which have to do with but
a few years are long. The works of Thucydides and Tacitus
are not like our compendiums of history, which merely touch
on great affairs, since want of space precludes any elaboration.
Tacitus treats of a comparatively short epoch, Thucydides
of a much shorter one: both histories are brief. Thucydides and Macaulay are examples of extremes. The Athe-

nian tells the story of twenty-four years in one volume;
the Englishman takes nearly five volumes of equal size for
his account of seventeen years. But it is safe to say that
Thucydides tells us as much that is worth knowing as
Macaulay. One is concise, the other is not. It is impossible
to paraphrase the fine parts of Thucydides, but Macaulay
lends himself readily to such an exercise. The thought of
the Athenian is so close that he has got rid of all redundancies
of expression: hence the effort to reproduce his ideas in
other words fails. The account of the plague in Athens
has been studied and imitated, and every imitation falls
short of the original not only in vividness but in brevity.
It is the triumph of art that in this and in other splendid
portions we wish more had been told. As the French say,
"the secret of wearying is to say all," and this the Athenian
thoroughly understood. Between our compendiums, which
tell too little, and our long general histories, which tell too
much, are Thucydides and Tacitus.

Again, it is a common opinion that our condensed histories lack life and movement. This is due in part to their
being written generally from a study of second-hand —
not original — materials. Those of the Athenian and the
Roman are mainly the original.

I do not think, however, that we may infer that we have
a much greater mass of materials, and thereby excuse our
modern prolixity. In written documents, of course, we exceed the ancients, for we have been flooded with these by
the art of printing. Yet any one who has investigated any
period knows how the same facts are told over and over
again, in different ways, by various writers; and if one can
get beyond the mass of verbiage and down to the really
significant original material, what a simplification of ideas
there is, what a lightening of the load! I own that this

process of reduction is painful, and thereby our work is made
more difficult than that of the ancients. A historian will
adapt himself naturally to the age in which he lives, and
Thucydides made use of the matter that was at his hand.
"Of the events of the war," he wrote, "I have not ventured
to speak from any chance information, nor according to any
notion of my own; I have described nothing but what I
either saw myself, or learned from others of whom I made
the most careful and particular inquiry. The task was a
laborious one, because eye-witnesses of the same occurrences
gave different accounts of them, as they remembered or
were interested in the actions of one side or the other." His
materials, then, were what he saw and heard. His books
and his manuscripts were living men. Our distinguished
military historian, John C. Ropes, whose untimely death we
deplore, might have written his history from the same sort
of materials; for he was contemporary with our Civil War,
and followed the daily events with intense interest. A
brother of his was killed at Gettysburg, and he had many
friends in the army. He paid at least one memorable visit
to Meade's headquarters in the field, and at the end of the
war had a mass of memories and impressions of the great
conflict. He never ceased his inquiries; he never lost a
chance to get a particular account from those who took
part in battles or campaigns; and before he began his Story
of the Civil War, he too could have said, "I made the most
careful and particular inquiry" of generals and officers on
both sides, and of men in civil office privy to the great
transactions. His knowledge drawn from living lips was
marvelous, and his conversation, when he poured this knowledge forth, often took the form of a flowing narrative in an
animated style. While there are not, so far as I remember,
any direct references in his two volumes to these memories,

or to memoranda of conversations which he had with living
actors after the close of the war drama, and while his main
authority is the Official Records of the Union and Confederate Armies, — which, no one appreciated better than he,
were unique historical materials, — nevertheless this personal knowledge trained his judgment and gave color to
his narrative.

It is pretty clear that Thucydides spent a large part of a
life of about threescore years and ten in gathering materials
and writing his history. The mass of facts which he set
down or stored away in his memory must have been enormous. He was a man of business, and had a home in
Thrace as well as in Athens, traveling probably at fairly
frequent intervals between the two places; but the main
portion of the first forty years of his life was undoubtedly
spent in Athens, where, during those glorious years of peace
and the process of beautifying the city, he received the best
education a man could get. To walk about the city and
view the buildings and statues was both directly and insensibly a refining influence. As Thucydides himself, in
the funeral oration of Pericles, said of the works which the
Athenian saw around him, "the daily delight of them
banishes gloom." There was the opportunity to talk with as
good conversers as the world has ever known; and he undoubtedly saw much of the men who were making history.
There was the great theater and the sublime poetry. In a
word, the life of Thucydides was adapted to the gathering of
a mass of historical materials of the best sort; and his daily
walk, his reading, his intense thought, gave him an intellectual grasp of the facts he has so ably handled. Of course
he was a genius, and he wrote in an effective literary style;
but seemingly his natural parts and acquired talents are
directed to this: a digestion of his materials, and a com-

pression of his narrative without taking the vigor out of his story in a manner I believe to be without parallel. He devoted a life to writing a volume. His years after the peace was broken, his career as a general, his banishment and enforced residence in Thrace, his visit to the countries of the Peloponnesian allies with whom Athens was at war, — all these gave him a signal opportunity to gather materials, and to assimilate them in the gathering. We may fancy him looking at an alleged fact on all sides, and turning it over and over in his mind; we know that he must have meditated long on ideas, opinions, and events; and the result is a brief, pithy narrative. Tradition hath it that Demosthenes copied out this history eight times, or even learned it by heart. Chatham, urging the removal of the forces from Boston, had reason to refer to the history of Greece, and, that he might impress it upon the lords that he knew whereof he spoke, declared, "I have read Thucydides."

Of Tacitus likewise is conciseness a well-known merit. Living in an age of books and libraries, he drew more from the written word than did Thucydides; and his method of working, therefore, resembled more our own. These are common expressions of his: "It is related by most of the writers of those times;" I adopt the account "in which the authors are agreed;" this account "agrees with those of the other writers." Relating a case of recklessness of vice in Messalina, he acknowledges that it will appear fabulous, and asserts his truthfulness thus: "But I would not dress up my narrative with fictions, to give it an air of marvel, rather than relate what has been stated to me or written by my seniors." He also speaks of the authority of tradition, and tells what he remembers "to have heard from aged men." He will not paraphrase the eloquence of Seneca after he had his veins opened, because the very words of the philosopher had been published; but when, a little later, Flavius the tribune came to die, the historian gives this report of his defiance of Nero. "I hated you," the tribune said to the emperor; "nor had you a soldier more true to you while you deserved to be loved. I began to hate you from the time you showed yourself the impious murderer of your mother and your wife, a charioteer, a stage-player, an incendiary." "I have given the very words," Tacitus adds, "because they were not, like those of Seneca, published, though the rough and vigorous sentiments of a soldier ought to be no less known." Everywhere we see in Tacitus, as in Thucydides, a dislike of superfluous detail, a closeness of thought, a compression of language. He was likewise a man of affairs, but his life work was his historical writings, which, had we all of them, would fill probably four moderate-sized octavo volumes.

To sum up, then: Thucydides and Tacitus are superior to the historians who have written in our century, because, by long reflection and studious method, they have better digested their materials and compressed their narrative. Unity in narration has been adhered to more rigidly. They stick closer to their subject. They are not allured into the fascinating bypaths of narration, which are so tempting to men who have accumulated a mass of facts, incidents, and opinions. One reason why Macaulay is so prolix is because he could not resist the temptation to treat events which had a picturesque side and which were suited to his literary style; so that, as John Morley says, "in many portions of his too elaborated history of William III. he describes a large number of events about which, I think, no sensible man can in the least care either how they happened, or whether indeed they happened at all or not." If I am right in my supposition that Thucydides and Tacitus had a mass of materials, they showed reserve and discretion in throwing a large part of them away, as not being necessary or important to the posterity for which they were writing. This could only be the result of a careful comparison of their materials, and of long meditation on their relative value. I suspect that they cared little whether a set daily task was accomplished or not; for if you propose to write only one large volume or four moderate-sized volumes in a lifetime, art is not too long nor is life too short.

Another superiority of the classical historians, as I reckon, arose from the fact that they wrote what was practically contemporaneous history. Herodotus was born 484 B.C., and the most important and accurate part of his history is the account of the Persian invasion which took place four years later. The case of Thucydides is more remarkable. Born in 471 B.C., he relates the events which happened between 435 and 411, when he was between the ages of thirty-six and sixty. Tacitus, born in 52 A.D., covered with his Annals and History the years between 14 and 96. "Herodotus and Thucydides belong to an age in which the historian draws from life and for life," writes Professor Jebb. It is manifestly easier to describe a life you know than one you must imagine, which is what you must do if you aim to relate events which took place before your own and your father's time. In many treatises which have been written demanding an extraordinary equipment for the historian, it is generally insisted that he shall have a fine constructive imagination; for how can he re-create his historic period unless he live in it? In the same treatises it is asserted that contemporary history cannot be written correctly, for impartiality in the treatment of events near at hand is impossible. Therefore the canon requires the quality of a great poet, and denies that there may be had the merit of a judge in a country where there are no great poets, but where

candid judges abound. Does not the common rating of
Thucydides and Tacitus refute the dictum that history within
the memory of men living cannot be written truthfully and
fairly? Given, then, the judicial mind, how much easier to
write it! The rare quality of a poet's imagination is no
longer necessary, for your boyhood recollections, your
youthful experiences, your successes and failures of manhood, the grandfather's tales, the parent's recollections,
the conversation in society, — all these put you in vital
touch with the life you seek to describe. These not only
give color and freshness to the vivifying of the facts you
must find in the record, but they are in a way materials
themselves, not strictly authentic, but of the kind that direct
you in search and verification. Not only is no extraordinary
ability required to write contemporary history, but the labor
of the historian is lightened, and Dryasdust is no longer his
sole guide. The funeral oration of Pericles is pretty nearly
what was actually spoken, or else it is the substance of the
speech written out in the historian's own words. Its in-
tensity of feeling and the fitting of it so well into the situation
indicate it to be a living contemporaneous document, and at
the same time it has that universal application which we
note in so many speeches of Shakespeare. A few years after
our Civil War, a lawyer in a city of the middle West, who had
been selected to deliver the Memorial Day oration, came
to a friend of his in despair because he could write nothing
but the commonplaces about those who had died for the
Union and for the freedom of a race which had been uttered
many times before, and he asked for advice. "Take the
funeral oration of Pericles for a model," was the reply.
"Use his words where they will fit, and dress up the rest to
suit our day." The orator was surprised to find how much
of the oration could be used bodily, and how much, with

adaptation, was germane to his subject. But slight alterations are necessary to make the opening sentence this:
"Most of those who have spoken here have commended the
law-giver who added this oration to our other customs;
it seemed to them a worthy thing that such an honor should
be given to the dead who have fallen on the field of battle."
In many places you may let the speech run on with hardly a
change. "In the face of death [these men] resolved to rely
upon themselves alone. And when the moment came they
were minded to resist and suffer rather than to fly and save
their lives; they ran away from the word of dishonor, but
on the battlefield their feet stood fast; and while for a moment they were in the hands of fortune, at the height, not of
terror, but of glory, they passed away. Such was the end of
these men; they were worthy of their country."

Consider for a moment, as the work of a contemporary, the
book which continues the account of the Sicilian expedition,
and ends with the disaster at Syracuse. "In the describing
and reporting whereof," Plutarch writes, "Thucydides hath
gone beyond himself, both for variety and liveliness of narration, as also in choice and excellent words." "There is no
prose composition in the world," wrote Macaulay, "which I
place so high as the seventh book of Thucydides. . . . I was
delighted to find in Gray's letters, the other day, this query to
Wharton: 'The retreat from Syracuse, — is it or is it not the
finest thing you ever read in your life?'" In the Annals of
Tacitus we have an account of part of the reign of Emperor
Nero, which is intense in its interest as the picture of a state
of society that would be incredible, did we not know that
our guide was a truthful man. One rises from a perusal of
this with the trite expression, "Truth is stranger than
fiction;" and one need only compare the account of Tacitus
with the romance of Quo Vadis to be convinced that true

history is more interesting than a novel. One of the most vivid impressions I ever had came immediately after reading the story of Nero and Agrippina in Tacitus, from a view of the statue of Agrippina in the National Museum at Naples.[1]

It will be worth our while now to sum up what I think may be established with sufficient time and care. Natural ability being presupposed, the qualities necessary for a historian are diligence, accuracy, love of truth, impartiality, the thorough digestion of his materials by careful selection and long meditating, and the compression of his narrative into the smallest compass consistent with the life of his story. He must also have a power of expression suitable for his purpose. All these qualities, we have seen, were possessed by Thucydides and Tacitus; and we have seen furthermore that, by bringing to bear these endowments and acquirements upon contemporary history, their success has been greater than it would have been had they treated a more distant period. Applying these considerations to the writing of history in America, it would seem that all we have to gain in method, in order that when the genius appears he shall rival the great Greek and the great Roman, is thorough assimilation of materials and rigorous conciseness in relation. I admit that the two things we lack are difficult to get as our own. In the collection of materials, in criticism and detailed analysis, in the study of cause and effect, in applying the principle of growth, of evolution, we certainly surpass the ancients. But if we live in the age of Darwin, we also live in an age of newspapers and magazines, when, as Lowell said, not only great events, but a vast "number of trivial incidents, are now recorded, and this dust of time gets

---

[1] Since this essay was first printed I have seen the authenticity of this portrait statue questioned.

in our eyes"; when distractions are manifold; when the desire
"to see one's name in print" and make books takes possession of us all.   If one has something like an original idea or
a fresh combination of truisms, one obtains easily a hearing.
The hearing once had, something of a success being made, the
writer is urged by magazine editors and by publishers for
more.   The good side of this is apparent.   It is certainly a
wholesome indication that a demand exists for many serious
books, but the evil is that one is pressed to publish his
thoughts before he has them fully matured.   The periods of
fruitful meditation out of which emerged the works of
Thucydides and Tacitus seem not to be a natural incident of
our time.   To change slightly the meaning of Lowell, "the
bustle of our lives keeps breaking the thread of that attention which is the material of memory, till no one has patience
to spin from it a continuous thread of thought."   We have
the defects of our qualities.   Nevertheless, I am struck
with the likeness between a common attribute of the Greeks
and Matthew Arnold's characterization of the Americans.
Greek thought, it is said, goes straight to the mark, and
penetrates like an arrow.   The Americans, Arnold wrote,
"think straight and see clear."   Greek life was adapted to
meditation.   American quickness and habit of taking the
short cut to the goal make us averse to the patient and elaborate method of the ancients.   In manner of expression,
however, we have improved.   The Fourth of July spread-
eagle oration, not uncommon even in New England in former
days, would now be listened to hardly anywhere without
merriment.   In a Lowell Institute lecture in 1855 Lowell
said, "In modern times, the desire for startling expression
is so strong that people hardly think a thought is good for
anything unless it goes off with a *pop*, like a ginger-beer
cork."   No one would thus characterize our present writing.

Between reserve in expression and reserve in thought there must be interaction. We may hope, therefore, that the trend in the one will become the trend in the other, and that we may look for as great historians in the future as in the past. The Thucydides or Tacitus of the future will write his history from the original materials, knowing that there only will he find the living spirit; but he will have the helps of the modern world. He will have at his hand monographs of students whom the professors of history in our colleges are teaching with diligence and wisdom, and he will accept these aids with thankfulness in his laborious search. He will have grasped the generalizations and methods of physical science, but he must know to the bottom his Thucydides and Tacitus. He will recognize in Homer and Shakespeare the great historians of human nature, and he will ever attempt, although feeling that failure is certain, to wrest from them their secret of narration, to acquire their art of portrayal of character. He must be a man of the world, but equally well a man of the academy. If, like Thucydides and Tacitus, the American historian chooses the history of his own country as his field, he may infuse his patriotism into his narrative. He will speak of the broad acres and their products, the splendid industrial development due to the capacity and energy of the captains of industry; but he will like to dwell on the universities and colleges, on the great numbers seeking a higher education, on the morality of the people, their purity of life, their domestic happiness. He will never be weary of referring to Washington and Lincoln, feeling that a country with such exemplars is indeed one to awaken envy, and he will not forget the brave souls who followed where they led. I like to think of the Memorial Day orator, speaking thirty years ago with his mind full of the Civil War and our Revolution, giving utterance to these noble words of Pericles: "I would have you day by day fix your eyes upon the greatness of your country, until you become filled with love of her; and when you are impressed by the spectacle of her glory, reflect that this empire has been acquired by men who knew their duty and had the courage to do it; who in the hour of conflict had the fear of dishonor always present to them; and who, if ever they failed in an enterprise, would not allow their virtues to be lost to their country, but freely gave their lives to her as the fairest offering which they could present at her feast. They received each one for himself a praise which grows not old, and the noblest of all sepulchers. For the whole earth is the sepulcher of illustrious men; not only are they commemorated by columns and inscriptions in their own country, but in foreign lands there dwells also an unwritten memorial of them, graven not on stone, but in the hearts of men."

CONCERNING THE WRITING OF HISTORY

Address delivered at the Meeting of the American Historical Association in Detroit, December, 1900.

CONCERNING THE WRITING OF HISTORY

CALLED on at the last moment, owing to the illness of Mr. Eggleston, to take the place of one whose absence can never be fully compensated, I present to you a paper on the writing of history. It is in a way a continuance of my inaugural address before this association one year ago, and despite the continuity of the thought I have endeavored to treat the same subject from a different point of view. While going over the same ground and drawing my lessons from the same historians, it is new matter so far as I have had the honor to present it to the American Historical Association.

A historian, to make a mark, must show some originality somewhere in his work. The originality may be in a method of investigation; it may be in the use of some hitherto inaccessible or unprinted material; it may be in the employment of some sources of information open to everybody, but not before used, or it may be in a fresh combination of well-known and well-elaborated facts. It is this last-named feature that leads Mr. Winsor to say, in speaking of the different views that may be honestly maintained from working over the same material, "The study of history is perennial." I think I can make my meaning clearer as to the originality one should try to infuse into historical work by drawing an illustration from the advice of a literary man as to the art of writing. Charles Dudley Warner once said to me, "Every one who writes should have something to add to the world's stock of knowledge or literary expression. If he falls un-

27

consciously into imitation or quotation, he takes away from his originality. No matter if some great writer has expressed the thought in better language than you can use, if you take his words you detract from your own originality. Express your thought feebly in your own way rather than with strength by borrowing the words of another."

This same principle in the art of authorship may be applied to the art of writing history. "Follow your own star," said Emerson, "and it will lead you to that which none other can attain. Imitation is suicide. You must take yourself for better or worse as your own portion." Any one who is bent upon writing history, may be sure that there is in him some originality, that he can add something to the knowledge of some period. Let him give himself to meditation, to searching out what epoch and what kind of treatment of that epoch is best adapted to his powers and to his training. I mean not only the collegiate training, but the sort of training one gets consciously or unconsciously from the very circumstances of one's life. In the persistence of thinking, his subject will flash upon him. Parkman, said Lowell, showed genius in the choice of his subject. The recent biography of Parkman emphasizes the idea which we get from his works — that only a man who lived in the virgin forests of this country and loved them, and who had traveled in the far West as a pioneer, with Indians for companions, could have done that work. Parkman's experience cannot be had by any one again, and he brought to bear the wealth of it in that fifty years' occupation of his. Critics of exact knowledge — such as Justin Winsor, for instance — find limitations in Parkman's books that may impair the permanence of his fame, but I suspect that his is the only work in American history that cannot and will not be written over again. The reason of it is that he had a unique life which has permeated his narrative, giving it the stamp of originality. No man whose training had been gained wholly in the best schools of Germany, France, or England could have written those books. A training racy of the soil was needed. "A practical knowledge," wrote Niebuhr, "must support historical jurisprudence, and if any one has got that he can easily master all scholastic speculations." A man's knowledge of everyday life in some way fits him for a certain field of historical study — in that field lies success. In seeking a period, no American need confine himself to his own country. "European history for Americans," said Motley, "has to be almost entirely rewritten."

I shall touch upon only two of the headings of historical originality which I have mentioned. The first that I shall speak of is the employment of some sources of information open to everybody, but not before used. A significant case of this in American history is the use which Doctor von Holst made of newspaper material. *Niles's Register,* a lot of newspaper cuttings, as well as speeches and state papers in a compact form, had, of course, been referred to by many writers who dealt with the period they covered, but in the part of his history covering the ten years from 1850 to 1860 von Holst made an extensive and varied employment of newspapers by studying the newspaper files themselves. As the aim of history is truth, and as newspapers fail sadly in accuracy, it is not surprising that many historical students believe that the examination of newspapers for any given period will not pay for the labor and drudgery involved; but the fact that a trained German historical scholar and teacher at a German university should have found some truth in our newspaper files when he came to write the history of our own country, gives to their use for that period the seal of scientific approval. Doctor von Holst used this material with pertinence and effect; his touch was nice. I used to wonder at his knowledge of the newspaper world, of the men who made and wrote our journals, until he told me that when he first came to this country one of his methods in gaining a knowledge of English was to read the advertisements in the newspapers. Reflection will show one what a picture of the life of a people this must be, in addition to the news columns.

No one, of course, will go to newspapers for facts if he can find those facts in better-attested documents. The haste with which the daily records of the world's doings are made up precludes sifting and revision. Yet in the decade between 1850 and 1860 you will find facts in the newspapers which are nowhere else set down. Public men of commanding position were fond of writing letters to the journals with a view to influencing public sentiment. These letters in the newspapers are as valuable historical material as if they were carefully collected, edited, and published in the form of books. Speeches were made which must be read, and which will be found nowhere but in the journals. The immortal debates of Lincoln and Douglas in 1858 were never put into a book until 1860, existing previously only in newspaper print. Newspapers are sometimes important in fixing a date and in establishing the whereabouts of a man. If, for example, a writer draws a fruitful inference from the alleged fact that President Lincoln went to see Edwin Booth play Hamlet in Washington in February, 1863, and if one finds by a consultation of the newspaper theatrical advertisements that Edwin Booth did not visit Washington during that month, the significance of the inference is destroyed. Lincoln paid General Scott a memorable visit at West Point in June, 1862. You may, if I remember correctly, search the books in vain to get at the exact date of this visit; but turn to the newspaper files and you find that the President left Washington at such an hour on such a day, arrived at Jersey City at a stated time, and made the transfer to the other railroad which took him to the station opposite West Point. The time of his leaving West Point and the hour of his return to Washington are also given.

The value of newspapers as an indication of public sentiment is sometimes questioned, but it can hardly be doubted that the average man will read the newspaper with the sentiments of which he agrees. "I inquired about newspaper opinion," said Joseph Chamberlain in the House of Commons last May. "I knew no other way of getting at popular opinion." During the years between 1854 and 1860 the daily journals were a pretty good reflection of public sentiment in the United States. Wherever, for instance, you found the *New York Weekly Tribune* largely read, Republican majorities were sure to be had when election day came. For fact and for opinion, if you knew the contributors, statements and editorials by them were entitled to as much weight as similar public expressions in any other form. You get to know Greeley and you learn to recognize his style. Now, an editorial from him is proper historical material, taking into account always the circumstances under which he wrote. The same may be said of Dana and of Hildreth, both editorial writers for the *Tribune,* and of the Washington despatches of J. S. Pike. It is interesting to compare the public letters of Greeley to the *Tribune* from Washington in 1856 with his private letters written at the same time to Dana. There are no misstatements in the public letters, but there is a suppression of the truth. The explanations in the private correspondence are clearer, and you need them to know fully how affairs looked in Washington to Greeley at the time; but this fact by no means detracts from the value of the public letters as historical material. I have found newspapers of greater value both for fact and opinion during the decade of 1850 to 1860 than for the period of the Civil War. A comparison of the newspaper accounts of battles with the history of them which may be drawn from the correspondence and reports in the Official Records of the War of the Rebellion will show how inaccurate and misleading was the war correspondence of the daily journals. It could not well be otherwise. The correspondent was obliged in haste to write the story of a battle of which he saw but a small section, and instead of telling the little part which he knew actually, he had to give to a public greedy for news a complete survey of the whole battlefield. This story was too often colored by his liking or aversion for the generals in command. A study of the confidential historical material of the Civil War, apart from the military operations, in comparison with the journalistic accounts, gives one a higher idea of the accuracy and shrewdness of the newspaper correspondents. Few important things were brewing at Washington of which they did not get an inkling. But I always like to think of two signal exceptions. Nothing ever leaked out in regard to the famous "Thoughts for the President's consideration," which Seward submitted to Lincoln in March, 1861, and only very incorrect guesses of the President's first emancipation proclamation, brought before his Cabinet in July, 1862, got into newspaper print.

Beware of hasty, strained, and imperfect generalizations. A historian should always remember that he is a sort of trustee for his readers. No matter how copious may be his notes, he cannot fully explain his processes or the reason of his confidence in one witness and not in another, his belief in one honest man against a half dozen untrustworthy men, without such prolixity as to make a general history unread-

able. Now, in this position as trustee he is bound to assert
nothing for which he has not evidence, as much as an executor of a will or the trustee for widows and orphans is
obligated to render a correct account of the moneys in his
possession. For this reason Grote has said, "An historian
is bound to produce the materials upon which he builds, be
they never so fantastic, absurd, or incredible." Hence the
necessity for footnotes. While mere illustrative and interesting footnotes are perhaps to be avoided, on account of
their redundancy, those which give authority for the statements in the text can never be in excess. Many good histories have undoubtedly been published where the authors
have not printed their footnotes; but they must have had,
nevertheless, precise records for their authorities. The advantage and necessity of printing the notes is that you furnish your critic an opportunity of finding you out if you have
mistaken or strained your authorities. Bancroft's example
is peculiar. In his earlier volumes he used footnotes, but
in volume vii he changed his plan and omitted notes,
whether of reference or explanation. Nor do you find them
in either of his carefully revised editions. "This is done,"
Bancroft wrote in the preface to his seventh volume, "not
from an unwillingness to subject every statement of fact,
even in its minutest details, to the severest scrutiny; but
from the variety and the multitude of the papers which
have been used and which could not be intelligently cited
without a disproportionate commentary." Again, Blaine's
"Twenty Years of Congress," a work which, properly weighed,
is not without historical value, is only to be read with great
care on account of his hasty and inaccurate generalizations.
There are evidences of good, honest labor in those two volumes, much of which must have been done by himself.
There is an aim at truth and impartiality, but many of his

general statements will seem, to any one who has gone over the original material, to rest on a slight basis. If Blaine had felt the necessity of giving authorities in a footnote for every statement about which there might have been a question, he certainly would have written an entirely different sort of a book.

My other head is the originality which comes from a fresh combination of known historical facts.

I do not now call to mind any more notable chapter which illustrates this than the chapter of Curtius, "The years of peace." One is perhaps better adapted for the keen enjoyment of it if he does not know the original material, for his suspicion that some of the inferences are strained and unwarranted might become a certainty. But accepting it as a mature and honest elaboration by one of the greatest historians of Greece of our day, it is a sample of the vivifying of dry bones and of a dovetailing of facts and ideas that makes a narrative to charm and instruct. You feel that the spirit of that age we all like to think and dream about is there, and if you have been so fortunate as to visit the Athens of to-day, that chapter, so great is the author's constructive imagination, carries you back and makes you for the moment live in the Athens of Pericles, of Sophocles, of Phidias and Herodotus.

With the abundance of materials for modern history, and, for that reason, our tendency to diffuseness, nothing is so important as a thorough acquaintance with the best classic models, such as Herodotus, Thucydides, and Tacitus. In Herodotus you have an example of an interesting story with the unity of the narrative well sustained in spite of certain unnecessary digressions. His book is obviously a life work and the work of a man who had an extensive knowledge gained by reading, social intercourse, and travel, and who brought his knowledge to bear upon his chosen task. That the history is interesting all admit, but in different periods of criticism stress is sometimes laid on the untrustworthy character of the narrative, with the result that there has been danger of striking Herodotus from the list of historical models; but such is the merit of his work that the Herodotus cult again revives, and, I take it, is now at its height. I received, six years ago, while in Egypt, a vivid impression of him whom we used to style the Father of History. Spending one day at the great Pyramids, when, after I had satisfied my first curiosity, after I had filled my eyes and mind with the novelty of the spectacle, I found nothing so gratifying to the historic sense as to gaze on those most wonderful monuments of human industry, constructed certainly 5000 years ago, and to read at the same time the account that Herodotus gave of his visit there about 2350 years before the date of my own. That same night I read in a modern and garish Cairo hotel the current number of the *London Times*. In it was an account of an annual meeting of the Royal Historical Society and a report of a formal and carefully prepared address of its president, whose subject was "Herodotus," whose aim was to point out the value of the Greek writer as a model to modern historians. The *Times*, for the moment laying aside its habitual attack on the then Liberal government, devoted its main leader to Herodotus — to his merits and the lessons he conveyed to the European writers. The article was a remarkable blending of scholarship and good sense, and I ended the day with the reflection of what a space in the world's history Herodotus filled, himself describing the work of twenty-six hundred years before his own time and being dilated on in 1894 by one of the most modern of nineteenth-century newspapers.

It is generally agreed, I think, that Thucydides is first in

order of time of philosophic historians, but it does not seem
to me that we have most to learn from him in the philosophic
quality. The tracing of cause and effect, the orderly sequence of events, is certainly better developed by moderns
than it has been by ancients. The influence of Darwin and
the support and proof which he gives to the doctrine of
evolution furnish a training of thought which was impossible
to the ancients; but Thucydides has digested his material
and compressed his narrative without taking the life out of
his story in a manner to make us despair, and this does not,
I take it, come from paucity of materials. A test which I
began to make as a study in style has helped me in estimating the solidity of a writer. Washington Irving formed his
style by reading attentively from time to time a page of
Addison and then, closing the book, endeavored to write out
the same ideas in his own words. In this way his style
became assimilated to that of the great English essayist.
I have tried the same mode with several writers. I found
that the plan succeeded with Macaulay and with Lecky. I
tried it again and again with Shakespeare and Hawthorne,
but if I succeeded in writing out the paragraph I found that
it was because I memorized their very words. To write
out their ideas in my own language I found impossible.
I have had the same result with Thucydides in trying to do
this with his description of the plague in Athens. Now, I
reason from this in the case of Shakespeare and Thucydides
that their thought was so concise they themselves got rid of
all redundancies; hence to effect the reproduction of their
ideas in any but their own language is practically impossible.

It is related of Macaulay somewhere in his "Life and
Letters," that in a moment of despair, when he instituted
a comparison between his manuscript and the work of

Thucydides, he thought of throwing his into the fire. I suspect that Macaulay had not the knack of discarding material on which he had spent time and effort, seeing how easily such events glowed under his graphic pen. This is one reason why he is prolix in the last three volumes. The first two, which begin with the famous introductory chapter and continue the story through the revolution of 1688 to the accession of William and Mary, seem to me models of historical composition so far as arrangement, orderly method, and liveliness of narration go. Another defect of Macaulay is that, while he was an omnivorous reader and had a prodigious memory, he was not given to long-continued and profound reflection. He read and rehearsed his reading in memory, but he did not give himself to "deep, abstract meditation" and did not surrender himself to "the fruitful leisures of the spirit." Take this instance of Macaulay's account of a journey: "The express train reached Hollyhead about 7 in the evening. I read between London and Bangor the lives of the emperors from Maximin to Carinus, inclusive, in the Augustine history, and was greatly amused and interested." On board the steamer: "I put on my greatcoat and sat on deck during the whole voyage. As I could not read, I used an excellent substitute for reading. I went through 'Paradise Lost' in my head. I could still repeat half of it, and that the best half. I really never enjoyed it so much." In Dublin: "The rain was so heavy that I was forced to come back in a covered car. While in this detestable vehicle I looked rapidly through the correspondence between Pliny and Trajan and thought that Trajan made a most creditable figure." It may be that Macaulay did not always digest his knowledge well. Yet in reading his "Life and Letters" you know that you are in company with a man who read many books and you give faith to Thackeray's remark, "Macaulay reads twenty books to write a sentence; he travels a hundred miles to make a line of description." It is a matter of regret that the progress of historical criticism and the scientific teaching of history have had the tendency to drive Macaulay out of the fashion with students, and I know not whether the good we used to get out of him thirty-five years ago can now be got from other sources. For I seem to miss something that we historical students had a generation ago — and that is enthusiasm for the subject. The enthusiasm that we had then had — the desire to compass all knowledge, the wish to gather the fruits of learning and lay them devoutly at the feet of our chosen muse — this enthusiasm we owed to Macaulay and to Buckle. Quite properly, no one reads Buckle now, and I cannot gainsay what John Morley said of Macaulay: "Macaulay seeks truth, not as she should be sought, devoutly, tentatively, with the air of one touching the hem of a sacred garment, but clutching her by the hair of the head and dragging her after him in a kind of boisterous triumph, a prisoner of war and not a goddess." It is, nevertheless, true that Macaulay and Buckle imparted a new interest to history.

I have spoken of the impression we get of Macaulay through reading his " Life and Letters." Of Carlyle, in reading the remarkable biography of him, we get the notion of a great thinker as well as a great reader. He was not as keen and diligent in the pursuit of material as Macaulay. He did not like to work in libraries; he wanted every book he used in his own study — padded as it was against the noises which drove him wild. H. Morse Stephens relates that Carlyle would not use a collection of documents relating to the French Revolution in the British Museum for the reason that the museum authorities would not have a private room reserved for him where he might study.   Rather than work in a room with other people, he neglected this valuable material.   But Carlyle has certainly digested and used his material well.   His "French Revolution" seems to approach the historical works of the classics in there being so much in a little space.   "With the gift of song," Lowell said, "Carlyle would have been the greatest of epic poets since Homer;" and he also wrote, Carlyle's historical compositions are no more history than the historical plays of Shakespeare.

The contention between the scientific historians and those who hold to the old models is interesting and profitable. One may enjoy the controversy and derive benefit from it without taking sides.   I suspect that there is truth in the view of both.   We may be sure that the long-continued study and approval by scholars of many ages of the works of Herodotus, Thucydides, and Tacitus implies historical merit on their part in addition to literary art.   It is, however, interesting to note the profound difference between President Woolsey's opinion of Thucydides and that of some of his late German critics.   Woolsey said, "I have such confidence in the absolute truthfulness of Thucydides that were he really chargeable with folly, as Grote alleges [in the affair of Amphipolis], I believe he would have avowed it."   On the other hand, a German critic, cited by Holm, says that Thucydides is a poet who invents facts partly in order to teach people how things ought to be done and partly because he liked to depict certain scenes of horror.   He says further, a narrative of certain occurrences is so full of impossibilities that it must be pure invention on the part of the historian.   Another German maintains that Thucydides has indulged in "a fanciful and half-romantic picture of events." But Holm, whom the scientific historians claim as one of their own, says, "Thucydides still remains a trustworthy

historical authority;" and, "On the whole, therefore, the old
view that he is a truthful writer is not in the least shaken."
Again Holm writes: "Attempts have been made to convict
Thucydides of serious inaccuracies, but without success.
On the other hand, the writer of this work [that is, the scientific historian, Holm] is able to state that he has followed
him topographically for the greater part of the sixth and
seventh books — and consequently for nearly one fourth
of the whole history — and has found that the more carefully his words are weighed and the more accurately the
ground is studied the clearer both the text and events become, and this is certainly high praise."   Holm and Percy
Gardner, both of whom have the modern method and have
studied diligently the historical evidence from coins and
inscriptions, placed great reliance on Herodotus, who, as
well as Thucydides and Tacitus, is taken by scholars as a
model of historical composition.

The sifting of time settles the reputations of historians.
Of the English of the eighteenth century only one historian
has come down to us as worthy of serious study.   Time is
wasted in reading Hume and Robertson as models, and no
one goes to them for facts.   But thirty years ago no course
of historical reading was complete without Hume.   In this
century the sifting process still goes on.   One loses little by
not reading Alison's "History of Europe."   But he was much
in vogue in the '50's.   *Harper's Magazine* published a part of
his history as a serial.   His rounded periods and bombastic
utterances were quoted with delight by those who thought
that history was not history unless it was bombastic.   Emerson says somewhere, "Avoid adjectives; let your nouns do
the work."   There was hardly a sentence in Alison which
did not traverse this rule.   One of his admirers told me that
the great merit of his style was his choiceness and aptness

in his use of adjectives. It is a style which now provokes
merriment, and even had Alison been learned and impartial,
and had he possessed a good method, his style for the present
taste would have killed his book. Gibbon is sometimes called
pompous, but place him by the side of Alison and what one
may have previously called pompousness one now calls
dignity.

Two of the literary historians of our century survive —
Carlyle and Macaulay. They may be read with care. We
may do as Cassius said Brutus did to him, observe all their
faults, set them in a note-book, learn and con them by rote;
nevertheless we shall get good from them. Oscar Browning
said — I am quoting H. Morse Stephens again — of Carlyle's
description of the flight of the king to Varennes, that
in every one of his details where a writer could go wrong,
Carlyle had gone wrong; but added that, although all the
details were wrong, Carlyle's account is essentially accurate.
No defense, I think, can be made of Carlyle's statement that
Marat was a "blear-eyed dog leach," nor of those statements from which you get the distinct impression that the
complexion of Robespierre was green; nevertheless, every
one who studies the French Revolution reads Carlyle, and he
is read because the reading is profitable. The battle descriptions in Carlyle's " Frederick the Great " are well worth reading. How refreshing they are after technical descriptions!
Carlyle said once, "Battles since Homer's time, when they
were nothing but fighting mobs, have ceased to be worth
reading about," but he made the modern battle interesting.

Macaulay is an honest partisan. You learn very soon how
to take him, and when distrust begins one has correctives
in Gardiner and Ranke. Froude is much more dangerous.
His splendid narrative style does not compensate for his
inaccuracies. Langlois makes an apt quotation from

Froude. "We saw," says Froude, of the city of Adelaide, in Australia, "below us in a basin, with the river winding through it, a city of 150,000 inhabitants, none of whom has ever known or ever will know one moment's anxiety as to the recurring regularity of three meals a day." Now for the facts. Langlois says: "Adelaide is built on an eminence; no river runs through it. When Froude visited it the population did not exceed 75,000, and it was suffering from a famine at the time." Froude was curious in his inaccuracies. He furnished the data which convict him of error. He quoted inaccurately the Simancas manuscripts and deposited correct copies in the British Museum. Carlyle and Macaulay are honest partisans and you know how to take them, but for constitutional inaccuracy such as Froude's no allowance can be made.

Perhaps it may be said of Green that he combines the merits of the scientific and literary historian. He has written an honest and artistic piece of work. But he is not infallible. I have been told on good authority that in his reference to the Thirty Years' War he has hardly stated a single fact correctly, yet the general impression you get from his account is correct. Saintsbury writes that Green has "out-Macaulayed Macaulay in reckless abuse" of Dryden. Stubbs and Gardiner are preëminently the scientific historians of England. Of Stubbs, from actual knowledge, I regret that I cannot speak, but the reputation he has among historical experts is positive proof of his great value. Of Gardiner I can speak with knowledge. Any one who desires to write history will do well to read every line Gardiner has written — not the text alone, but also the notes. It is an admirable study in method which will bear important fruit. But because Gibbon, Gardiner, and Stubbs should be one's chief reliance, it does not follow that one may

neglect Macaulay, Carlyle, Tacitus, Thucydides, and Herodotus. Gardiner himself has learned much from Macaulay
and Carlyle. All of them may be criticised on one point or
another, but they all have lessons for us.

We shall all agree that the aim of history is to get at the
truth and express it as clearly as possible. The differences
crop out when we begin to elaborate our meaning. "This
I regard as the historian's highest function," writes Tacitus,
"to let no worthy action be uncommemorated, and to hold
out the reprobation of posterity as a terror to evil words
and deeds;" while Langlois and the majority of the scholars
of Oxford are of the opinion that the formation and expression of ethical judgments, the approval or condemnation of
Julius Cæsar or of Cæsar Borgia is not a thing within the
historian's province. Let the controversy go on! It is
well worth one's while to read the presentations of the subject from the different points of view. But infallibility
will nowhere be found. Mommsen and Curtius in their detailed investigations received applause from those who adhered rigidly to the scientific view of history, but when they
addressed the public in their endeavor, it is said, to produce an effect upon it, they relaxed their scientific rigor;
hence such a chapter as Curtius's "The years of peace," and
in another place his transmuting a conjecture of Grote into
an assertion; hence Mommsen's effusive panegyric of Cæsar.
If Mommsen did depart from the scientific rules, I suspect
that it came from no desire of a popular success, but rather
from the enthusiasm of much learning. The examples of
Curtius and Mommsen show probably that such a departure
from strict impartiality is inherent in the writing of general
history, and it comes, I take it, naturally and unconsciously.
Holm is a scientific historian, but on the Persian Invasion
he writes: "I have followed Herodotus in many passages

which are unauthenticated and probably even untrue, because he reproduces the popular traditions of the Greeks." And again: "History in the main ought only to be a record of facts, but now and then the historian may be allowed to display a certain interest in his subject." These expressions traverse the canons of scientific history as much as the sayings of the ancient historiographers themselves. But because men have warm sympathies that cause them to color their narratives, shall no more general histories be written? Shall history be confined to the printing of original documents and to the publication of learned monographs in which the discussion of authorities is mixed up with the relation of events? The proper mental attitude of the general historian is to take no thought of popularity. The remark of Macaulay that he would make his history take the place of the last novel on my lady's table is not scientific. The audience which the general historian should have in mind is that of historical experts — men who are devoting their lives to the study of history. Words of approval from them are worth more than any popular recognition, for theirs is the enduring praise. Their criticism should be respected; there should be unceasing effort to avoid giving them cause for fault-finding. No labor should be despised which shall enable one to present things just as they are. Our endeavor should be to think straight and see clear. An incident should not be related on insufficient evidence because it is interesting, but an affair well attested should not be discarded because it happens to have a human interest. I feel quite sure that the cardinal aim of Gardiner was to be accurate and to proportion his story well. In this he has succeeded; but it is no drawback that he has made his volumes interesting. Jacob D. Cox, who added to other accomplishments that of being learned in the law, and who looked upon

Gardiner with such reverence that he called him the Chief Justice, said there was no reason why he should read novels, as he found Gardiner's history more interesting than any romance. The scientific historians have not revolutionized historical methods, but they have added much. The process of accretion has been going on since, at any rate, the time of Herodotus, and the canons for weighing evidence and the synthesis of materials are better understood now than ever before, for they have been reduced from many models. I feel sure that there has been a growth in candor. Compare the critical note to a later edition which Macaulay wrote in 1857, maintaining the truth of his charge against William Penn, with the manly way in which Gardiner owns up when an error or insufficient evidence for a statement is pointed out. It is the ethics of the profession to be forward in correcting errors. The difference between the old and the new lies in the desire to have men think you are infallible and the desire to be accurate.

THE PROFESSION OF HISTORIAN

Lecture read before the History Club of Harvard University, April
27, 1908, and at Yale, Columbia, and Western Reserve Universities.

THE PROFESSION OF HISTORIAN

I AM assuming that among my audience there are some students who aspire to become historians. To these especially my discourse is addressed.

It is not to be expected that I should speak positively and in detail on matters of education. Nevertheless, a man of sixty who has devoted the better part of his life to reading, observation, and reflection must have gained, if only through a perception of his own deficiencies, some ideas that should be useful to those who have life's experience before them. Hence, if a Freshman should say to me, I wish to be a historian, tell me what preliminary studies you would advise, I should welcome the opportunity. From the nature of the case, the history courses will be sought and studied in their logical order and my advice will have to do only with collateral branches of learning.

In the first place, I esteem a knowledge of Latin and French of the highest importance. By a knowledge of French, I mean that you should be able to read it substantially as well as you read English, so that when you have recourse to a dictionary it will be a French dictionary and not one of the French-English kind. The historical and other literature that is thus opened up to you enables you to live in another world, with a point of view impossible to one who reads for pleasure only in his own tongue. To take two instances: Molière is a complement to Shakespeare, and the man who knows his Molière as he does his Shakespeare has made a propitious beginning in that study of human character which must be understood if he desires to write a history that shall gain readers. "I have known and loved Molière," said Goethe, "from my youth and have learned from him during my whole life. I never fail to read some of his plays every year, that I may keep up a constant intercourse with what is excellent. It is not merely the perfectly artistic treatment which delights me; but particularly the amiable nature, the highly formed mind of the poet. There is in him a grace and a feeling for the decorous, and a tone of good society, which his innate beautiful nature could only attain by daily intercourse with the most eminent men of his age." [1]

My other instance is Balzac. In reading him for pleasure, as you read Dickens and Thackeray, you are absorbing an exact and fruitful knowledge of French society of the Restoration and of Louis Philippe. Moreover you are still pursuing your study of human character under one of the acute critics of the nineteenth century. Balzac has always seemed to me peculiarly French; his characters belong essentially to Paris or to the provinces. I associate Eugénie Grandet with Saumur in the Touraine and César Birotteau with the Rue St. Honoré in Paris; and all his other men and women move naturally in the great city or in the provinces which he has given them for their home. A devoted admirer however tells me that in his opinion Balzac has created universal types; the counterpart of some of his men may be seen in the business and social world of Boston, and the peculiarly sharp and dishonest transaction which brought César Birotteau to financial ruin was here exactly reproduced.

The French language and literature seem to possess the merits which ours lack; and the writer of history cannot

[1] Conversations of Goethe, Eng. trans., 230.

afford to miss the lessons he will receive by a constant reading of the best French prose.

I do not ask the Freshman who is going to be a historian to realize Macaulay's ideal of a scholar, to "read Plato with his feet on the fender," [1] but he should at least acquire a pretty thorough knowledge of classical Latin, so that he can read Latin, let me say, as many of us read German, that is with the use of a lexicon and the occasional translation of a sentence or a paragraph into English to arrive at its exact meaning. Of this, I can speak from the point of view of one who is deficient. The reading of Latin has been for me a grinding labor and I would have liked to read with pleasure in the original, the History and Annals of Tacitus, Cæsar's Gallic and Civil wars and Cicero's Orations and Private Letters even to the point of following Macaulay's advice, "Soak your mind with Cicero." [1] These would have given me, I fancy, a more vivid impression of two periods of Roman history than I now possess. Ferrero, who is imparting a fresh interest to the last period of the Roman republic, owes a part of his success, I think, to his thorough digestion and effective use of Cicero's letters, which have the faculty of making one acquainted with Cicero just as if he were a modern man. During a sojourn on the shores of Lake Geneva, I read two volumes of Voltaire's private correspondence, and later, while passing the winter in Rome, the four volumes of Cicero's letters in French. I could not help thinking that in the republic of letters one was not in time at a far greater distance from Cicero than from Voltaire. While the impression of nearness may have come from reading both series of letters in French, or because, to use John Morley's words, "two of the most perfect masters of the art of letter writing were Cicero and Voltaire," [2]

[1] Trevelyan, I, 86.   [2] Life of Gladstone, II, 181.

there is a decided flavor of the nineteenth century in Cicero's words to a good liver whom he is going to visit. "You must not reckon," he wrote, "on my eating your hors d'œuvre. I have given them up entirely. The time has gone by when I can abuse my stomach with your olives and your Lucanian sausages." [1]

To repeat then, if the student, who is going to be a historian, uses his acquisitive years in obtaining a thorough knowledge of French and Latin, he will afterwards be spared useless regrets. He will naturally add German for the purpose of general culture and, if languages come easy, perhaps Greek. "Who is not acquainted with another language," said Goethe, "knows not his own." A thorough knowledge of Latin and French is a long stride towards an efficient mastery of English. In the matter of diction, the English writer is rarely in doubt as to words of Anglo-Saxon origin, for these are deep-rooted in his childhood and his choice is generally instinctive. The difficulties most persistently besetting him concern words that come from the Latin or the French; and here he must use reason or the dictionary or both. The author who has a thorough knowledge of Latin and French will argue with himself as to the correct diction, will follow Emerson's advice, "Know words etymologically; pull them apart; see how they are made; and use them only where they fit." [2] As it is in action through life, so it is in writing; the conclusions arrived at by reason are apt to be more valuable than those which we accept on authority. The reasoned literary style is more virile than that based on the dictionary. A judgment arrived at by argument sticks in the memory, while it is necessary for the user of the dictionary constantly to invoke authority, so that the writer who reasons out the meaning

---

[1] III, 51.   [2] Talks with Emerson, 23.

of words may constantly accelerate his pace, for the doubt
and decision of yesterday is to-day a solid acquirement, ingrained in his mental being. I have lately been reading a
good deal of Gibbon and I cannot imagine his having had
frequent recourse to a dictionary. I do not remember even
an allusion either in his autobiographies or in his private
letters to any such aid. Undoubtedly his thorough knowledge of Latin and French, his vast reading of Latin, French,
and English books, enabled him to dispense with the thumb-
ing of a dictionary and there was probably a reasoning
process at the back of every important word. It is difficult,
if not impossible, to improve on Gibbon by the substitution
of one word for another.

A rather large reading of Sainte-Beuve gives me the same
impression. Indeed his literary fecundity, the necessity of
having the Causerie ready for each Monday's issue of the
Constitutionnel or the *Moniteur*, precluded a study of words
while composing, and his rapid and correct writing was undoubtedly due to the training obtained by the process of
reasoning. Charles Sumner seems to be an exception to
my general rule. Although presumably he knew Latin
well, he was a slave to dictionaries. He generally had five
at his elbow (Johnson, Webster, Worcester, Walker, and
Pickering) and when in doubt as to the use of a word he
consulted all five and let the matter be decided on the American democratic principle of majority rule.[1] Perhaps this
is one cause of the stilted and artificial character of Sumner's
speeches which, unlike Daniel Webster's, are not to be thought
of as literature. One does not associate dictionaries with
Webster. Thus had I written the sentence without thinking
of a not infrequent confusion between Noah and Daniel
Webster, and this confusion reminded me of a story which

[1] My Vol. II, 142, n. 2.

John Fiske used to tell with gusto and which some of you
may not have heard.   An English gentleman remarked to an
American: "What a giant intellect that Webster of yours
had!   To think of so great an orator and statesman writing
that dictionary!   But I felt sure that one who towered so
much above his fellows would come to a bad end and I was
not a bit surprised to learn that he had been hanged for the
murder of Dr. Parkman."

To return to my theme: One does not associate dictionaries with Daniel Webster.   He was given to preparing
his speeches in the solitudes of nature, and his first Bunker
Hill oration, delivered in 1825, was mainly composed while
wading in a trout stream and desultorily fishing for trout.[1]
Joe Jefferson, who loved fishing as well as Webster, used to
say, "The trout is a gentleman and must be treated as such."
Webster's companion might have believed that some such
thought as this was passing through the mind of the great
Daniel as, standing middle deep in the stream, he uttered
these sonorous words: "Venerable men! You have come down
to us from a former generation.   Heaven has bounteously
lengthened out your lives that you might behold this joyous
day."   I think Daniel Webster for the most part reasoned
out his choice of words; he left the dictionary work to
others.   After delivery, he threw down the manuscript of
his eulogy on Adams and Jefferson and said to a student in
his law office, "There, Tom, please to take that discourse and
weed out the Latin words."[2]

When doubtful as to the use of words, I should have been
helped by a better knowledge of Latin and enabled very often
to write with a surer touch.   Though compelled to resort
frequently to the dictionary, I early learned to pay little
attention to the definition but to regard with care the illus-

[1] Curtis, I, 250.   [2] *Ibid.*, I, 252.

trative meaning in the citations from standard authors. When I began writing I used the Imperial Dictionary, an improvement over Webster in this respect. Soon the Century Dictionary began to appear, and best of all the New English Dictionary on historical principles edited by Murray and Bradley and published by the Clarendon Press at Oxford. A study of the mass of quotations in these two dictionaries undoubtedly does much to atone for the lack of linguistic knowledge; and the tracing of the history of words, as it is done in the Oxford dictionary, makes any inquiry as to the meaning of a word fascinating work for the historian. Amongst the multiplicity of aids for the student and the writer no single one is so serviceable as this product of labor and self-sacrifice, fostered by the Clarendon Press, to whom, all writers in the English language owe a debt of gratitude.

Macaulay had a large fund of knowledge on which he might base his reasoning, and his indefatigable mind welcomed any outside assistance. He knew Greek and Latin thoroughly and a number of other languages, but it is related of him that he so thumbed his copy of Johnson's Dictionary that he was continually sending it to the binder. In return for his mastery of the languages, the dictionaries are fond of quoting Macaulay. If I may depend upon a rough mental computation, no prose writer of the nineteenth century is so frequently cited. "He never wrote an obscure sentence in his life," said John Morley; [1] and this is partly due to his exact use of words. There is never any doubt about his meaning. Macaulay began the use of Latin words at an early age. When four and a half years old he was asked if he had got over the toothache, to which question came this reply, "The agony is abated."

Mathematics beyond arithmetic are of no use to the his-

[1] Miscellanies, I, 275.

torian and may be entirely discarded. I do not ignore John Stuart Mill's able plea for them, some words of which are worth quoting. "Mathematical studies," he said, "are of immense benefit to the student's education by habituating him to precision. It is one of the peculiar excellences of mathematical discipline that the mathematician is never satisfied with an *à peu près*. He requires the *exact* truth. . . . The practice of mathematical reasoning gives wariness of the mind; it accustoms us to demand a sure footing." [1] Mill, however, is no guide except for exceptionally gifted youth. He began to learn Greek when he was three years old, and by the time he had reached the age of twelve had read a good part of Latin and Greek literature and knew elementary geometry and algebra thoroughly.

The three English historians who have most influenced thought from 1776 to 1900 are those whom John Morley called "great born men of letters" [2] — Gibbon, Macaulay, and Carlyle; and two of these despised mathematics. "As soon as I understood the principles," wrote Gibbon in his "Autobiography," "I relinquished forever the pursuit of the Mathematics; nor can I lament that I desisted before my mind was hardened by the habit of rigid demonstration, so destructive of the finer feelings of moral evidence, which must however determine the actions and opinions of our lives." [3] Macaulay, while a student at Cambridge, wrote to his mother: "Oh, for words to express my abomination of mathematics . . . .'Discipline' of the mind! Say rather starvation, confinement, torture, annihilation! . . . I feel myself becoming a personification of Algebra, a living trigonometrical canon, a walking table of logarithms. All my perceptions of elegance and beauty gone, or at least going. . . . Fare-

---

[1] Exam. of Sir W. Hamilton's Philosophy, II, 310, 311.
[2] Gladstone, I, 195.　　　　[3] p. 142.

well then Homer and Sophocles and Cicero." [1] I must in
fairness state that in after life Macaulay regretted his lack of
knowledge of mathematics and physics, but his career and
Gibbon's demonstrate that mathematics need have no place
on the list of the historian's studies. Carlyle, however,
showed mathematical ability which attracted the attention
of Legendre and deemed himself sufficiently qualified to
apply, when he was thirty-nine years old, for the professorship of Astronomy at the University of Edinburgh. He did
not succeed in obtaining the post but, had he done so, he
"would have made," so Froude his biographer thinks, "the
school of Astronomy at Edinburgh famous throughout Europe." [2] When fifty-two, Carlyle said that "the man who
had mastered the first forty-seven propositions of Euclid
stood nearer to God than he had done before." [3] I may cap
this with some words of Emerson, who in much of his
thought resembled Carlyle: "What hours of melancholy
my mathematical works cost! It was long before I learned
that there is something wrong with a man's brain who loves
them." [4]

Mathematics are of course the basis of many studies,
trades, and professions and are sometimes of benefit as a
recreation for men of affairs. Devotion to Euclid undoubtedly added to Lincoln's strength, but the necessary range
of knowledge for the historian is so vast that he cannot spend
his evenings and restless nights in the solution of mathematical problems. In short, mathematics are of no more
use to him than is Greek to the civil or mechanical engineer.

In the category with mathematics must be placed a detailed study of any of the physical or natural sciences. I
think that a student during his college course should have

---

[1] Trevelyan, I, 91. [2] Froude, II, 317.
[3] Nichol, 20. [4] Talks with Emerson, 162.

a year's work in a chemical laboratory or else, if his taste inclines him to botany, geology, or zoölogy, a year's training of his observing powers in some one of these studies. For he ought to get, while at an impressible age, a superficial knowledge of the methods of scientific men, as a basis for his future reading. We all know that science is moving the world and to keep abreast with the movement is a necessity for every educated man. Happily, there are scientific men who popularize their knowledge. John Fiske, Huxley, and Tyndall presented to us the theories and demonstrations of science in a literary style that makes learning attractive. Huxley and Tyndall were workers in laboratories and gave us the results of their patient and long-continued experiments. It is too much to expect that every generation will produce men of the remarkable power of expression of Huxley and John Fiske, but there will always be clear writers who will delight in instructing the general public in language easily understood. In an address which I delivered eight or nine years ago before the American Historical Association, I cheerfully conceded that, in the realm of intellectual endeavor, the natural and physical sciences should have the precedence of history. The question with us now is not which is the nobler pursuit, but how is the greatest economy of time to be compassed for the historian. My advice is in the line of concentration. Failure in life arises frequently from intellectual scattering; hence I like to see the historical student getting his physical and natural science at second-hand.

The religious and political revolutions of the last four hundred years have weakened authority; but in intellectual development I believe that in general an important advantage lies in accepting the dicta of specialists. In this respect our scientific men may teach us a lesson. One not infrequently meets a naturalist or a physician, who possesses an excellent knowledge of history, acquired by reading the works of general historians who have told an interesting story. He would laugh at the idea that he must verify the notes of his author and read the original documents, for he has confidence that the interpretation is accurate and truthful. This is all that I ask of the would-be historian. For the sake of going to the bottom of things in his own special study, let him take his physical and natural science on trust and he may well begin to do this during his college course. As a manner of doing this, there occur to me three interesting biographies, the Life of Darwin, the Life of Huxley, and the Life of Pasteur, which give the important part of the story of scientific development during the last half of the nineteenth century. Now I believe that a thorough mastery of these three books will be worth more to the historical student than any driblets of science that he may pick up in an unsystematic college course.

With this elimination of undesirable studies — undesirable because of lack of time — there remains ample time for those studies which are necessary for the equipment of a historian; to wit, languages, histories, English, French, and Latin literature, and as much of economics as his experienced teachers advise. Let him also study the fine arts as well as he can in America, fitting himself for an appreciation of the great works of architecture, sculpture, and painting in Europe which he will recognize as landmarks of history in their potent influence on the civilization of mankind. Let us suppose that our hypothetical student has marked out on these lines his college course of four years, and his graduate course of three. At the age of twenty-five he will then have received an excellent college education. The university with its learned and hard-working teachers, its wealth, its varied and whole-

some traditions has done for him the utmost possible.
Henceforward his education must depend upon himself
and, unless he has an insatiable love of reading, he had better
abandon the idea of becoming a historian; for books, pam-
phlets, old newspapers, and manuscripts are the stock of his
profession and to them he must show a single-minded devotion. He must love his library as Pasteur did his laboratory and must fill with delight most of the hours of the day
in reading or writing. To this necessity there is no alternative. Whether it be in general preparation or in the
detailed study of a special period, there is no end to the material which may be read with advantage. The young man
of twenty-five can do no better than to devote five years of
his life to general preparation. And what enjoyment he
has before him! He may draw upon a large mass of histories and biographies, of books of correspondence, of poems,
plays, and novels; it is then for him to select with discrimination, choosing the most valuable, as they afford
him facts, augment his knowledge of human nature, and
teach him method and expression. "A good book," said
Milton, "is the precious life blood of a master spirit,"
and every good book which wins our student's interest
and which he reads carefully will help him directly or
indirectly in his career. And there are some books which
he will wish to master, as if he were to be subjected
to an examination on them. As to these he will be guided
by strong inclination and possibly with a view to the subject of his magnum opus; but if these considerations be
absent and if the work has not been done in the university,
I cannot too strongly recommend the mastery of Gibbon's
"Decline and Fall" and Bryce's "Holy Roman Empire."
Gibbon merits close study because his is undoubtedly the
greatest history of modern times and because it is, in the

words of Carlyle, a splendid bridge from the old world to the new. He should be read in the edition of Bury, whose scholarly introduction gives a careful and just estimate of Gibbon and whose notes show the results of the latest researches. This edition does not include Guizot's and Milman's notes, which seem to an old-fashioned reader of Gibbon like myself worthy of attention, especially those on the famous Fifteenth and Sixteenth Chapters. Bryce's "Holy Roman Empire" is a fitting complement to Gibbon, and the intellectual possession of the two is an education in itself which will be useful in the study of any period of history that may be chosen.

The student who reads Gibbon will doubtless be influenced by his many tributes to Tacitus and will master the Roman historian. I shall let Macaulay furnish the warrant for a close study of Thucydides. "This day," Macaulay said, when in his thirty-fifth year, "I finished Thucydides after reading him with inexpressible interest and admiration. He is the greatest historian that ever lived." Again during the same year he wrote: "What are all the Roman historians to the great Athenian? I do assure you there is no prose composition in the world, not even the oration on the Crown, which I place so high as the seventh book of Thucydides. It is the *ne plus ultra* of human art. I was delighted to find in Gray's letters the other day this query to Wharton: 'The retreat from Syracuse — is or is it not the finest thing you ever read in your life?' . . . Most people read all the Greek they ever read before they are five and twenty. They never find time for such studies afterwards until they are in the decline of life; and then their knowledge of the language is in great measure lost, and cannot easily be recovered. Accordingly, almost all the ideas that people have of Greek literature are ideas formed while they were still very young. A young man, whatever his genius may be, is no judge of such a writer as Thucydides. I had no high opinion of him ten years ago. I have now been reading him with a mind accustomed to historical researches and to political affairs and I am astonished at my own former blindness and at his greatness." [1]

I have borrowed John Morley's words, speaking of Gibbon, Macaulay, and Carlyle as "three great born men of letters." Our student cannot therefore afford to miss a knowledge of Macaulay's History, but the Essays, except perhaps three or four of the latest ones, need not be read. In a preface to the authorized edition of the Essays, Macaulay wrote that he was "sensible of their defects," deemed them "imperfect pieces," and did not think that they were "worthy of a permanent place in English literature." For instance, his essay on Milton contained scarcely a paragraph which his matured judgment approved. Macaulay's peculiar faults are emphasized in his Essays and much of the harsh criticism which he has received comes from the glaring defects of these earlier productions. His history, however, is a great book, shows extensive research, a sane method and an excellent power of narration; and when he is a partisan, he is so honest and transparent that the effect of his partiality is neither enduring nor mischievous.

I must say further to the student: read either Carlyle's "French Revolution" or his "Frederick the Great," I care not which, although it is well worth one's while to read both. If your friends who maintain that history is a science convince you that the "French Revolution" is not history, as perhaps they may, read it as a narrative poem. Truly Carlyle spoke rather like a poet than a historian when he wrote to his wife (in his forty-first

[1] Trevelyan, I, 379, 387, 409.

year): "A hundred pages more and this cursed book is flung out of me. I mean to write with force of fire till that consummation; above all with the speed of fire. . . . It all stands pretty fair in my head, nor do I mean to investigate much more about it, but to splash down what I know in large masses of colors, that it may look like a smoke-and-flame conflagration in the distance, which it is." [1] It was Carlyle's custom to work all of the morning and take a solitary walk in Hyde Park in the afternoon, when looking upon the gay scene, the display of wealth and fashion, "seeing," as he said, "all the carriages dash hither and thither and so many human bipeds cheerily hurrying along," he said to himself: "There you go, brothers, in your gilt carriages and prosperities, better or worse, and make an extreme bother and confusion, the devil very largely in it. . . . Not one of you could do what I am doing, and it concerns you too, if you did but know it." [2] When the book was done he wrote to his brother, "It is a wild, savage book, itself a kind of French Revolution." [3] From its somewhat obscure style it requires a slow perusal and careful study, but this serves all the more to fix it in the memory causing it to remain an abiding influence.

There are eight volumes of "Frederick the Great," containing, according to Barrett Wendell's computation, over one million words; and this eighteenth-century tale, with its large number of great and little characters, its "mass of living facts" impressed Wendell chiefly with its unity. "Whatever else Carlyle was," he wrote, "the unity of this enormous book proves him, when he chose to be, a Titanic artist." [4] Only those who have striven for unity in a narrative can appreciate the tribute contained in these words. It was a

[1] Froude, III, 64, 65. [2] Ibid., II, 385; III, 59.
[3] Ibid., III, 73. [4] English Composition, 158.

struggle, too, for Carlyle. Fifty-six years old when he conceived the idea of Frederick, his nervousness and irritability were a constant torment to himself and his devoted wife. Many entries in his journal tell of his "dismal continual wrestle with Friedrich," [1] perhaps the most characteristic of which is this: "My Frederick looks as if it would never take shape in me; in fact the problem is to burn away the immense dungheap of the eighteenth century, with its ghastly cants, foul, blind sensualities, cruelties, and *inanity* now fallen *putrid*, rotting inevitably towards annihilation; to destroy and extinguish all that, having got to know it, and to know that it must be rejected for evermore; after which the perennial portion, pretty much Friedrich and Voltaire so far as I can see, may remain conspicuous and capable of being delineated." [2]

The student, who has become acquainted with the works of Gibbon, Macaulay, and Carlyle, will wish to know something of the men themselves and this curiosity may be easily and delightfully gratified. The autobiographies of Gibbon, the Life of Macaulay by Sir George Trevelyan, the History of Carlyle's Life by Froude, present the personality of these historians in a vivid manner. Gibbon has himself told of all his own faults and Froude has omitted none of Carlyle's, so that these two books are useful aids in a study of human nature, in which respect they are real adjuncts of Boswell's Johnson. Gibbon, Carlyle, and Macaulay had an insatiable love of reading; in their solitary hours they were seldom without books in their hands. Valuable instruction may be derived from a study of their lives from their suggestions of books, helpful in the development of a historian. They knew how to employ their odd moments, and Gibbon and Macaulay were adepts in the art of desultory reading. Sainte-

---

[1] Letters of Jane Carlyle, II, 31.   [2] Froude's Carlyle, IV, 125.

Beuve makes a plea for desultory reading in instancing Tocqueville's lack of it, so that he failed to illustrate and animate his pages with its fruits, the result being, in the long run, great monotony.[1] As a relief to the tired brain, without a complete loss of time, the reading at hazard, even browsing in a library, has its place in the equipment of a historian.

One of the most striking examples of self-education in literature is Carlyle's seven years, from the age of thirty-two to thirty-nine, passed at Craigenputtock where his native inclination was enforced by his physical surroundings. Craigenputtock, wrote Froude, is "the dreariest spot in all the British dominions. The nearest cottage is more than a mile from it; the elevation, 700 feet above the sea, stunts the trees and limits the garden produce to the hardiest vegetables. The house is gaunt and hungry-looking." [2] The place realized Tennyson's words, "O, the dreary, dreary moorland." Here Carlyle read books, gave himself over to silent meditation, and wrote for his bread, although a man who possessed an adequate income could not have been more independent in thought than he was, or more averse to writing to the order of editors of reviews and magazines. With no outside distractions, books were his companions as well as his friends. As you read Froude's intimate biography, it comes upon you, as you consider Carlyle's life in London, what a tremendous intellectual stride he had made while living in this dreary solitude of Craigenputtock. It was there that he continued his development under the intellectual influence of Goethe, wrote " Sartor Resartus " and conceived the idea of writing the story of the French Revolution. Those seven years, as you trace their influence during the rest of his life, will ever be a tribute to the concentrated, bookish labors of bookish men.

[1] Causeries du Lundi, XV, 95.   [2] Froude, II, 19.

It is often said that some practical experience in life is necessary for the training of a historian; that only thus can he arrive at a knowledge of human nature and become a judge of character; that, while the theory is occasionally advanced that history is a series of movements which may be described without taking individuals into account, as a matter of fact, one cannot go far on this hypothesis without running up against the truth that movements have motors and the motors are men. Hence we are to believe the dictum that the historian needs that knowledge of men which is to be obtained only by practical dealings with them. It is true that Gibbon's service in the Hampshire militia and his membership in the House of Commons were of benefit to the historian of the Roman Empire. Grote's business life, Macaulay's administrative work in India, and the parliamentary experience of both were undoubtedly of value to their work as historians, but there are excellent historians who have never had any such training. Carlyle is an example, and Samuel R. Gardiner is another. Curiously enough, Gardiner, who was a pure product of the university and the library, has expressed sounder judgments on many of the prominent men of the seventeenth century than Macaulay. I am not aware that there is in historical literature any other such striking contrast as this, for it is difficult to draw the line closely between the historian and the man of affairs, but Gardiner's example is strengthened in other historians' lives sufficiently to warrant the statement that the historian need not be a man of the world. Books are written by men and treat of the thoughts and actions of men and a good study may be made of human character without going beyond the walls of a library.

Drawing upon my individual experience again I feel that the two authors who have helped me most in this study of human character are Shakespeare and Homer. I do not mean that in the modern world we meet Hamlet, Iago, Macbeth, and Shylock, but when we perceive "the native hue of resolution sicklied o'er with the pale cast of thought," when we come in contact with the treachery of a seeming friend, with unholy ambition and insensate greed, we are better able to interpret them on the page of history from having grasped the lessons of Shakespeare to mankind. A constant reading of Shakespeare will show us unchanging passions and feelings; and we need not make literal contrasts, as did the British matron who remarked of "Antony and Cleopatra" that it was "so unlike the home life of our beloved queen." Bernard Shaw, who has said much in detraction of Shakespeare, writes in one of his admiring moods, "that the imaginary scenes and people he has created become more real to us than our actual life — at least until our knowledge and grip of actual life begins to deepen and glow beyond the common. When I was twenty," Shaw continues, "I knew everybody in Shakespeare from Hamlet to Abhorson, much more intimately than I knew my living contemporaries; and to this day, if the name of Pistol or Polonius catches my eye in a newspaper, I turn to the passage with curiosity." [1]

Homer's character of Ulysses is a link between the ancient and the modern world. One feels that Ulysses would be at home in the twentieth century and would adapt himself to the conditions of modern political life. Perhaps, indeed, he would have preferred to his militant age our industrial one where prizes are often won by craft and persuasive eloquence rather than by strength of arm. The story of Ulysses is a signal lesson in the study of human character, and receives a luminous commentary in Shakespeare's adaptation of it.

[1] Dramatic Opinions, II, 53.

The advice which Ulysses gives to Achilles[1] is a piece of worldly wisdom and may well be acted on by those who desire advancement in life and are little scrupulous in regard to means. The first part of Goethe's "Faust" is another book which has profoundly affected my view of life. I read it first when seventeen years old and have continually re-read it; and, while I fail to comprehend it wholly, and, although it does not give me the same kind of knowledge of human character that I derive from Shakespeare's plays, I carry away from it abiding impressions from the contact that it affords with one of the greatest of human minds.

All this counsel of mine, as to the reading of the embryo historian is, of course, merely supplementary, and does not pretend to be exhaustive. I am assuming that during his undergraduate and graduate course the student has been advised to read, either wholly or in part, most of the English, German, and French scientific historians of the past fifty years, and that he has become acquainted in a greater or less degree with all the eminent American historians. My own experience has been that a thorough knowledge of one book of an author is better than a superficial acquaintance with all of his works. The only book of Francis Parkman's which I have read is his "Montcalm and Wolfe," parts of which I have gone over again and again. One chapter, pervaded with the scenery of the place, I have read on Lake George, three others more than once at Quebec, and I feel that I know Parkman's method as well as if I had skimmed all his volumes. But I believe I was careful in my selection, for in his own estimation, and in that of the general public, "Montcalm and Wolfe" is his best work. So with Motley,

[1] " Time hath, my lord, a wallet at his back
Wherein he puts alms for oblivion,
A great-sized monster of ingratitudes:" etc.

I have read nothing but the "Dutch Republic," but that I have read through twice carefully. I will not say that it is the most accurate of his works, but it is probably the most interesting and shows his graphic and dashing style at its best. An admirer of Stubbs told me that his "Lectures and Addresses on Mediæval and Modern History" would give me a good idea of his scholarship and literary manner and that I need not tackle his magnum opus. But those lectures gave me a taste for more and, undeterred by the remark of still another admirer that nobody ever read his "Constitutional History" through, I did read one volume with interest and profit, and I hope at some future time to read the other two. On the other hand, I have read everything that Samuel R. Gardiner has written except "What Gunpowder Plot Was." Readers differ. There are fast readers who have the faculty of getting just what they want out of a book in a brief time and they retain the thing which they have sought. Assuredly I envy men that power. For myself, I have never found any royal road to learning, have been a slow reader, and needed a re-reading, sometimes more than one, to acquire any degree of mastery of a book. Macaulay used to read his favorite Greek and Latin classics over and over again and presumably always with care, but modern books he turned off with extraordinary speed. Of Buckle's large volume of the "History of Civilization" Macaulay wrote in his journal: "I read Buckle's book all day, and got to the end, skipping, of course. A man of talent and of a good deal of reading, but paradoxical and incoherent." [1] John Fiske, I believe, was a slow reader, but he had such a remarkable power of concentration that what he read once was his own. Of this I can give a notable instance. At a meeting in Boston a number of years ago of the

_____
[1] Trevelyan, II, 388, n.

Military Historical Society of Massachusetts, Colonel William R. Livermore read a learned and interesting paper on Napoleon's Campaigns in Northern Italy, and a few men, among whom were Fiske and John C. Ropes, remained after supper to discuss the paper. The discussion went well into details and was technical. Fiske had as much to say as any one and met the military critics on their own ground, holding his own in this interchange of expert opinions. As we returned to Cambridge together, I expressed my surprise at his wide technical knowledge. "It is all due to one book," he said. "A few summers ago I had occasion to read Sir Edward Hamley's 'Operations of War' and for some reason or other everything in it seemed to sink into my mind and to be there retained, ready for use, as was the case to-night with his references to the Northern Italian campaigns."

Outside of ordinary historical reading, a book occurs to me which is well worth a historian's mastery. I am assuming that our hypothetical student has read Goethe's "Faust," "Werther," and "Wilhelm Meister," and desires to know something of the personality of this great writer. He should, therefore, read Eckermann's "Conversations with Goethe," in which he will find a body of profitable literary criticism, given out in a familiar way by the most celebrated man then living. The talks began when he was seventy-three and continued until near his death, ten years later; they reveal his maturity of judgment. Greek, Roman, German, English, French, Spanish, and Italian authors are taken up from time to time and discussed with clearness and appreciation, running sometimes to enthusiasm. As a guide to the best reading extant up to 1832 I know nothing better. Eckermann is inferior as a biographer to Boswell, and his book is neither so interesting nor amusing; but Goethe was far greater than Johnson, and his talk is cosmopolitan and broad, while Johnson's is apt to be insular and narrow. "One should not study contemporaries and competitors," Goethe said, "but the great men of antiquity, whose works have for centuries received equal homage and consideration. . . . Let us study Molière, let us study Shakespeare, but above all things, the old Greeks and always the Greeks." [1] Here is an opinion I like to dwell upon: "He who will work aright must never rail, must not trouble himself at all about what is ill done, but only to do well himself. For the great point is, not to pull down, but to build up and in this humanity finds pure joy." [2] It is well worth our while to listen to a man so great as to be free from envy and jealousy, but this was a lesson Carlyle could not learn from his revered master. It is undoubtedly his broad mind in connection with his wide knowledge which induced Sainte-Beuve to write that Goethe is "the greatest of modern critics and of critics of all time." [3]

All of the conversations did not run upon literature and writers. Although Goethe never visited either Paris or London, and resided for a good part of his life in the little city of Weimar, he kept abreast of the world's progress through books, newspapers, and conversations with visiting strangers. No statesman or man of business could have had a wider outlook than Goethe, when on February 21, 1827, he thus spoke: "I should wish to see England in possession of a canal through the Isthmus of Suez. . . . And it may be foreseen that the United States, with its decided predilection to the West will, in thirty or forty years, have occupied and peopled the large tract of land beyond the Rocky Mountains. It may furthermore be foreseen that along the whole coast of the Pacific Ocean where nature has already formed the most capacious and secure harbors,

[1] Eng. trans., 236.   [2] *Ibid.*, 115.   [3] Nouveaux Lundis, III, 265.

important commercial towns will gradually arise, for the furtherance of a great intercourse between China and the East Indies and the United States. In such a case, it would not only be desirable, but almost necessary, that a more rapid communication should be maintained between the eastern and western shores of North America, both by merchant ships and men-of-war than has hitherto been possible with the tedious, disagreeable, and expensive voyage around Cape Horn. . . . It is absolutely indispensable for the United States to effect a passage from the Gulf of Mexico to the Pacific Ocean, and I am certain that they will do it. Would that I might live to see it!" [1]

"Eckermann's book," wrote Sainte-Beuve, "is the best biography of Goethe; that of Lewes, for the facts; that of Eckermann, for the portrait from the inside and the physiognomy. The soul of a great man breathes in it." [2]

I have had frequent occasion to speak of Sainte-Beuve and I cannot recommend our student too strongly to read from time to time some of his critical essays. His best work is contained in the fifteen volumes of "Causeries du Lundi" and in the thirteen volumes of "Nouveaux Lundis" which were articles written for the daily newspapers, the *Constitutionnel*, the *Moniteur*, and the *Temps*, when, between the ages of forty-five and sixty-five, he was at the maturity of his powers. Considering the very high quality of the work, the quantity is enormous, and makes us call to mind the remark of Goethe that "genius and fecundity are very closely allied." Excluding Goethe, we may safely, I think, call Sainte-Beuve the greatest of modern critics, and there is enough of resemblance between historical and literary criticism to warrant a study by the historian of these remarkable essays. "The root of everything in his criticism," wrote

---

[1] Eng. trans., 222.   [2] Nouveaux Lundis, III, 328.

Matthew Arnold, "is his single-hearted devotion to truth. What he called 'fictions' in literature, in politics, in religion, were not allowed to influence him." And Sainte-Beuve himself has said, "I am accustomed incessantly to call my judgments in question anew and to recast my opinions the moment I suspect them to be without validity."[1] The writer who conforms to such a high standard is an excellent guide for the historian and no one who has made a study of these Causeries can help feeling their spirit of candor and being inspired to the attempt to realize so high an ideal.

Sainte-Beuve's essays deal almost entirely with French literature and history, which were the subjects he knew best. It is very desirable for us Anglo-Saxons to broaden our minds and soften our prejudices by excursions outside of our own literature and history, and with Goethe for our guide in Germany, we can do no better than to accept Sainte-Beuve for France. Brunetière wrote that the four literary men of France in the nineteenth century who had exercised the most profound influence were Sainte-Beuve, Balzac, Victor Hugo, and Auguste Comte.[2] I have already recommended Balzac, who portrays the life of the nineteenth century; and Sainte-Beuve, in developing the thought of the same period, gives us a history of French literature and society. Moreover, his volumes are valuable to one who is studying human character by the means of books. "Sainte-Beuve had," wrote Henry James, "two passions which are commonly assumed to exclude each other, the passion for scholarship and the passion for life. He valued life and literature equally for the light they threw on each other; to his mind, one implied the other; he was unable to conceive of them apart."[3]

Supposing the student to have devoted five years to this

<hr/>

[1] Enc. Brit.   [2] Balzac, 309.   [3] Brander Matthews, *Cent. Mag.*, 1901.

general preparation and to have arrived at the age of thirty, which Motley, in similar advice to an aspiring historian, fixed as the earliest age at which one should devote himself to his special work, he is ready to choose a period and write a history, if indeed his period has not already suggested itself during his years of general preparation. At all events it is doubtless that his own predilection will fix his country and epoch and the only counsel I have to offer is to select an interesting period. As to this, opinions will differ; but I would say for example that the attractive parts of German history are the Reformation, the Thirty Years' War, the epoch of Frederick the Great, and the unification of Germany which we have witnessed in our own day. The French Revolution is to me the most striking period in modern annals, whilst the history of the Directory is dull, relieved only by the exploits of Napoleon; but when Napoleon becomes the chief officer of state, interest revives and we follow with unflagging attention the story of this master of men, for which there is a superabundance of material, in striking contrast with the little that is known about his Titanic predecessors, Alexander and Cæsar, in the accounts of whose careers conjecture must so frequently come to the aid of facts to construct a continuous story. The Restoration and the reign of Louis Philippe would for me be dull periods were they not illumined by the novels of Balzac; but from the Revolution of 1848 to the fall of the Second Empire and the Commune, a wonderful drama was enacted. In our own history the Revolutionary War, the framing of the Constitution, and Washington's administrations seem to me replete with interest which is somewhat lacking for the period between Washington and the slavery conflict. "As to special history," wrote Motley to the aspiring historian, "I should be inclined rather to direct your attention to that of the last three and a half centuries."[1] Discussing the subject before the advanced historical students of Harvard a number of years ago, I gave an extension to Motley's counsel by saying that ancient history had better be left to the Germans. I was fresh from reading Holm's History of Greece and was impressed with his vast learning, elaboration of detail, and exhaustive treatment of every subject which seemed to me to require a steady application and patience, hardly consonant with the American character. But within the past five years Ferrero, an Italian, has demonstrated that others besides Germans are equal to the work by writing an interesting history of Rome, which intelligent men and scholars discuss in the same breath with Mommsen's. Courageously adopting the title "Grandeur and Decadence of Rome" which suggests that of Montesquieu, Ferrero has gleaned the well-reaped field from the appearance of Julius Cæsar to the reign of Augustus[2] in a manner to attract the attention of the reading public in Italy, France, England, and the United States. There is no reason why an American should not have done the same. "All history is public property," wrote Motley in the letter previously referred to. "All history may be rewritten and it is impossible that with exhaustive research and deep reflection you should not be able to produce something new and valuable on almost any subject."[3]

After the student has chosen his period I have little advice to offer him beyond what I have previously given in two formal addresses before the American Historical Association, but a few additional words may be useful. You will evolve your own method by practice and by comparison with the methods of other historians. "Follow your own star."

[1] Letter of April 4, 1864, *Harper's Mag.*, June, 1889.
[2] I speak of the first four volumes.   [3] *L.c.*

If you feel impelled to praise or blame as do the older historians, if it is forced upon you that your subject demands such treatment, proceed fearlessly, so that you do nothing for effect, so that you do not sacrifice the least particle of truth for a telling statement. If, however, you fall naturally into the rigorously judicial method of Gardiner you may feel your position sure. It is well, as the scientific historians warn you, to be suspicious of interesting things, but, on the other hand, every interesting incident is not necessarily untrue. If you have made a conscientious search for historical material and use it with scrupulous honesty, have no fear that you will transgress any reasonable canon of historical writing.

An obvious question to be put to a historian is, What plan do you follow in making notes of your reading? Langlois, an experienced teacher and tried scholar, in his introduction to the "Study of History," condemns the natural impulse to set them down in notebooks in the order in which one's authorities are studied, and says, "Every one admits nowadays that it is advisable to collect materials on separate cards or slips of paper,"[1] arranging them by a systematic classification of subjects. This is a case in point where writers will, I think, learn best from their own experience. I have made my notes mainly in notebooks on the plan which Langlois condemns, but by colored pencil-marks of emphasis and summary, I keep before me the prominent facts which I wish to combine; and I have found this, on the whole, better than the card system. For I have aimed to study my authorities in a logical succession. First I go over the period in some general history, if one is to be had; then I read very carefully my original authorities in the order of their estimated importance, making

[1] p. 103.

copious excerpts. Afterwards I skim my second-hand materials. Now I maintain that it is logical and natural to have the extracts before me in the order of my study. When unusually careful and critical treatment has been required, I have drawn off my memoranda from the note-books to cards, classifying them according to subjects. Such a method enables me to digest thoroughly my materials, but in the main I find that a frequent re-perusal of my notes answers fully as well and is an economy of time.

Carlyle, in answer to an inquiry regarding his own procedure, has gone to the heart of the matter. "I go into the business," he said, "with all the intelligence, patience, silence, and other gifts and virtues that I have . . . and on the whole try to keep the whole matter simmering in the *living* mind and memory rather than laid up in paper bundles or otherwise laid up in the inert way. For this certainly turns out to be a truth; only what you at last *have living* in your own memory and heart is worth putting down to be printed; this alone has much chance to get into the living heart and memory of other men. And here indeed, I believe, is the essence of all the rules I have ever been able to devise for myself. I have tried various schemes of arrangement and artificial helps to remembrance," but the gist of the matter is, "to keep the thing you are elaborating as much as possible actually *in* your own living mind; in order that this same mind, as much awake as possible, may have a chance to make something of it!" [1]

The objection may be made to my discourse that I have considered our student as possessing the purse of Fortunatus and have lost sight of Herbert Spencer's doctrine that a very important part of education is to fit a man to acquire the means of living. I may reply that there are a number

[1] New Letters, II, 11.

of Harvard students who will not have to work for their bread and whose parents would be glad to have them follow the course that I have recommended. It is not too much to hope, therefore, that among these there are, to use Huxley's words, "glorious sports of nature" who will not be "corrupted by luxury" but will become industrious historians. To others who are not so fortunately situated, I cannot recommend the profession of historian as a means of gaining a livelihood. Bancroft and Parkman, who had a good deal of popularity, spent more money in the collection and copying of documents than they ever received as income from their histories. A young friend of mine, at the outset of his career and with his living in part to be earned, went for advice to Carl Schurz, who was very fond of him. "What is your aim?" asked Mr. Schurz. "I purpose being a historian," was the reply. "Aha!" laughed Schurz, "you are adopting an aristocratic profession, one which requires a rent-roll." Every aspiring historian has, I suppose, dreamed of that check of £20,000, which Macaulay received as royalty on his history for its sale during the year 1856,[1] but no such dream has since been realized.

Teaching and writing are allied pursuits. And the teacher helps the writer, especially in history, through the necessary elaboration and digestion of materials. Much excellent history is given to the world by college professors. Law and medicine are too exacting professions with too large a literature of their own to leave any leisure for historical investigation. If one has the opportunity to get a good start, or, in the talk of the day, the right sort of a "pull," I can recommend business as a means of gaining a competence which shall enable one to devote one's whole time to a favorite pursuit. Grote was a banker until he reached

[1] Life, II, 345.

the age of forty-nine when he retired from the banking house and began the composition of the first volume of his history. Henry C. Lea was in the active publishing business until he was fifty-five, and as I have already frequently referred to my own personal experience, I may add that I was immersed in business between the ages of twenty-two and thirty-seven. After three years of general and special preparation I began my writing at forty. The business man has many free evenings and many journeys by rail, as well as a summer vacation, when devotion to a line of study may constitute a valuable recreation. Much may be done in odd hours in the way of preparation for historical work, and a business life is an excellent school for the study of human character.

NEWSPAPERS AS HISTORICAL SOURCES

A paper read before the American Historical Association in Washington on December 29, 1908; printed in the *Atlantic Monthly*, May, 1909.

NEWSPAPERS AS HISTORICAL SOURCES

THE impulse of an American writer in justifying the use of newspapers as historical materials is to adopt an apologetic tone. It is somewhat curious that such should be the case, for newspapers satisfy so many canons of historical evidence. They are contemporary, and, being written without knowledge of the end, cannot bolster any cause without making a plain showing of their intent. Their object is the relation of daily events; and if their relation is colored by honest or dishonest partisanship, this is easily discernible by the critic from the internal evidence and from an easily acquired knowledge of a few external facts. As the journals themselves say, their aim is to print the news; and much of the news is present politics. Moreover, the newspaper itself, its news and editorial columns, its advertisements, is a graphic picture of society.

When Aulard, in his illuminating criticism of Taine, writes that the journals are a very important source of the history of the French Revolution, provided they are revised and checked by one another, the statement seems in accordance with the canons of historical writing; and when he blames Taine for using two journals only and neglecting ten others which he names, the impression on the mind is the same as if Taine were charged with the neglect of evidence of another class. One would hardly attempt to justify Taine by declaring that all journals are inaccurate, partisan, and dishonest, and that the omission was a merit, not a defect. Leaving out of account the greater size and diffuseness of the modern journal, the dictum of Aulard would seem to apply to any period of history.

Why is it then that some American students fall consciously or unconsciously into an apologetic tone when they attempt to justify the use of newspapers as historical sources? I suppose it is because of the attitude of cultivated society to the newspaper of to-day. Society calls the ordinary newspaper sensational and unreliable; and, if neither, its accounts are so diffuse and badly proportioned as to weary the seeker after the facts of any given transaction. Despite the disfavor into which the American newspaper has fallen in certain circles, I suspect that it has only exaggerated these defects, and that the journals of different democracies have more resemblances than diversities. The newspaper that caters to the "masses" will never suit the "classes," and the necessity for a large circulation induces it to furnish the sheet which the greatest number of readers desire.

But this does not concern the historian. He does not make his materials. He has to take them as they are. It would undoubtedly render his task easier if all men spoke and wrote everywhere with accuracy and sincerity; but his work would lose much of its interest. Take the newspaper for what it is, a hasty gatherer of facts, a hurried commentator on the same, and it may well constitute a part of historical evidence.

When, in 1887, I began the critical study of the History of the United States from 1850 to 1860, I was struck with the paucity of material which would serve the purpose of an animated narrative. The main facts were to be had in the state papers, the Statutes, the *Congressional Globe* and documents, the records of national conventions and platforms, and the tabulated results of elections. But there was much less private correspondence than is available for the early history of our country; and, compared with the period of

the Civil War and later, a scarcity of biographies and reminiscences, containing personal letters of high historical
value. Since I wrote my first two volumes, much new matter concerning the decade of 1850 to 1860 has been published.
The work of the American Historical Association, and of
many historical societies, the monographs of advanced university students, have thrown light upon this, as they
have upon other periods, with the result that future delvers
in this field can hardly be so much struck with the paucity
of material as I was twenty-one years ago.

Boy though I was during the decade of 1850 to 1860, I had
a vivid remembrance of the part that the newspaper played
in politics, and the thought came to me that the best way
to arrive at the spirit of the times was to steep my mind in
journalistic material; that there was the secret of living
over again that decade, as the Abolitionist, the Republican,
the Whig, and the Democrat had actually lived in it. In
the critical use of such sources, I was helped by the example
of von Holst, who employed them freely in his volumes
covering the same period, and by the counsel and collaboration of my friend Edward G. Bourne, whose training was
in the modern school. For whatever training I had beyond
that of self came from the mastery, under the guidance of
teachers, of certain general historians belonging to an epoch
when power of expression was as much studied as the collecting and sifting of evidence.

While considering my materials, I was struck with a
statement cited by Herbert Spencer as an illustration in his
"Philosophy of Style": "A modern newspaper statement,
though probably true, if quoted in a book as testimony,
would be laughed at; but the letter of a court gossip, if
written some centuries ago, is thought good historical evidence." At about the same time, I noticed that Motley

used as one of his main authorities for the battle of St. Quentin the manuscript of an anonymous writer. From these two circumstances, it was a logical reflection that some historians might make an exaggerated estimate of the value of manuscript material because it reposed in dusty archives and could be utilized only by severe labor and long patience; and that, imbued with this idea, other historians for other periods might neglect the newspaper because of its ready accessibility.

These several considerations justified a belief, arrived at from my preliminary survey of the field, that the use of newspapers as sources for the decade of 1850 to 1860 was desirable. At each step of my pretty thorough study of them, I became more and more convinced that I was on the right track. I found facts in them which I could have found nowhere else. The public meeting is a great factor in the political life of this decade, and is most fully and graphically reported in the press. The newspaper, too, was a vehicle for personal accounts of a quasi-confidential nature, of which I can give a significant example. In an investigation that Edward Bourne made for me during the summer of 1889, he came across in the *Boston Courier* an inside account of the Whig convention of 1852, showing, more conclusively than I have seen elsewhere, the reason of the failure to unite the conservative Whigs, who were apparently in a majority, on Webster. From collateral evidence we were convinced that it was written by a Massachusetts delegate; and the *Springfield Republican*, which copied the account, furnished a confirmation of it. It was an interesting story, and I incorporated it in my narrative.

I am well aware that Dr. Dryasdust may ask, What of it? The report of the convention shows that Webster received a very small vote and that Scott was nominated. Why waste time and words over the "might have been"? I can plead only the human interest in the great Daniel Webster ardently desiring that nomination, Rufus Choate advocating it in sublime oratory, the two antislavery delegates from Massachusetts refusing their votes for Webster, thus preventing a unanimous Massachusetts, and the delegates from Maine, among whom was Webster's godson William P. Fessenden, coldly refusing their much-needed aid.

General Scott, having received the nomination, made a stumping tour in the autumn through some of the Western States. No accurate account of it is possible without the newspapers, yet it was esteemed a factor in his overwhelming defeat, and the story of it is well worth preserving as data for a discussion of the question, Is it wise for a presidential candidate to make a stumping tour during his electoral campaign?

The story of the formation of the Republican party, and the rise of the Know-nothings, may possibly be written without recourse to the newspapers, but thorough steeping in such material cannot fail to add to the animation and accuracy of the story. In detailed history and biographical books, dates, through mistakes of the writer or printer, are frequently wrong; and when the date was an affair of supreme importance, I have sometimes found a doubt resolved by a reference to the newspaper, which, from its strictly contemporary character, cannot in such a matter lead one astray.

I found the newspapers of value in the correction of logical assumptions, which frequently appear in American historical and biographical books, especially in those written by men who bore a part in public affairs. By a logical assumption, I mean the statement of a seemingly necessary consequence which apparently ought to follow some well-attested fact or condition. A striking instance of this occurred during the political campaign of 1856, when "bleeding Kansas" was a thrilling catchword used by the Republicans, whose candidate for president was Frémont. In a year and a half seven free-state men had been killed in Kansas by the border ruffians, and these outrages, thoroughly ventilated, made excellent campaign ammunition. But the Democrats had a *tu quoque* argument which ought to have done much towards eliminating this question from the canvass.

On the night of May 24, 1856, five pro-slavery men, living on the Pottawatomie Creek, were deliberately and foully murdered by John Brown and seven of his disciples; and, while this massacre caused profound excitement in Kansas and Missouri, it seems to have had no influence east of the Mississippi River, although the fact was well attested. A Kansas journalist of 1856, writing in 1879, made this logical assumption: "The opposition press both North and South took up the damning tale . . . of that midnight butchery on the Pottawatomie. . . . Whole columns of leaders from week to week, with startling headlines, liberally distributed capitals, and frightful exclamation points, filled all the newspapers." And it was his opinion that, had it not been for this massacre, Frémont would have been elected.

But I could not discover that the massacre had any influence on the voters in the pivotal states. I examined, or had examined, the files of the *New York Journal of Commerce, New York Herald, Philadelphia Pennsylvanian, Washington Union*, and *Cleveland Plain Dealer*, all Democratic papers except the *New York Herald*, and I was struck with the fact that substantially no use was made of the massacre as a campaign argument. Yet could anything have been more logical than the assumption that the Democrats would have been equal to their opportunity and spread far and wide such a story? The facts in the case show therefore that cause and effect in actual American history are not always the same as the statesman may conceive them in his cabinet or the historian in his study.

In the newspapers of 1850 to 1860 many speeches, and many public, and some private, letters of conspicuous public men are printed; these are valuable material for the history of the decade, and their use is in entire accordance with modern historical canons.

I have so far considered the press in its character of a register of facts; but it has a further use for historical purposes, since it is both a representative and guide of public sentiment. Kinglake shows that the *Times* was the potent influence which induced England to invade the Crimea; Bismarck said in 1877 that the press "was the cause of the last three wars"; Lord Cromer writes, "The people of England as represented by the press insisted on sending General Gordon to the Soudan, and accordingly to the Soudan he was sent;" and it is current talk that the yellow journals brought on the Spanish-American War. Giving these statements due weight, can a historian be justified in neglecting the important influence of the press on public opinion?

As reflecting and leading popular sentiment during the decade of 1850 to 1860, the newspapers of the Northern States were potent. I own that many times one needs no further index to public sentiment than our frequent elections, but in 1854 conditions were peculiar. The repeal of the Missouri Compromise had outraged the North and indicated that a new party must be formed to resist the extension of slavery. In the disorganization of the Democratic party, and the effacement of the Whig, nowhere may the new movement so well be traced as in the news and editorial columns of the newspapers, and in the speeches of the Northern leaders, many of these indeed being printed nowhere else than in the press. What journals and what journalists there were in those days! Greeley and Dana of the *New York Tribune;* Bryant and Bigelow of the *Evening Post;* Raymond of the *Times;* Webb of the *Courier and Enquirer;* Bowles of the *Springfield Republican;* Thurlow Weed of the *Albany Journal;* Schouler of the *Cincinnati Gazette,* — all inspired by their opposition to the spread of slavery, wrote with vigor and enthusiasm, representing the ideas of men who had burning thoughts without power of expression, and guiding others who needed the constant iteration of positive opinions to determine their political action.

The main and cross currents which resulted in the formation of the compact Republican party of 1856 have their principal record in the press, and from it, directly or indirectly, must the story be told. Unquestionably the newspapers had greater influence than in an ordinary time, because the question was a moral one and could be concretely put. Was slavery right or wrong? If wrong, should not its extension be stopped? That was the issue, and all the arguments, constitutional and social, turned on that point.

The greatest single journalistic influence was the *New York Weekly Tribune* which had in 1854 a circulation of 112,000, and many times that number of readers. These readers were of the thorough kind, reading all the news, all the printed speeches and addresses, and all the editorials, and pondering as they read. The questions were discussed in their family circles and with their neighbors, and, as differences arose, the *Tribune,* always at hand, was consulted and re-read. There being few popular magazines during this decade, the weekly newspaper, in some degree, took their place; and, through this medium, Greeley and his able coadjutors spoke to the people of New York and of the West, where New England ideas predominated, with a power never before or since known in this country. When Motley was studying the old letters and documents of the sixteenth century in the archives of Brussels, he wrote: "It is something to read the real *bona fide* signs manual of such fellows as William of Orange, Count Egmont, Alexander Farnese, Philip the Second, Cardinal Granville and the rest of them. It gives a 'realizing sense,' as the Americans have it." I had somewhat of the same feeling as I turned over the pages of the bound volumes of the *Weekly Tribune,* reading the editorials and letters of Greeley, the articles of Dana and Hildreth. I could recall enough of the time to feel the influence of this political bible, as it was termed, and I can emphatically say that if you want to penetrate into the thoughts, feelings, and ground of decision of the 1,866,000 men who voted for Lincoln in 1860, you should study with care the *New York Weekly Tribune.*

One reason why the press was a better representative of opinion during the years from 1854 to 1860 than now is that there were few, if any, independent journals. The party man read his own newspaper and no other; in that, he found an expression of his own views. And the party newspaper in the main printed only the speeches and arguments of its own side. Greeley on one occasion was asked by John Russell Young, an associate, for permission to reprint a speech of Horatio Seymour in full as a matter of news. "Yes," Greeley said, "I will print Seymour's speech when the *World* will print those of our side."

Before the war, Charleston was one of the most interesting cities of the country. It was a small aristocratic community, with an air of refinement and distinction. The story of Athens proclaims that a large population is not necessary to exercise a powerful influence on the world; and, after the election of Lincoln in 1860, the 40,000 people of Charleston, or rather the few patricians who controlled its fate and that of South Carolina, attracted the attention of the whole country. The story of the secession movement of November and December, 1860, cannot be told with correctness and life without frequent references to the *Charleston Mercury* and the *Charleston Courier*. The *Mercury* especially was an index of opinion, and so vivid is its daily chronicle of events that the historian is able to put himself in the place of those ardent South Carolinians and understand their point of view.

For the history of the Civil War, newspapers are not so important. The other material is superabundant, and in choosing from the mass of it, the newspapers, so far as affairs at the North are concerned, need only be used in special cases, and rarely for matters of fact. The accounts of campaigns and battles, which filled so much of their space, may be ignored, as the best possible authorities for these are the one hundred and twenty-eight volumes of the United States government publication, the "Official Records of the Union and Confederate armies." The faithful study of the correspondence and the reports in these unique volumes is absolutely essential to a comprehension of the war; and it is a labor of love. When one thinks of the mass of manuscripts students of certain periods of European history have been obliged to read, the American historian is profoundly grateful to his government, that at a cost to itself of nearly three million dollars,[1] it has furnished him this priceless material in neatly printed volumes with excellent indexes. The serious student can generally procure these volumes

---

[1] $2,858,514, without including the pay of army officers detailed from time to time for duty in connection with the work. Official Records, 130, V.

gratis through the favor of his congressman; or, failing in this, may purchase the set at a moderate price, so that he is not obliged to go to a public library to consult them.

Next to manuscript material, the physical and mental labor of turning over and reading bound volumes of newspapers is the most severe, and I remember my feeling of relief at being able to divert my attention from what Edward L. Pierce called this back-breaking and eye-destroying labor, much of it in public libraries, to these convenient books in my own private library. A mass of other materials, notably Nicolay and Hay's contributions, military narratives, biographies, private correspondence, to say nothing of the Congressional publications, render the student fairly independent of the newspapers. But I did myself make, for certain periods, special researches among them to ascertain their influence on public sentiment; and I also found them very useful in my account of the New York draft riots of 1863. It is true the press did not accurately reflect the gloom and sickness of heart at the North after the battle of Chancellorsville, for the reason that many editors wrote for the purpose of keeping up the hopes of their readers. In sum, the student may congratulate himself that a continuous study of the Northern newspapers for the period of the Civil War is unnecessary, for their size and diffuseness are appalling.

But what I have said about the press of the North will not apply to that of the South. Though strenuous efforts have been made, with the diligent coöperation of Southern men, to secure the utmost possible amount of Confederate material for the "Official Records," it actually forms only about twenty-nine per cent of the whole matter. Other historical material is also less copious. For example, there is no record of the proceedings of the Confederate Congress, like the

Globe; there are no reports of committees, like that of the Committee on the Conduct of the War; and even the journal of the Congress was kept on loose memoranda, and not written up until after the close of the war. With the exception of this journal, which has been printed by our government, and the "Statutes at Large," our information of the work of the Confederate Congress comes from the newspapers and some books of biography and recollections. The case of the Southern States was peculiar, because they were so long cut off from intercourse with the outer world, owing to the efficient Federal blockade; and the newspaper in its local news, editorials, and advertisements, is important material for portraying life in the Confederacy during the Civil War. Fortunately for the student, the Southern newspaper was not the same voluminous issue as the Northern, and, if it had not been badly printed, its use would be attended with little difficulty. Owing to the scarcity of paper, many of the newspapers were gradually reduced in size, and in the end were printed on half-sheets, occasionally one on brown paper, and another on wall paper; even the white paper was frequently coarse, and this, with poor type, made the news-sheet itself a daily record of the waning fortunes of the Confederacy.

In the history of Reconstruction the historian may be to a large extent independent of the daily newspaper. For the work of reconstruction was done by Congress, and Congress had the full support of the Northern people, as was shown by the continuous large Republican majority which was maintained. The debates, the reports, and the acts of Congress are essential, and little else is required except whatever private correspondence may be accessible. Congress represented public sentiment of the North, and if one desires newspaper opinion, one may find it in many pithy expressions on the floor of the House or the Senate. For the congressman and the senator are industrious newspaper readers. They are apt to read some able New York journal which speaks for their party, and the congressman will read the daily and weekly newspapers of his district, and the senator the prominent ones of his state which belong to his party.

For the period which covered Reconstruction, from 1865 to 1877, I used the *Nation* to a large extent. Its bound volumes are convenient to handle in one's own library, and its summary of events is useful in itself, and as giving leads to the investigation of other material. Frequently its editorials have spoken for the sober sense of the people with amazing success. As a constant reader of the *Nation* since 1866, I have felt the fascination of Godkin, and have been consciously on guard against it. I tried not to be led away by his incisive statements and sometimes uncharitable judgments. But whatever may be thought of his bias, he had an honest mind, and was incapable of knowingly making a false statement; and this, with his other qualities, makes his journal excellent historical material. After considering with great care some friendly criticism, I can truly say that I have no apology to make for the extent to which I used the *Nation*.

Recurring now to the point with which I began this discussion, — that learned prejudice against employing newspapers as historical material, — I wish to add that, like all other evidence, they must be used with care and skepticism, as one good authority is undoubtedly better than a dozen poor ones. An anecdote I heard years ago has been useful to me in weighing different historical evidence. A Pennsylvania-Dutch justice of the peace in one of the interior townships of Ohio had a man arraigned before him for stealing a pig. One witness swore that he distinctly saw the theft committed; eight swore that they never saw the accused steal a pig, and the verdict was worthy of Dogberry. "I discharge the accused," said the justice. "The testimony of eight men is certainly worth more than the testimony of one."

Private and confidential correspondence is highly valuable historical material, for such utterances are less constrained and more sincere than public declarations; but all men cannot be rated alike. Some men have lied as freely in private letters as in public speeches; therefore the historian must get at the character of the man who has written the letter and the influences surrounding him; these factors must count in any satisfactory estimate of his accuracy and truth. The newspaper must be subjected to similar tests. For example, to test an article or public letter written by Greeley or Godkin, the general situation, the surrounding influences, and the individual bias must be taken into account, and, when allowance is made for these circumstances, as well as for the public character of the utterance, it may be used for historical evidence. For the history of the last half of the nineteenth century just such material — the material of the fourth estate — must be used. Neglect of it would be like neglect of the third estate in the history of France for the eighteenth century.

In the United States we have not, politically speaking, either the first or second estates, but we have the third and fourth estates with an intimate connection between the two. Lord Cromer said, when writing of the sending of Gordon to the Soudan, "Newspaper government has certain disadvantages;" and this he emphasized by quoting a wise remark of Sir George Cornewall Lewis, "Anonymous authorship places the public under the direction of guides who have no sense of personal responsibility." Nevertheless this newspaper government must be reckoned with. The duty of the historian is, not to decide if the newspapers are as good as they ought to be, but to measure their influence on the present, and to recognize their importance as an ample and contemporary record of the past.

SPEECH PREPARED FOR THE COMMENCEMENT DINNER AT HARVARD UNIVERSITY

June 26, 1901 (not delivered).

SPEECH PREPARED FOR THE COMMENCEMENT DINNER AT HARVARD UNIVERSITY

THANKING heartily the governing boards of Harvard College for the honor conferred upon me, I shall say, on this my first admission to the circle of the Harvard alumni, a word on the University as it appears to one whose work has lain outside of it. The spirit of the academy in general and especially of this University impels men to get to the bottom of things, to strive after exact knowledge; and this spirit permeates my own study of history in a remarkable degree. "The first of all Gospels is this," said Carlyle, "that a lie cannot endure forever." This is the gospel of historical students. A part of their work has been to expose popular fallacies, and to show up errors which have been made through partiality and misguided patriotism or because of incomplete investigation. Men of my age are obliged to unlearn much. The youthful student of history has a distinct advantage over us in that he begins with a correct knowledge of the main historical facts. He does not for example learn what we all used to learn — that in the year 1000 the appearance of a fiery comet caused a panic of terror to fall upon Christendom and gave rise to the belief that the end of the world was at hand. Nor is he taught that the followers of Peter the Hermit in the first crusade were a number of spiritually minded men and women of austere morality. It is to the University that we owe it that we are seeing things as they are in history, that the fables, the fallacies, and the exaggerations are disappearing from the books.

To regard the past with accuracy and truth is a preparation for envisaging the present in the same way. For this attitude towards the past and the present gained by college students of history, and for other reasons which it is not necessary here to detail, the man of University training has, other things being equal, this advantage over him who lacks it, that in life in the world he will get at things more certainly and state them more accurately.

"A university," said Lowell, "is a place where nothing useful is taught." By utility Lowell undoubtedly meant, to use the definition which Huxley puts into the average Englishman's mouth, "that by which we get pudding or praise or both." A natural reply to the statement of Lowell is that great numbers of fathers every year, at a pecuniary sacrifice, send their sons to college with the idea of fitting them better to earn their living, in obedience to the general sentiment of men of this country that there is a money value to college training. But the remark of Lowell suggests another object of the University which, to use the words of Huxley again, is "to catch the exceptional people, the glorious sports of nature, and turn them to account for the good of society." This appeals to those imbued with the spirit of the academy who frankly acknowledge, in the main, our inferiority in the scholarship, which produces great works of literature and science, to England, Germany, and France, and who with patriotic eagerness wish that we may reach the height attained in the older countries. To recur to my own study again, should we produce a historian or historical writer the equal of Gibbon, Mommsen, Carlyle, or Macaulay there would be a feeling of pride in our historical genius which would make itself felt at every academical and historical gathering. We have something of that sentiment in regard to Francis Parkman, our most original

historian. But it may be that the historical field of Parkman is too narrow to awaken a world-wide interest and I
suspect that the American who will be recognized as the
equal of Gibbon, Mommsen, Carlyle, or Macaulay must secure that recognition by writing of some period of European
history better than the Englishman, German, or Frenchman
has written of it. He must do it not only in the way of
scientific history, in which in his field Henry Charles Lea has
won so much honor for himself and his country, but he
must bring to bear on his history that quality which
has made the historical writings of Gibbon, Carlyle, and
Macaulay literature.

EDWARD GIBBON

Lecture read at Harvard University, April 6, 1908, and printed in *Scribner's Magazine*, June, 1909.

EDWARD GIBBON

No English or American lover of history visits Rome without bending reverent footsteps to the Church of Santa Maria in Ara Cœli. Two visits are necessary, as on the first you are at once seized by the sacristan, who can conceive of no other motive for entering this church on the Capitol Hill than to see the miraculous Bambino — the painted doll swaddled in gold and silver tissue and "crusted over with magnificent diamonds, emeralds, and rubies." When you have heard the tale of what has been called "the oldest medical practitioner in Rome," of his miraculous cures, of these votive offerings, the imaginary picture you had conjured up is effaced; and it is better to go away and come a second time when the sacristan will recognize you and leave you to yourself. Then you may open your Gibbon's Autobiography and read that it was the subtle influence of Italy and Rome that determined the choice, from amongst many contemplated subjects of historical writing, of "The Decline and Fall of the Roman Empire." "In my Journal," wrote Gibbon, "the place and moment of conception are recorded; the 15th of October, 1764, in the close of the evening, as I sat musing in the Church of the Franciscan friars while they were singing vespers in the Temple of Jupiter on the ruins of the Capitol." [1] Gibbon was twenty-seven when he made this fruitful visit of eighteen weeks to Rome, and his first impression, though often quoted, never loses interest, showing, as it does, the enthusiasm of an unemotional man. "At the distance of twenty-five years,"

[1] Autobiography, 270.

he wrote, "I can neither forget nor express the strong emotions which agitated my mind as I first approached and entered the *Eternal City*. After a sleepless night, I trod with a lofty step the ruins of the Forum; each memorable spot where Romulus *stood* or Cicero spoke or Cæsar fell was at once present to my eye."

The admirer of Gibbon as he travels northward will stop at Lausanne and visit the hotel which bears the historian's name. Twice have I taken luncheon in the garden where he wrote the last words of his history; and on a third visit, after lunching at another inn, I could not fail to admire the penetration of the Swiss concierge. As I alighted, he seemed to divine at once the object of my visit, and before I had half the words of explanation out of my mouth, he said, "Oh, yes. It is this way. But I cannot show you anything but a spot." I have quoted from Gibbon's Autobiography the expression of his inspiration of twenty-seven; a fitting companion-piece is the reflection of the man of fifty. "I have presumed to mark the moment of conception," he wrote; "I shall now commemorate the hour of my final deliverance. It was on the day, or rather the night, of the 27th of June, 1787, between the hours of eleven and twelve, that I wrote the last lines of the last page in a summer-house in my garden. . . . I will not dissemble the first emotions of joy on the recovery of my freedom and perhaps the establishment of my fame. But my pride was soon humbled, and a sober melancholy was spread over my mind by the idea that I had taken my everlasting leave of an old and agreeable companion." [1]

Although the idea was conceived when Gibbon was twenty-seven, he was thirty-one before he set himself seriously at work to study his material. At thirty-six he began the

[1] Autobiography, 333.

composition, and he was thirty-nine, when, in February, 1776, the first quarto volume was published. The history had an immediate success. "My book," he wrote, "was on every table and almost on every toilette; the historian was crowned by the taste or fashion of the day." [1] The first edition was exhausted in a few days, a second was printed in 1776, and next year a third. The second and third volumes, which ended the history of the Western empire, were published in 1781, and seven years later the three volumes devoted to the Eastern empire saw the light. The last sentence of the work, written in the summer-house at Lausanne, is, "It was among the ruins of the Capitol that I first conceived the idea of a work which has amused and exercised near twenty years of my life, and which, however inadequate to my own wishes, I finally deliver to the curiosity and candor of the public."

This is a brief account of one of the greatest historical works, if indeed it is not the greatest, ever written. Let us imagine an assemblage of English, German, and American historical scholars called upon to answer the question, Who is the greatest modern historian? No doubt can exist that Gibbon would have a large majority of the voices; and I think a like meeting of French and Italian scholars would indorse the verdict. "Gibbon's work will never be excelled," declared Niebuhr.[2] "That great master of us all," said Freeman, "whose immortal tale none of us can hope to displace." [3] Bury, the latest editor of Gibbon, who has acutely criticised and carefully weighed "The Decline and Fall," concludes "that Gibbon is behind date in many details. But in the main things he is still our master, above and beyond date." [4] His work wins plaudits from those

[1] Autobiography, 311.
[2] Lectures, 763.
[3] Chief Periods European Hist., 75.
[4] Introduction, lxvii.

who believe that history in its highest form should be literature and from those who hold that it should be nothing
more than a scientific narrative. The disciples of Macaulay
and Carlyle, of Stubbs and Gardiner, would be found voting
in unison in my imaginary Congress. Gibbon, writes Bury,
is "the historian and the man of letters," thus ranking with
Thucydides and Tacitus. These three are put in the highest
class, exemplifying that "brilliance of style and accuracy
of statement are perfectly compatible in an historian." [1]
Accepting this authoritative classification it is well worth
while to point out the salient differences between the ancient
historians and the modern. From Thucydides we have
twenty-four years of contemporary history of his own country. If the whole of the Annals and History of Tacitus
had come down to us, we should have had eighty-three
years; as it is, we actually have forty-one of nearly contemporary history of the Roman Empire. Gibbon's tale covers
1240 years. He went far beyond his own country for his
subject, and the date of his termination is three centuries
before he was born. Milman spoke of "the amplitude, the
magnificence, and the harmony of Gibbon's design," [2] and
Bury writes, "If we take into account the vast range of his
work, his accuracy is amazing." [3] Men have wondered and
will long wonder at the brain with such a grasp and with
the power to execute skillfully so mighty a conception. "The
public is seldom wrong" in their judgment of a book, wrote
Gibbon in his Autobiography,[4] and, if that be true at the
time of actual publication to which Gibbon intended to
apply the remark, how much truer it is in the long run of
years. "The Decline and Fall of the Roman Empire" has
had a life of over one hundred and thirty years, and there is
no indication that it will not endure as long as any interest

[1] Introduction, xxxi.   [2] Preface, ix.   [3] Introduction, xli.   [4] p. 324.

is taken in the study of history. "I have never presumed
to accept a place in the triumvirate of British historians,"
said Gibbon, referring to Hume and Robertson. But in our
day Hume and Robertson gather dust on the shelf, while
Gibbon is continually studied by students and read by serious men.

A work covering Gibbon's vast range of time would have
been impossible for Thucydides or Tacitus. Historical skepticism had not been fully enough developed. There had
not been a sufficient sifting and criticism of historical materials for a master's work of synthesis. And it is probable
that Thucydides lacked a model. Tacitus could indeed have
drawn inspiration from the Greek, while Gibbon had lessons
from both, showing a profound study of Tacitus and a
thorough acquaintance with Thucydides.

If circumstances then made it impossible for the Greek
or the Roman to attempt history on the grand scale of Gibbon, could Gibbon have written contemporary history with
accuracy and impartiality equal to his great predecessors?
This is one of those delightful questions that may be ever
discussed and never resolved. When twenty-three years
old, arguing against the desire of his father that he should
go into Parliament, Gibbon assigned, as one of the reasons,
that he lacked "necessary prejudices of party and of nation"; [1] and when in middle life he embraced the fortunate
opportunity of becoming a member of the House of Commons, he thus summed up his experience, "The eight sessions
that I sat in Parliament were a school of civil prudence, the
first and most essential virtue of an historian." [2] At the
end of this political career, Gibbon, in a private letter to
an intimate Swiss friend, gave the reason why he had embraced it. "I entered Parliament," he said, "without

---

[1] Letters, I, 23.   [2] Autobiography, 310.

patriotism, and without ambition, and I had no other aim
than to secure the comfortable and honest place of a *Lord of
Trade*. I obtained this place at last. I held it for three
years, from 1779 to 1782, and the net annual product of it,
being £750 sterling, increased my revenue to the level of
my wants and desires." [1] His retirement from Parliament
was followed by ten years' residence at Lausanne, in the first
four of which he completed his history. A year and a half
after his removal to Lausanne, he referred, in a letter to his
closest friend, Lord Sheffield, to the "abyss of your cursed
politics," and added: "I never was a very warm patriot
and I grow every day a citizen of the world. The scramble
for power and profit at Westminster or St. James's, and the
names of Pitt and Fox become less interesting to me than
those of Cæsar and Pompey." [2]

These expressions would seem to indicate that Gibbon
might have written contemporary history well and that the
candor displayed in "The Decline and Fall" might not have
been lacking had he written of England in his own time.
But that subject he never contemplated. When twenty-
four years old he had however considered a number of English periods and finally fixed upon Sir Walter Raleigh for
his hero; but a year later, he wrote in his journal: "I
shrink with terror from the modern history of England,
where every character is a problem, and every reader a
friend or an enemy; where a writer is supposed to hoist a
flag of party and is devoted to damnation by the adverse
faction. . . . I must embrace a safer and more extensive
theme." [3]

How well Gibbon knew himself! Despite his coolness
and candor, war and revolution revealed his strong Tory
prejudices, which he undoubtedly feared might color any

[1] *Letters*, II, 36.   [2] *Ibid.*, 127.   [3] *Autobiography*, 196.

history of England that he might undertake. "I took my seat," in the House of Commons, he wrote, "at the beginning of the memorable contest between Great Britain and America; and supported with many a sincere and *silent* vote the rights though perhaps not the interests of the mother country." [1] In 1782 he recorded the conclusion: "The American war had once been the favorite of the country, the pride of England was irritated by the resistance of her colonies, and the executive power was driven by national clamor into the most vigorous and coercive measures." But it was a fruitless contest. Armies were lost; the debt and taxes were increased; the hostile confederacy of France, Spain and Holland was disquieting. As a result the war became unpopular and Lord North's ministry fell. Dr. Johnson thought that no nation not absolutely conquered had declined so much in so short a time. "We seem to be sinking," he said. "I am afraid of a civil war." Dr. Franklin, according to Horace Walpole, said "he would furnish Mr. Gibbon with materials for writing the History of the Decline of the British Empire." With his country tottering, the self-centered but truthful Gibbon could not avoid mention of his personal loss, due to the fall of his patron, Lord North. "I was stripped of a convenient salary," he said, "after having enjoyed it about three years." [2]

The outbreak of the French Revolution intensified his conservatism. He was then at Lausanne, the tranquillity of which was broken up by the dissolution of the neighboring kingdom. Many Lausanne families were terrified by the menace of bankruptcy. "This town and country," Gibbon wrote, "are crowded with noble exiles, and we sometimes

---

[1] Autobiography, 310. "I am more and more convinced that we have both the right and power on our side." Letters, I, 248.

[2] Hill's ed. Gibbon Autobiography, 212, 213, 314.

count in an assembly a dozen princesses and duchesses." [1]
Bitter disputes between them and the triumphant Democrats disturbed the harmony of social circles. Gibbon espoused the cause of the royalists. "I beg leave to subscribe my assent to Mr. Burke's creed on the Revolution of France," he wrote. "I admire his eloquence, I approve his politics, I adore his chivalry, and I can almost excuse his reverence for Church establishments." [2] Thirteen days after the massacre of the Swiss guard in the attack on the Tuileries in August, 1792, Gibbon wrote to Lord Sheffield, "The last revolution of Paris appears to have convinced almost everybody of the fatal consequences of Democratical principles which lead by a path of flowers into the abyss of hell." [3] Gibbon, who was astonished by so few things in history, wrote Sainte-Beuve, was amazed by the French Revolution. [4] Nothing could be more natural. The historian in his study may consider the fall of dynasties, social upheavals, violent revolutions, and the destruction of order without a tremor. The things have passed away. The events furnish food for his reflections and subjects for his pen, while sanguine uprisings at home or in a neighboring country in his own time inspire him with terror lest the oft-prophesied dissolution of society is at hand. It is the difference between the earthquake in your own city and the one 3000 miles away. As Gibbon's pocket-nerve was sensitive, it may be he was also thinking of the £1300 he had invested in 1784 in the new loan of the King of France, deeming the French funds as solid as the English. [5]

It is well now to repeat our dictum that Gibbon is the greatest modern historian, but, in reasserting this, it is no more than fair to cite the opinions of two dissentients —

---

[1] Letters, II, 249.   [2] Autobiography, 342.   [3] Letters, II, 310.
[4] Causeries du Lundi, viii, 469.   [5] Letters, II, 98.

the great literary historians of the nineteenth century, Macaulay and Carlyle. "The truth is," wrote Macaulay in his diary, "that I admire no historians much except Herodotus, Thucydides, and Tacitus. . . . There is merit no doubt in Hume, Robertson, Voltaire, and Gibbon. Yet it is not the thing. I have a conception of history more just, I am confident, than theirs."[1] "Gibbon," said Carlyle in a public lecture, is "a greater historian than Robertson but not so great as Hume. With all his swagger and bombast, no man ever gave a more futile account of human things than he has done of the decline and fall of the Roman Empire; assigning no profound cause for these phenomena, nothing but diseased nerves, and all sorts of miserable motives, to the actors in them."[2] Carlyle's statement shows envious criticism as well as a prejudice in favor of his brother Scotchman. It was made in 1838, since when opinion has raised Gibbon to the top, for he actually lives while Hume is read perfunctorily, if at all. Moreover among the three — Gibbon, Macaulay, and Carlyle — whose works are literature as well as history, modern criticism has no hesitation in awarding the palm to Gibbon.

Before finally deciding upon his subject Gibbon thought of "The History of the Liberty of the Swiss" and "The History of the Republic of Florence under the House of Medicis,"[3] but in the end, as we have seen, he settled on the later history of the Roman Empire, showing, as Lowell said of Parkman, his genius in the choice of his subject. His history really begins with the death of Marcus Aurelius, 180 A.D., but the main narrative is preceded by three excellent introductory chapters, covering in Bury's edition eighty-two pages. After the completion of his work, he regretted

[1] Trevelyan, II, 232.   [2] Lectures on the Hist. of Literature, 185.
[3] Autobiography, 196.

that he had not begun it at an earlier period. On the first page of his own printed copy of his book where he announces his design, he has entered this marginal note: "Should I not have given the *history* of that fortunate period which was interposed between two iron ages? Should I not have deduced the decline of the Empire from the Civil Wars that ensued after the Fall of Nero or even from the tyranny which succeeded the reign of Augustus? Alas! I should; but of what avail is this tardy knowledge?"[1] We may echo Gibbon's regret that he had not commenced his history with the reign of Tiberius, as, in his necessary use of Tacitus, we should have had the running comment of one great historian on another, of which we have a significant example in Gibbon's famous sixteenth chapter wherein he discusses Tacitus's account of the persecution of the Christians by Nero. With his power of historic divination, he would have so absorbed Tacitus and his time that the history would almost have seemed a collaboration between two great and sympathetic minds. "Tacitus," he wrote, "very frequently trusts to the curiosity or reflection of his readers to supply those intermediate circumstances and ideas, which, in his extreme conciseness, he has thought proper to suppress."[2] How Gibbon would have filled those gaps! Though he was seldom swayed by enthusiasm, his admiration of the Roman historian fell little short of idolatry. His references in "The Decline and Fall" are many, and some of them are here worth recalling to mind. "In their primitive state of simplicity and independence," he wrote, "the Germans were surveyed by the discerning eye and delineated by the masterly pencil of Tacitus, the first of historians who applied the science of philosophy to the study of facts."[3] Again he speaks of him as "the philosophic historian whose

[1] Bury's ed., xxxv. [2] Decline and Fall, Smith's ed., 236. [3] *Ibid.*, I, 349.

writings will instruct the last generation of mankind." [1]
And in Chapter XVI he devoted five pages to citation from,
and comment on, Tacitus, and paid him one of the most
splendid tributes one historian ever paid another. "To
collect, to dispose, and to adorn a series of fourscore years
in an immortal work, every sentence of which is pregnant
with the deepest observations and the most lively images,
was an undertaking sufficient to exercise the genius of Tacitus himself during the greatest part of his life." [2] So much
for admiration. That, nevertheless, Gibbon could wield the
critical pen at the expense of the historian he rated so highly,
is shown by a marginal note in his own printed copy of "The
Decline and Fall." It will be remembered that Tacitus
published his History and wrote his Annals during the reign
of Trajan, whom he undoubtedly respected and admired.
He referred to the reigns of Nerva and Trajan in suggested
contrast to that of Domitian as "times when men were
blessed with the rare privilege of thinking with freedom, and
uttering what they thought." [3] It fell to both Tacitus and
Gibbon to speak of the testament of Augustus which, after
his death, was read in the Senate: and Tacitus wrote, Augustus "added a recommendation to keep the empire within
fixed limits," on which he thus commented, "but whether
from apprehension for its safety, or jealousy of future rivals,
is uncertain." [4] Gibbon thus criticised this comment: "Why
must rational advice be imputed to a base or foolish motive?
To what cause, error, malevolence, or flattery, shall I ascribe
the unworthy alternative? Was the historian dazzled by
Trajan's conquests?" [5]

The intellectual training of the greatest modern historian
is a matter of great interest. "From my early youth,"

[1] Decline and Fall, Smith's ed., II, 35.   [2] II, 235.   [3] History, I, 1.
[4] Annals, I, 11.   [5] Bury's introduction, xxxv.

wrote Gibbon in his Autobiography, "I aspired to the character of an historian." [1] He had "an early and invincible
love of reading" which he said he "would not exchange for
the treasures of India" and which led him to a "vague and
multifarious" perusal of books. Before he reached the age
of fifteen he was matriculated at Magdalen College, giving
this account of his preparation. "I arrived at Oxford,"
he said, "with a stock of erudition that might have puzzled
a Doctor and a degree of ignorance of which a schoolboy would
have been ashamed." [2] He did not adapt himself to the
life or the method of Oxford, and from them apparently
derived no benefit. "I spent fourteen months at Magdalen
College," he wrote; "they proved the fourteen months the
most idle and unprofitable of my whole life." [3] He became
a Roman Catholic. It was quite characteristic of this
bookish man that his conversion was effected, not by the
emotional influence of some proselytizer, but by the reading of books. English translations of two famous works of
Bossuet fell into his hands. "I read," he said, "I applauded,
I believed . . . and I surely fell by a noble hand." Before
a priest in London, on June 8, 1753, he privately "abjured
the errors of heresy" and was admitted into the "pale of
the church." But at that time this was a serious business
for both priest and proselyte. For the rule laid down by
Blackstone was this, "Where a person is reconciled to the
see of Rome, or procures others to be reconciled, the offence
amounts to High-Treason." This severe rule was not enforced, but there were milder laws under which a priest
might suffer perpetual imprisonment and the proselyte's
estate be transferred to his nearest relations. Under such
laws prosecutions were had and convictions obtained.
Little wonder was it when Gibbon apprised his father in

[1] Autobiography, 193. [2] Ibid., 48, 59. [3] Ibid., 67.

an "elaborate controversial epistle" of the serious step
which he had taken, that the elder Gibbon should be astonished and indignant. In his passion he divulged the
secret which effectually closed the gates of Magdalen College to his son,[1] who was packed off to Lausanne and "settled
under the roof and tuition" of a Calvinist minister.[2] Edward Gibbon passed nearly five years at Lausanne, from the
age of sixteen to that of twenty-one, and they were fruitful
years for his education. It was almost entirely an affair
of self-training, as his tutor soon perceived that the student
had gone beyond the teacher and allowed him to pursue his
own special bent. After his history was published and his
fame won, he recorded this opinion: "In the life of every
man of letters there is an æra, from a level, from whence
he soars with his own wings to his proper height, and the
most important part of his education is that which he bestows on himself." [3] This was certainly true in Gibbon's
case. On his arrival at Lausanne he hardly knew any
French, but before he returned to England he thought spontaneously in French and understood, spoke, and wrote it
better than he did his mother tongue.[4] He read Montesquieu frequently and was struck with his "energy of style
and boldness of hypothesis." Among the books which
"may have remotely contributed to form the historian of the
Roman Empire" were the Provincial Letters of Pascal,
which he read "with a new pleasure" almost every year.
From them he said, "I learned to manage the weapon of
grave and temperate irony, even on subjects of ecclesiastical
solemnity." As one thinks of his chapters in "The Decline
and Fall" on Julian, one is interested to know that during
this period he was introduced to the life and times of this

---

[1] Autobiography, 86 et seq.; Hill's ed., 69, 291.   [2] Autobiography, 131.
[3] Ibid., 137.   [4] Ibid., 134.

Roman emperor by a book written by a French abbé. He read Locke, Grotius, and Puffendorf, but unquestionably his greatest knowledge, mental discipline, and peculiar mastery of his own tongue came from his diligent and systematic study of the Latin classics. He read nearly all of the historians, poets, orators, and philosophers, going over for a second or even a third time Terence, Virgil, Horace, and Tacitus. He mastered Cicero's Orations and Letters so that they became ingrained in his mental fiber, and he termed these and his other works, "a library of eloquence and reason." "As I read Cicero," he wrote, "I applauded the observation of Quintilian, that every student may judge of his own proficiency by the satisfaction which he receives from the Roman orator." And again, "Cicero's epistles may in particular afford the models of every form of correspondence from the careless effusions of tenderness and friendship to the well-guarded declaration of discreet and dignified resentment."[1] Gibbon never mastered Greek as he did Latin; and Dr. Smith, one of his editors, points out where he has fallen into three errors from the use of the French or Latin translation of Procopius instead of consulting the original.[2] Indeed he himself has disclosed one defect of self-training. Referring to his youthful residence at Lausanne, he wrote: "I worked my way through about half the Iliad, and afterwards interpreted alone a large portion of Xenophon and Herodotus. But my ardor, destitute of aid and emulation, was gradually cooled and, from the barren task of searching words in a lexicon, I withdrew to the free and familiar conversation of Virgil and Tacitus."[3]

All things considered, however, it was an excellent training for a historian of the Roman Empire. But all except the

---

[1] Autobiography, 139–142.   [2] V, 108, 130, 231.   [3] Autobiography, 141.

living knowledge of French he might have had in his "elegant apartment in Magdalen College" just as well as in his "ill-contrived and ill-furnished small chamber" in "an old inconvenient house," situated in a "narrow gloomy street, the most unfrequented of an unhandsome town"; [1] and in Oxford he would have had the "aid and emulation" of which at Lausanne he sadly felt the lack.

The Calvinist minister, his tutor, was a more useful guide for Gibbon in the matter of religion than in his intellectual training. Through his efforts and Gibbon's "private reflections," Christmas Day, 1754, one year and a half after his arrival at Lausanne, was witness to his reconversion, as he then received the sacrament in the Calvinistic Church. "The articles of the Romish creed," he said, had "disappeared like a dream"; and he wrote home to his aunt, "I am now a good Protestant and am extremely glad of it." [2]

An intellectual and social experience of value was his meeting with Voltaire, who had set up a theater in the neighborhood of Lausanne for the performance mainly of his own plays. Gibbon seldom failed to procure a ticket to these representations. Voltaire played the parts suited to his years; his declamation, Gibbon thought, was old-fashioned, and "he expressed the enthusiasm of poetry rather than the feelings of nature." "The parts of the young and fair," he said, "were distorted by Voltaire's fat and ugly niece." Despite this criticism, these performances fostered a taste for the French theater, to the abatement of his idolatry for Shakespeare, which seemed to him to be "inculcated from our infancy as the first duty of an Englishman." [3] Personally, Voltaire and Gibbon did not get on well together. Dr. Hill suggests that Voltaire may have slighted the "English youth," and if this is correct, Gibbon

[1] Autobiography, 132.   [2] Hill's ed., 89, 293.   [3] Autobiography, 149.

was somewhat spiteful to carry the feeling more than thirty years.   Besides the criticism of the acting, he called Voltaire "the envious bard" because it was only with much reluctance and ill-humor that he permitted the performance of Iphigenie of Racine.   Nevertheless, Gibbon is impressed with the social influence of the great Frenchman.   "The wit and philosophy of Voltaire, his table and theatre," he wrote, "refined in a visible degree the manners of Lausanne, and however addicted to study, I enjoyed my share of the amusements of society.   After the theatrical representations, I sometimes supped with the actors: I was now familiar in some, and acquainted in many, houses; and my evenings were generally devoted to cards and conversation, either in private parties or numerous assemblies." [1]

Gibbon was twenty-one when he returned to England. Dividing his time between London and the country, he continued his self-culture.   He read English, French, and Latin, and took up the study of Greek.   "Every day, every hour," he wrote, "was agreeably filled"; and "I was never less alone than when by myself." [2]   He read repeatedly Robertson and Hume, and has in the words of Sainte-Beuve left a testimony so spirited and so delicately expressed as could have come only from a man of taste who appreciated Xenophon. [3]   "The perfect composition, the nervous language," wrote Gibbon, "the well-turned periods of Dr. Robertson inflamed me to the ambitious hope that I might one day tread in his footsteps; the calm philosophy, the careless inimitable beauties of his friend and rival, often forced me to close the volume with a mixed sensation of delight and despair." [4]   He made little progress in London society and his solitary evenings were passed with his books,

<hr>

[1] Autobiography, 149.   [2] *Ibid.*, 161.
[3] Causeries du Lundi, VIII, 445.   [4] Autobiography, 167.

but he consoled himself by thinking that he lost nothing by a withdrawal from a "noisy and expensive scene of crowds without company, and dissipation without pleasure." At twenty-four he published his "Essay on the Study of Literature," begun at Lausanne and written entirely in French. This possesses no interest for the historical student except to know the bare fact of the writing and publication as a step in the intellectual development of the historian. Sainte-Beuve in his two essays on Gibbon devoted three pages to an abstract and criticism of it, perhaps because it had a greater success in France than in England; and his opinion of Gibbon's language is interesting. "The French," Sainte-Beuve wrote, "is that of one who has read Montesquieu much and imitates him; it is correct, but artificial French."[1]

Then followed two and a half years' service in the Hampshire militia. But he did not neglect his reading. He mastered Homer, whom he termed "the Bible of the ancients," and in the militia he acquired "a just and indelible knowledge" of what he called "the first of languages." And his love for Latin abided also: "On every march, in every journey, Horace was always in my pocket and often in my hand."[2] Practical knowledge he absorbed almost insensibly. "The daily occupations of the militia," he wrote, "introduced me to the science of Tactics" and led to the study of "the precepts of Polybius and Cæsar." In this connection occurs the remark which admirers of Gibbon will never tire of citing: "A familiar view of the discipline and evolutions of a modern battalion gave me a clearer notion of the Phalanx and the Legion; and the Captain of the Hampshire Grenadiers (the reader may smile) has not been useless to the historian of the decline and fall of the

[1] Causeries du Lundi, VIII, 446.   [2] Autobiography, Hill's ed., 142.

Roman Empire."[1] The grand tour followed his militia service. Three and a half months in Paris, and a revisit to Lausanne preceded the year that he passed in Italy. Of the conception of the History of the Decline and Fall, during his stay in Rome, I have already spoken.

On his return to England, contemplating "the decline and fall of Rome at an awful distance," he began, in collaboration with the Swiss Deyverdun, his bosom friend, a history of Switzerland written in French. During the winter of 1767, the first book of it was submitted to a literary society of foreigners in London. As the author was unknown the strictures were free and the verdict unfavorable. Gibbon was present at the meeting and related that "the momentary sensation was painful," but, on cooler reflection, he agreed with his judges and intended to consign his manuscript to the flames. But this, as Lord Sheffield, his literary executor and first editor, shows conclusively, he neglected to do.[2] This essay of Gibbon's possesses interest for us, inasmuch as David Hume read it, and wrote to Gibbon a friendly letter, in which he said: "I have perused your manuscript with great pleasure and satisfaction. I have only one objection, derived from the language in which it is written. Why do you compose in French, and carry faggots into the wood, as Horace says with regard to Romans who wrote in Greek?"[3] This critical query of Hume must have profoundly influenced Gibbon. Next year he began to work seriously on "The Decline and Fall" and five years later began the composition of it in English. It does not appear that he had any idea of writing his magnum opus in French.

In this rambling discourse, in which I have purposely avoided relating the life of Gibbon in anything like a

[1] Autobiography, 258.   [2] Ibid., 277.   [3] Ibid.

chronological order, we return again and again to the great History. And it could not well be otherwise. For if Edward Gibbon could not have proudly said, I am the author of "six volumes in quartos" [1] he would have had no interest for us. Dr. Hill writes, "For one reader who has read his 'Decline and Fall,' there are at least a score who have read his Autobiography, and who know him, not as the great historian, but as a man of a most original and interesting nature." [2] But these twenty people would never have looked into the Autobiography had it not been the life of a great historian; indeed the Autobiography would never have been written except to give an account of a great life work. "The Decline and Fall," therefore, is the thing about which all the other incidents of his life revolve. The longer this history is read and studied, the greater is the appreciation of it. Dean Milman followed Gibbon's track through many portions of his work, and read his authorities, ending with a deliberate judgment in favor of his "general accuracy." "Many of his seeming errors," he wrote, "are almost inevitable from the close condensation of his matter." [3] Guizot had three different opinions based on three various readings. After the first rapid perusal, the dominant feeling was one of interest in a narrative, always animated in spite of its extent, always clear and limpid in spite of the variety of objects. During the second reading, when he examined particularly certain points, he was somewhat disappointed; he encountered some errors either in the citations or in the facts and especially shades and strokes of partiality which led him to a comparatively rigorous judgment. In the ensuing complete third reading, the first impression, doubtless corrected by the second, but not destroyed, survived and was main-

[1] Letters, II, 279.   [2] Preface, x.   [3] Smith's ed., I, xi.

tained; and with some restrictions and reservations, Guizot declared that, concerning that vast and able work, there remained with him an appreciation of the immensity of research, the variety of knowledge, the sagacious breadth and especially that truly philosophical rectitude of a mind which judges the past as it would judge the present.[1] Mommsen said in 1894: "Amid all the changes that have come over the study of the history of the Roman Empire, in spite of all the rush of the new evidence that has poured in upon us and almost overwhelmed us, in spite of changes which must be made, in spite of alterations of view, or alterations even in the aspect of great characters, no one would in the future be able to read the history of the Roman Empire unless he read, possibly with a fuller knowledge, but with the broad views, the clear insight, the strong grasp of Edward Gibbon." [2]

It is difficult for an admirer of Gibbon to refrain from quoting some of his favorite passages. The opinion of a great historian on history always possesses interest. History, wrote Gibbon, is "little more than the register of the crimes, follies, and misfortunes of mankind." Again, "Wars and the administration of public affairs are the principal subjects of history." And the following cannot fail to recall a similar thought in Tacitus, "History undertakes to record the transactions of the past for the instruction of future ages." [3] Two references to religion under the Pagan empire are always worth repeating. "The various modes of worship which prevailed in the Roman world," he wrote, "were all considered by the people as equally true; by the philosopher as equally false; and by the magistrate as equally useful." "The fashion of incredulity was com-

---

[1] Causeries du Lundi, VIII, 453. [2] *London Times*, November 16, 1894.
[3] Smith's ed., I, 215, 371; II, 230.

municated from the philosopher to the man of pleasure or business, from the noble to the plebeian, and from the master to the menial slave who waited at his table and who equally listened to the freedom of his conversation." [1] Gibbon's idea of the happiest period of mankind is interesting and characteristic. "If," he wrote, "a man were called to fix the period in the history of the world during which the condition of the human race was most happy and prosperous, he would, without hesitation, name that which elapsed from the death of Domitian to the accession of Commodus." [2] This period was from A.D. 96 to 180, covering the reigns of Nerva, Trajan, Hadrian, Antoninus Pius, and Marcus Aurelius. Professor Carter, in a lecture in Rome in 1907, drew, by a modern comparison, a characterization of the first three named. When we were studying in Germany, he said, we were accustomed to sum up the three emperors, William I, Frederick III, and William II, as der greise Kaiser, der weise Kaiser, und der reise Kaiser. The characterizations will fit well Nerva, Trajan, and Hadrian. Gibbon speaks of the "restless activity" of Hadrian, whose life "was almost a perpetual journey," and who during his reign visited every province of his empire. [3]

A casual remark of Gibbon's, "Corruption [is] the most infallible symptom of constitutional liberty," [4] shows the sentiment of the eighteenth century. The generality of the history becomes specific in a letter to his father, who has given him hopes of a seat in Parliament. "This seat," so Edward Gibbon wrote, "according to the custom of our venal country was to be bought, and fifteen hundred pounds were mentioned as the price of purchase." [5]

Gibbon anticipated Captain Mahan. In speaking of a

---

[1] Smith's ed., I, 165; II, 205.   [2] *Ibid.*, I, 216.   [3]*Ibid.*, I, 144.
[4] *Ibid.*, III, 78.   [5] Letters, I, 23.

naval battle between the fleet of Justinian and that of the
Goths in which the galleys of the Eastern empire gained a
signal victory, he wrote, "The Goths affected to depreciate
an element in which they were unskilled; but their own
experience confirmed the truth of a maxim, that the master
of the sea will always acquire the dominion of the land." [1]
But Gibbon's anticipation was one of the frequent cases
where the same idea has occurred to a number of men of
genius, as doubtless Captain Mahan was not aware of this
sentence any more than he was of Bacon's and Raleigh's epit-
omes of the theme which he has so originally and brilliantly
treated.[2]

No modern historian has been the subject of so much
critical comment as Gibbon.   I do not know how it will
compare in volume with either of the similar examinations
of Thucydides and Tacitus; but the criticism is of a different sort.   The only guarantee of the honesty of Tacitus,
wrote Sainte-Beuve, is Tacitus himself; [3] and a like remark
will apply to Thucydides.   But a fierce light beats on Gibbon.   His voluminous notes furnish the critics the materials on which he built his history, which, in the case of
the ancient historians, must be largely a matter of conjecture.   With all the searching examination of "The Decline
and Fall," it is surprising how few errors have been found
and, of the errors which have been noted, how few are really
important.   Guizot, Milman, Dr. Smith, Cotter Morison,
Bury, and a number of lesser lights have raked his text and
his notes with few momentous results.   We have, writes
Bury, improved methods over Gibbon and "much new material of various kinds," but "Gibbon's historical sense
kept him constantly right in dealing with his sources";

---

[1] Smith's ed., V, 230.   [2] See Mahan's From Sail to Steam, 276.
[3] Causeries du Lundi, I, 153.

and "in the main things he is still our master."[1] The man is generally reflected in his book. That Gibbon has been weighed and not found wanting is because he was as honest and truthful as any man who ever wrote history. The autobiographies and letters exhibit to us a transparent man, which indeed some of the personal allusions in the history might have foreshadowed. "I have often fluctuated and shall *tamely* follow the Colbert Ms.," he wrote, where the authenticity of a book was in question.[2] In another case "the scarcity of facts and the uncertainty of dates" opposed his attempt to describe the first invasion of Italy by Alaric.[3] In the beginning of the famous Chapter XLIV which is "admired by jurists as a brief and brilliant exposition of the principles of Roman law,"[4] Gibbon wrote, "Attached to no party, interested only for the truth and candor of history, and directed by the most temperate and skillful guides, I enter with just diffidence on the subject of civil law."[5] In speaking of the state of Britain between 409 and 449, he said, "I owe it to myself and to historic truth to declare that some *circumstances* in this paragraph are founded only on conjecture and analogy."[6] Throughout his whole work the scarcity of materials forces Gibbon to the frequent use of conjecture, but I believe that for the most part his conjectures seem reasonable to the critics. Impressed with the correctness of his account of the Eastern empire a student of the subject once told me that Gibbon certainly possessed the power of wise divination.

Gibbon's striving after precision and accuracy is shown in some marginal corrections he made in his own printed copy of "The Decline and Fall." On the first page in his first

---

[1] Introduction, xlv, l, lxvii.   [2] Smith's ed., III, 14.   [3] *Ibid.*, IV, 31.
[4] Bury, lii.   [5] Smith's ed., V, 258.   [6] *Ibid.*, IV, 132 n.

printed edition and as it now stands, he said, "To deduce the most important circumstances of its decline and fall: a revolution which will ever be remembered and is still felt by the nations of the earth." For this the following is substituted: "To prosecute the decline and fall of the empire of Rome: of whose language, religion, and laws the impression will be long preserved in our own and the neighboring countries of Europe." He thus explains the change: "Mr. Hume told me that, in correcting his history, he always labored to reduce superlatives and soften positives. Have Asia and Africa, from Japan to Morocco, any feeling or memory of the Roman Empire?"

On page 6, Bury's edition, the text is, "The praises of Alexander, transmitted by a succession of poets and historians, had kindled a dangerous emulation in the mind of Trajan." We can imagine that Gibbon reflected, What evidence have I that Trajan had read these poets and historians? Therefore he made this change: "Late generations and far distant climates may impute their calamities to the immortal author of the Iliad. The spirit of Alexander was inflamed by the praises of Achilles; and succeeding heroes have been ambitious to tread in the footsteps of Alexander. Like him, the Emperor Trajan aspired to the conquest of the East." [1]

The "advertisement" to the first octavo edition published in 1783 is an instance of Gibbon's truthfulness. He wrote, "Some alterations and improvements had presented themselves to my mind, but I was unwilling to injure or offend the purchasers of the preceding editions." Then he seems to reflect that this is not quite the whole truth and adds, "Perhaps I may stand excused if, amidst the avocations of a busy winter, I have preferred the pleasures of

[1] Bury's ed., xxxv, xxxvi.

composition and study to the minute diligence of revising a former publication." [1]

The severest criticism that Gibbon has received is on his famous chapters XV and XVI which conclude his first volume in the original quarto edition of 1776. We may disregard the flood of contemporary criticism from certain people who were excited by what they deemed an attack on the Christian religion. Dean Milman, who objected seriously to much in these chapters, consulted these various answers to Gibbon on the first appearance of his work with, according to his own confession, little profit. [2] "Against his celebrated fifteenth and sixteenth chapters," wrote Buckle, "all the devices of controversy have been exhausted; but the only result has been, that while the fame of the historian is untarnished, the attacks of his enemies are falling into complete oblivion. The work of Gibbon remains; but who is there who feels any interest in what was written against him?" [3] During the last generation, however, criticism has taken another form and scientific men now do not exactly share Buckle's gleeful opinion. Both Bury and Cotter Morison state or imply that well-grounded exceptions may be taken to Gibbon's treatment of the early Christian church. He ignored some facts; his combination of others, his inferences, his opinions are not fair and unprejudiced. A further grave objection may be made to the tone of these two chapters: sarcasm pervades them and the Gibbon sneer has become an apt characterization.

Francis Parkman admitted that he was a reverent agnostic, and if Gibbon had been a reverent free-thinker these two chapters would have been far different in tone. Lecky

[1] Smith's ed., I, xxi.   [2] Smith's ed., I, xvii.
[3] History of Civilization, II, 308 n.

regarded the Christian church as a great institution worthy
of reverence and respect although he stated the central
thesis of Gibbon with emphasis just as great. Of the conversion of the Roman Empire to Christianity, Lecky wrote,
"it may be boldly asserted that the assumption of a moral
or intellectual miracle is utterly gratuitous. Never before
was a religious transformation so manifestly inevitable." [1]
Gibbon's sneering tone was a characteristic of his time.
There existed during the latter part of the eighteenth century, wrote Sir James Mackintosh, "an unphilosophical
and indeed fanatical animosity against Christianity." But
Gibbon's private defense is entitled to consideration as
placing him in a better light. "The primitive church, which
I have treated with some freedom," he wrote to Lord Sheffield in 1791, "was itself at that time an innovation, and
I was attached to the old Pagan establishment." [2] "Had I
believed," he said in his Autobiography, "that the majority of English readers were so fondly attached to the
name and shadow of Christianity, had I foreseen that the
pious, the timid, and the prudent would feel, or affect to
feel, with such exquisite sensibility, I might perhaps have
softened the two invidious chapters." [3]

On the other hand Gibbon's treatment of Julian the Apos-
tate is in accordance with the best modern standard. It
might have been supposed that a quasi-Pagan, as he avowed
himself, would have emphasized Julian's virtues and ignored his weaknesses as did Voltaire, who invested him with
all the good qualities of Trajan, Cato, and Julius Cæsar, without their defects. [4] Robertson indeed feared that he might
fail in this part of the history; [5] but Gibbon weighed Julian
in the balance, duly estimating his strength and his weak-

[1] Morals, I, 419.　　　[2] Letters, II, 237.　　　[3] Autobiography, 316.
[4] Cotter Morison, 118.　　　[5] Sainte-Beuve, 458.

ness, with the result that he has given a clear and just account in his best and most dignified style.[1]

Gibbon's treatment of Theodora, the wife of Justinian, is certainly open to objection. Without proper sifting and a reasonable skepticism, he has incorporated into his narrative the questionable account with all its salacious details which Procopius gives in his Secret History, Gibbon's love of a scandalous tale getting the better of his historical criticism. He has not neglected to urge a defense. "I am justified," he wrote, "in painting the manners of the times; the vices of Theodora form an essential feature in the reign and character of Justinian. . . . My English text is chaste, and all licentious passages are left in the obscurity of a learned language."[2] This explanation satisfies neither Cotter Morison nor Bury, nor would it hold for a moment as a justification of a historian of our own day. Gibbon is really so scientific, so much like a late nineteenth-century man, that we do right to subject him to our present-day rigid tests.

There has been much discussion about Gibbon's style, which we all know is pompous and Latinized. On a long reading his rounded and sonorous periods become wearisome, and one wishes that occasionally a sentence would terminate with a small word, even a preposition. One feels as did Dickens after walking for an hour or two about the handsome but "distractingly regular" city of Philadelphia. "I felt," he wrote, "that I would have given the world for a crooked street."[3] Despite the pomposity, Gibbon's style is correct, and the exact use of words is a marvel. It is rare, I think, that any substitution or change of words will improve upon the precision of the text. His

---

[1] Cotter Morison, 120.   [2] Autobiography, 337 n.
[3] American Notes, Chap. VII.

compression and selection of salient points are remarkable.
Amid some commonplace philosophy he frequently rises
to a generalization as brilliant as it is truthful.   Then, too,
one is impressed with the dignity of history; one feels that
Gibbon looked upon his work as very serious, and thought
with Thucydides, "My history is an everlasting possession,
not a prize composition which is heard and forgotten."

To a writer of history few things are more interesting than
a great historian's autobiographical remarks which relate
to the composition of his work.   "Had I been more indigent
or more wealthy," wrote Gibbon in his Autobiography,
"I should not have possessed the leisure or the perseverance
to prepare and execute my voluminous history." [1]   "Not-
withstanding the hurry of business and pleasure," he wrote
from London in 1778, "I steal some moments for the Roman
Empire." [2]   Between the writing of the first three and the
last three volumes, he took a rest of "near a twelvemonth"
and gave expression to a thought which may be echoed by
every studious writer, "Yet in the luxury of freedom, I
began to wish for the daily task, the active pursuit which
gave a value to every book and an object to every inquiry." [3]
Every one who has written a historical book will sympathize
with the following expression of personal experience as he approached the completion of "The Decline and Fall": "Let no
man who builds a house or writes a book presume to say when
he will have finished.   When he imagines that he is drawing near to his journey's end, Alps rise on Alps, and he continually finds something to add and something to correct." [4]

Plain truthful tales are Gibbon's autobiographies.   The
style is that of the history, and he writes of himself as frankly
as he does of any of his historical characters.   His fail-

[1] p. 155.   [2] Letters, I, 331.
[3] Autobiography, 325.   [4] Letters, II, 143.

ings — what he has somewhere termed "the amiable weaknesses of human nature" — are disclosed with the openness of a Frenchman. All but one of the ten years between 1783 and 1793, between the ages of 46 and 56, he passed at Lausanne. There he completed "The Decline and Fall," and of that period he spent from August, 1787, to July, 1788, in England to look after the publication of the last three volumes. His life in Lausanne was one of study, writing, and agreeable society, of which his correspondence with his English friends gives an animated account. The two things one is most impressed with are his love for books and his love for Madeira. "Though a lover of society," he wrote, "my library is the room to which I am most attached." [1] While getting settled at Lausanne, he complains that his boxes of books "loiter on the road." [2] And then he harps on another string. "Good Madeira," he writes, "is now become essential to my health and reputation;" [3] yet again, "If I do not receive a supply of Madeira in the course of the summer, I shall be in great shame and distress." [4] His good friend in England, Lord Sheffield, regarded his prayer and sent him a hogshead of "best old Madeira" and a tierce, containing six dozen bottles of "finest Malmsey," and at the same time wrote: 'You will remember that a hogshead is on his travels through the torrid zone for you. . . . No wine is meliorated to a greater degree by keeping than Madeira, and you latterly appeared so ravenous for it, that I must conceive you wish to have a stock." [5] Gibbon's devotion to Madeira bore its penalty. At the age of forty-eight he sent this account to his stepmother: "I was in hopes that my old Enemy the Gout had given over the attack, but the Villain, with his ally the winter, con-

[1] Letters, II, 130.   [2] Ibid., 89.   [3] Ibid., 211.   [4] Ibid., 217.
[5] Ibid., II, 232.

vinced me of my error, and about the latter end of March I found myself a prisoner in my library and my great chair. I attempted twice to rise, he twice knocked me down again and kept possession of both my feet and knees longer (I must confess) than he ever had done before." [1]　Eager to finish his history, he lamented that his "long gout" lost him "three months in the spring." Thus as you go through his correspondence, you find that orders for Madeira and attacks of gout alternate with regularity. Gibbon apparently did not connect the two as cause and effect, as in his autobiography he charged his malady to his service in the Hampshire militia, when "the daily practice of hard and even excessive drinking" had sown in his constitution "the seeds of the gout." [2]

Gibbon has never been a favorite with women, owing largely to his account of his early love affair. While at Lausanne, he had heard much of "the wit and beauty and erudition of Mademoiselle Curchod" and when he first met her, he had reached the age of twenty. "I saw and loved," he wrote. "I found her learned without pedantry, lively in conversation, pure in sentiment, and elegant in manners. . . . She listened to the voice of truth and passion. . . . At Lausanne I indulged my dream of felicity"; and indeed he appeared to be an ardent lover. "He was seen," said a contemporary, "stopping country people near Lausanne and demanding at the point of a naked dagger whether a more adorable creature existed than Suzanne Curchod." [3] On his return to England, however, he soon discovered that his father would not hear of this alliance, and he thus related the sequence: "After a painful struggle, I yielded to my fate. . . . I sighed as a lover, I obeyed as a son." [4]　From

---

[1] Letters, II, 129.　　　　[2] Ibid., 189.
[3] Ibid., I, 40.　　　　[4] Autobiography, pp. 151, 239.

England he wrote to Mademoiselle Curchod breaking off the engagement. Perhaps it is because of feminine criticism that Cotter Morison indulges in an elaborate defense of Gibbon, which indeed hardly seems necessary. Rousseau, who was privy to the love affair, said that "Gibbon was too cold-blooded a young man for his taste or for Mademoiselle Curchod's happiness." [1] Mademoiselle Curchod a few years later married Necker, a rich Paris banker, who under Louis XVI held the office of director-general of the finances. She was the mother of Madame de Staël, was a leader of the literary society in Paris and, despite the troublous times, must have led a happy life. One delightful aspect of the story is the warm friendship that existed between Madame Necker and Edward Gibbon. This began less than a year after her marriage. "The Curchod (Madame Necker) I saw at Paris," he wrote to his friend Holroyd. "She was very fond of me and the husband particularly civil. Could they insult me more cruelly? Ask me every evening to supper; go to bed, and leave me alone with his wife — what an impertinent security!" [2]

If women read the Correspondence as they do the Autobiography, I think that their aversion to the great historian would be increased by these confiding words to his stepmother, written when he was forty-nine: "The habits of female conversation have sometimes tempted me to acquire the piece of furniture, a wife, and could I unite in a single Woman the virtues and accomplishments of half a dozen

[1] Letters, I, 41.

[2] Letters, I, 81. In 1790 Madame de Staël, then at Coppet, wrote: "Nous possédons dans ce château M. Gibbon, l'ancien amoreux de ma mère, celui qui voulait l'épouser. Quand je le vois, je me demande si je serais née de son union avec ma mère: je me reponds que non et qu'il suffisait de mon père seul pour que je vinsse au monde." — Hill's ed., 107, n. 2.

of my acquaintance, I would instantly pay my addresses to the Constellation." [1]

I have always been impressed with Gibbon's pride at being the author of "six volumes in quartos"; but as nearly all histories now are published in octavo, I had not a distinct idea of the appearance of a quarto volume until the preparation of this essay led me to look at different editions of Gibbon in the Boston Athenæum. There I found the quartos, the first volume of which is the third edition, published in 1777 [it will be remembered that the original publication of the first volume was in February, 1776]. The volume is $11\frac{1}{4}$ inches long by 9 inches wide and is much heavier than our very heavy octavo volumes. With this volume in my hand I could appreciate the remark of the Duke of Gloucester when Gibbon brought him the second volume of the "Decline and Fall." Laying the quarto on the table he said, "Another d—d thick square book! Always scribble, scribble, scribble! Eh! Mr. Gibbon?" [2]

During my researches at the Athenæum, I found an octavo edition, the first volume of which was published in 1791, and on the cover was written, "Given to the Athenæum by Charles Cabot. Received December 10, 1807." This was the year of the foundation of the Athenæum. On the quarto of 1777 there was no indication, but the scholarly cataloguer informed me that it was probably also received in 1807. Three later editions than these two are in this library, the last of which is Bury's of 1900 to which I have constantly referred. Meditating in the quiet alcove, with the two early editions of Gibbon before me, I found an answer to the comment of H. G. Wells in his book "The Future in America" which I confess had somewhat irritated me. Thus wrote Wells: "Frankly I grieve over Boston as a

[1] Letters, II, 143.   [2] Birkbeck Hill's ed., 127.

great waste of leisure and energy, as a frittering away of moral and intellectual possibilities. We give too much to the past. . . . We are obsessed by the scholastic prestige of mere knowledge and genteel remoteness." [1] Pondering this iconoclastic utterance, how delightful it is to light upon evidence in the way of well-worn volumes that, since 1807, men and women here have been carefully reading Gibbon, who, as Dean Milman said, "has bridged the abyss between ancient and modern times and connected together the two worlds of history." [2] A knowledge of "The Decline and Fall" is a basis for the study of all other history; it is a mental discipline, and a training for the problems of modern life. These Athenæum readers did not waste their leisure, did not give too much to the past. They were supremely right to take account of the scholastic prestige of Gibbon, and to endeavor to make part of their mental fiber this greatest history of modern times.

I will close with a quotation from the Autobiography, which in its sincerity and absolute freedom from literary cant will be cherished by all whose desire is to behold "the bright countenance of truth in the quiet and still air of delightful studies." "I have drawn a high prize in the lottery of life," wrote Gibbon. "I am disgusted with the affectation of men of letters, who complain that they have renounced a substance for a shadow and that their fame affords a poor compensation for envy, censure, and persecution. My own experience at least has taught me a very different lesson: twenty happy years have been animated by the labor of my history; and its success has given me a name, a rank, a character in the world, to which I should not otherwise have been entitled. . . . D'Alembert relates that as he was walking in the gardens of Sans-souci

<hr />

[1] p. 235.   [2] Smith's ed., I, vii.

with the King of Prussia, Frederick said to him, 'Do you see that old woman, a poor weeder, asleep on that sunny bank? She is probably a more happy Being than either of us.'" Now the comment of Gibbon: "The King and the Philosopher may speak for themselves; for my part I do not envy the old woman." [1]

[1] Autobiography, 343, 346.

SAMUEL RAWSON GARDINER

A paper read before the Massachusetts Historical Society at the
March meeting of 1902, and printed in the *Atlantic Monthly*,
May, 1902.

SAMUEL RAWSON GARDINER

It is my purpose to say a word of Samuel Rawson Gardiner, the English historian, who died February 23, 1902, and who in his research and manner of statement represents fitly the scientific school of historical writers. He was thorough in his investigation, sparing neither labor nor pains to get at the truth. It may well enough be true that the designedly untruthful historian, like the undevout astronomer, is an anomaly, for inaccuracy comes not from purpose, but from neglect. Now Gardiner went to the bottom of things, and was not satisfied until he had compassed all the material within his reach. As a matter of course he read many languages. Whether his facts were in Spanish, Italian, French, German, Dutch, Swedish, or English made apparently no difference. Nor did he stop at what was in plain language. He read a diary written chiefly in symbols, and many letters in cipher. A large part of his material was in manuscript, which entailed greater labor than if it had been in print. As one reads the prefaces to his various volumes and his footnotes, amazement is the word to express the feeling that a man could have accomplished so much in forty-seven years. One feels that there is no one-sided use of any material. The Spanish, the Venetian, the French, the Dutch nowhere displaces the English. In Froude's Elizabeth one gets the impression that the Simancas manuscripts furnish a disproportionate basis of the narrative; in Ranke's England, that the story is made up too much from the Venetian archives. Gardiner himself copied many Simancas manuscripts in Spain, and he studied the archives in Venice, Paris, Brussels, and Rome, but these, and all the other great mass of foreign material, are kept adjunctive to that found in his own land. My impression from a study of his volumes is that more than half of his material is in manuscript, but because he has matter which no one else had ever used, he does not neglect the printed pages open to every one. To form "a judgment on the character and aims of Cromwell," he writes, "it is absolutely necessary to take Carlyle's monumental work as a starting point;"[1] yet, distrusting Carlyle's printed transcripts, he goes back to the original speeches and letters themselves. Carlyle, he says, "amends the text without warning" in many places; these emendations Gardiner corrects, and out of the abundance of his learning he stops a moment to show how Carlyle has misled the learned Dr. Murray in attributing to Cromwell the use of the word "communicative" in its modern meaning, when it was on the contrary employed in what is now an obsolete sense.[2]

Gardiner's great work is the History of England from 1603 to 1656. In the revised editions there are ten volumes called the "History of England, from the Accession of James I to the Outbreak of the Civil War," and four volumes on the Great Civil War. Since this revision he has published three volumes on the History of the Commonwealth and the Protectorate. He was also the author of a number of smaller volumes, a contributor to the Encyclopædia Britannica and the Dictionary of National Biography, and for ten years editor-in-chief of the *English Historical Review*.

I know not which is the more remarkable, the learning, accuracy, and diligence of the man, or withal his modesty.

---

[1] History of the Great Civil War, I, viii.
[2] History of the Commonwealth and the Protectorate, III, 27.

With his great store of knowledge, the very truthfulness of his soul impels him to be forward in admitting his own mistakes. Lowell said in 1878 that Darwin was "almost the only perfectly disinterested lover of truth" he had ever encountered. Had Lowell known the historian as we know him, he would have placed Gardiner upon the same elevation. In the preface to the revised ten-volume edition he alludes to the "defects" of his work. "Much material," he wrote, "has accumulated since the early volumes were published, and my own point of view is not quite the same as it was when I started with the first years of James I."[1] The most important contribution to this portion of his period had been Spedding's edition of Bacon's Letters and Life. In a note to page 208 of his second volume he tells how Spedding's arguments have caused him to modify some of his statements, although the two regard the history of the seventeenth century differently. Writing this soon after the death of Spedding, to which he refers as "the loss of one whose mind was so acute and whose nature was so patient and kindly," he adds, "It was a true pleasure to have one's statements and arguments exposed to the testing fire of his hostile criticism." Having pointed out later some inaccuracies in the work of Professor Masson, he accuses himself. "I have little doubt," he writes, "that if my work were subjected to as careful a revision, it would yield a far greater crop of errors."[2]

Gardiner was born in 1829. Soon after he was twenty-six years old he conceived the idea of writing the history of England from the accession of James I to the restoration of Charles II. It was a noble conception, but his means were small. Having married, as his first wife, the youngest daughter of Edward Irving, the enthusiastic founder of the

[1] History, I, v.   [2] Ibid., IX, viii.

Catholic Apostolic Church, he became an Irvingite. Because he was an Irvingite, his university, — he was a son of Oxford, — so it is commonly said, would give him no position whereby he might gain his living. Nevertheless, Gardiner studied and toiled, and in 1863 published two volumes entitled "A History of England from the Accession of James I to the Disgrace of Chief Justice Coke." Of this work only one hundred and forty copies were sold. Still he struggled on. In 1869 two volumes called "Prince Charles and the Spanish Marriage" were published and sold five hundred copies. Six years later appeared two volumes entitled "A History of England under the Duke of Buckingham and Charles I." This installment paid expenses, but no profit. One is reminded of what Carlyle said about the pecuniary rewards of literary men in England: "Homer's Iliad would have brought the author, had he offered it to Mr. Murray on the half-profit system, say five-and-twenty guineas. The Prophecies of Isaiah would have made a small article in a review which . . . could cheerfully enough have remunerated him with a five-pound note." The first book from which Gardiner received any money was a little volume for the Epochs of Modern History Series on the Thirty Years' War, published in 1874. Two more installments of the history appearing in 1877 and 1881 made up the first edition of what is now our ten-volume history, but in the meantime some of the volumes went out of print. It was not until 1883, the year of the publication of the revised edition, that the value of his labors was generally recognized. During this twenty-eight years, from the age of twenty-six to fifty-four, Gardiner had his living to earn. He might have recalled the remark made, I think, by either Goldsmith or Lamb, that the books which will live are not those by which we ourselves can live. Therefore Gardiner got his bread by teaching. He became a professor in King's College, London, and he lectured on history for the London Society for the Extension of University Teaching, having large audiences all over London, and being well appreciated in the East End. He wrote schoolbooks on history. Finally success came twenty-eight years after his glorious conception, twenty years after the publication of his first volume. He had had a hard struggle for a living with money coming in by driblets. Bread won in such a way is come by hard, yet he remained true to his ideal. His potboilers were good and honest books; his brief history on the Thirty Years' War has received the praise of scholars. Recognition brought him money rewards. In 1882 Mr. Gladstone bestowed upon him a civil list pension of £150 a year. Two years later All Souls College, Oxford, elected him to a research fellowship; when this expired Merton made him a fellow. Academic honors came late. Not until 1884, when he was fifty-five, did he take his degree of M.A. Edinburgh conferred upon him an LL.D., and Göttingen a Ph.D.; but he was sixty-six when he received the coveted D.C.L. from his own university. The year previous Lord Rosebery offered him the Regius Professorship of History at Oxford, but he declined it because the prosecution of his great work required him to be near the British Museum. It is worthy of mention that in 1874, nine years before he was generally appreciated in England, the Massachusetts Historical Society elected him a corresponding member.[1]

During the latter part of his life Gardiner resided in the country near London, whence it took him about an hour to reach the British Museum, where he did his work. He labored on his history from eleven o'clock to half-past four, with an intermission of half an hour for luncheon. He did

[1] He was transferred to the roll of honorary members in October, 1896.

not dictate to a stenographer, but wrote everything out. Totally unaccustomed to collaboration, he never employed a secretary or assistant of any kind. In his evenings he did no serious labor; he spent them with his family, attended to his correspondence, or read a novel. Thus he wrought five hours daily. What a brain, and what a splendid training he had given himself to accomplish such results in so short a working day!

In the preface to his first volume of the "History of the Commonwealth," published in 1894, Gardiner said that he was "entering upon the third and last stage of a task the accomplishment of which seemed to me many years ago to be within the bounds of possibility." One more volume bringing the history down to the death of Cromwell would have completed the work, and then Mr. Charles H. Firth, a fellow of All Souls College, Oxford, was to take up the story. Firth now purposes to begin his narrative with the year 1656. Gardiner's mantle has fallen on worthy shoulders.

Where historical scholars congregate in England and America, Gardiner is highly esteemed. But the critics must have their day. They cannot attack him for lack of diligence and accuracy, which according to Gibbon, the master of us all, are the prime requisites of a historian, so they assert that he was deficient in literary style, he had no dramatic power, his work is not interesting and will not live. Gardiner is the product solely of the university and the library. You may visualize him at Oxford, in the British Museum, or at work in the archives on the Continent, but of affairs and of society by personal contact he knew nothing. In short, he was not a man of the world, and the histories must be written, so these critics aver, by those who have an actual knowledge by experience of their fellow-men. It is profitable to examine these dicta by the light of concrete examples. Froude saw much of society, and was a man of the world. He wrote six volumes on the reign of Elizabeth, from which we get the distinct impression that the dominant characteristics of Elizabeth were meanness, vacillation, selfishness, and cruelty. Gardiner in an introductory chapter of forty-three pages restores to us the great queen of Shakespeare, who brought upon her land "a thousand, thousand blessings." She loved her people well, he writes, and ruled them wisely. She "cleared the way for liberty, though she understood it not." [1] Elsewhere he speaks of "her high spirit and enlightened judgment." [2] The writer who has spent his life in the library among dusty archives estimates the great ruler more correctly than the man of the world. We all know Macaulay, a member of Parliament, a member of the Supreme Council of India, a cabinet minister, a historian of great merit, a brilliant man of letters. In such a one, according to the principles laid down by these critics, we should expect to find a supreme judge of men. Macaulay in his essays and the first chapter of the History painted Wentworth and Laud in the very blackest of colors, which "had burned themselves into the heart of the people of England." Gardiner came. Wentworth and Laud, he wrote, were controlled by a "noble ambition," which was "not stained with personal selfishness or greed." [3] "England may well be proud of possessing in Wentworth a nobler if a less practical statesman than Richelieu, of the type to which the great cardinal belonged." [4] Again Wentworth was "the high-minded, masterful statesman, erring gravely through defects of temper and knowledge." [5] From Macaulay we carry away the impression that Wentworth was very wicked and that Cromwell was very good. Gardiner

[1] History, I, 43.   [2] Ibid., VIII, 36.   [3] Ibid., 67.   [4] Ibid., 215.
[5] Ibid., IX, 229.

loved Cromwell not less than did Macaulay, but thus he speaks of his government: "Step by step the government of the Commonwealth was compelled . . . to rule by means which every one of its members would have condemned if they had been employed by Charles or Wentworth." Is it not a triumph for the bookish man that in his estimate of Wentworth and Laud he has with him the consensus of the historical scholars of England?

What a change there has been in English opinion of Cromwell in the last half century! Unquestionably that is due to Carlyle more than to any other one man, but there might have been a reaction from the conception of the hero worshiper had it not been supported and somewhat modified by so careful and impartial a student as Gardiner.

The alteration of sentiment toward Wentworth and Laud is principally due to Gardiner, that toward Cromwell is due to him in part. These are two of the striking results, but they are only two of many things we see differently because of the single-minded devotion of this great historian. We know the history in England from 1603 to 1656 better than we do that of any other period of the world; and for this we are indebted mainly to Samuel Rawson Gardiner.

WILLIAM E. H. LECKY

A paper read before the Massachusetts Historical Society at the
November meeting of 1903.

WILLIAM E. H. LECKY

AMAZEMENT was the feeling of the reading world on learning that the author of the History of Rationalism was only twenty-seven, and the writer of the History of European Morals only thirty-one. The sentiment was that a prodigy of learning had appeared, and a perusal of these works now renders comprehensible the contemporary astonishment. The Morals (published in 1869) is the better book of the two, and, if I may judge from my own personal experience, it may be read with delight when young, and re-read with respect and advantage at an age when the enthusiasms of youth have given way to the critical attitude of experience. Grant all the critics say of it, that the reasoning by which Lecky attempts to demolish the utilitarian theory of morals is no longer of value, and that it lacks the consistency of either the orthodox or the agnostic, that there is no new historical light, and that much of the treatise is commonplace, nevertheless the historical illustrations and disquisitions, the fresh combination of well-known facts are valuable for instruction and for a new point of view. His analysis of the causes of the decline and fall of the Roman Empire is drawn, of course, from Gibbon, but I have met those who prefer the interesting story of Lecky to the majestic sweep of the great master. Much less brilliant than Buckle's "History of Civilization," the first volume of which appeared twelve years earlier, the Morals has stood better the test of time.

The intellectual biography of so precocious a writer is interesting, and fortunately it has been related by Lecky himself. When he entered Trinity College, Dublin, in 1856, "Mill was in the zenith of his fame and influence"; Hugh Miller was attempting to reconcile the recent discoveries of geology with the Mosaic cosmogony. "In poetry," wrote Lecky, "Tennyson and Longfellow reigned, I think with an approach to equality which has not continued." In government the orthodox political economists furnished the theory and the Manchester school the practice. All this intellectual fermentation affected this inquiring young student; but at first Bishop Butler's Analogy and sermons, which were then much studied at Dublin, had the paramount influence. Of the living men, Archbishop Whately, then at Dublin, held sway. Other writers whom he mastered were Coleridge, Newman, and Emerson, Pascal, Bossuet, Rousseau, and Voltaire, Dugald Stewart, and Mill. In 1857 Buckle burst upon the world, and proved a stimulus to Lecky as well as to most serious historical students. The result of these studies, Lecky relates, was his History of Rationalism, published in the early part of 1865.

The claim made by many of Lecky's admirers, that he was a philosophic historian, as distinct from literary historians like Carlyle and Macaulay, and scientific like Stubbs and Gardiner, has injured him in the eyes of many historical students who believe that if there be such a thing as the philosophy of history the narrative ought to carry it naturally. To interrupt the relation of events or the delineation of character with parading of trite reflections or with rashly broad generalizations is neither science nor art. Lecky has sometimes been condemned by students who, revolting at the term "philosophy" in connection with history, have failed to read his greatest work, the "History of England in the Eighteenth Century." This is a decided advance on the History of Morals, and shows honest investigation in original material, much of it manuscript, and an excellent power of generalization widely different from that which exhibits itself in a paltry philosophy. These volumes are a real contribution to historical knowledge. Parts of them which I like often to recur to are the account of the ministry of Walpole, the treatment of "parliamentary corruption," of the condition of London, and of "national tastes and manners." His Chapter IX, which relates the rise of Methodism, has a peculiarly attractive swing and go, and his use of anecdote is effective.

Chapter XX, on the "Causes of the French Revolution," covering one hundred and forty-one pages, is an ambitious effort, but it shows a thorough digestion of his material, profound reflection, and a lively presentation of his view. Mr. Morse Stephens believes that it is idle to attempt to inquire into the causes of this political and social overturn. If a historian tells the *how*, he asserts he should not be asked to tell the *why*. This is an epigrammatic statement of a tenet of the scientific historical school of Oxford, but men will always be interested in inquiring why the French Revolution happened, and such chapters as this of Lecky, a blending of speculation and narrative, will hold their place. These volumes have much well and impartially written Irish history, and being published between 1878 and 1890, at the time when the Irish question in its various forms became acute, they attracted considerable attention from the political world. Gladstone was an admirer of Lecky, and said in a chat with John Morley: "Lecky has real insight into the motives of statesmen. Now Carlyle, so mighty as he is in flash and penetration, has no eye for motives. Macaulay, too, is so caught by a picture, by color, by surface, that he is seldom to be counted on for just account of motive." The Irish chapters furnished arguments for the

Liberals, but did not convert Lecky himself to the policy of home rule. When Gladstone and his party adopted it, he became a Liberal Unionist, and as such was elected in 1895 a member of the House of Commons by Dublin University. In view of the many comments that he was not successful in parliamentary life, I may say that the election not only came to him unsought, but that he recognized that he was too old to adapt himself to the atmosphere of the House of Commons; he accepted the position in the belief which was pressed. upon him by many friends that he could in Parliament be useful to the University.

Within less than three years have we commemorated in this hall three great English historians — Stubbs, Gardiner, and Lecky. The one we honor to-day was the most popular of the three. Not studied so much at the seats of learning, he is better known to journalists, to statesmen, to men of affairs, in short to general readers. Even our Society made him an honorary member fourteen years before it so honored Gardiner, although Gardiner was the older man and two volumes of his history had been published before Lecky's Rationalism, and two volumes more in the same year as the Morals. One year after it was published, Rationalism went into a third edition. Gardiner's first volumes sold one hundred and forty copies. It must, however, be stated that the Society recognized Gardiner's work as early as 1874 by electing him a corresponding member.

It is difficult to guess how long Lecky will be read. His popularity is distinct. He was the rare combination of a scholar and a man of the world, made so by his own peculiar talent and by lucky opportunities. He was not obliged to earn his living. In early life, by intimate personal intercourse, he drew intellectual inspiration from Dean Milman, and later he learned practical politics through his friendship with Lord Russell. He knew well Herbert Spencer, Huxley, and Tyndall. In private conversation he was a very interesting man. His discourse ran on books and on men; he turned from one to the other and mixed up the two with a ready familiarity. He went much into London society, and though entirely serious and without having, so far as I know, a gleam of humor, he was a fluent and entertaining talker.

Mr. Lecky was vitally interested in the affairs of this country, and sympathized with the North during our Civil War. He once wrote to me: "I am old enough to remember vividly your great war, and was then much with an American friend — a very clever lawyer named George Bemis — whom I came to know very well at Rome. . . . I was myself a decided Northerner, but the 'right of revolution' was always rather a stumbling block." Talking with Mr. Lecky in 1895, not long after the judgment of the United States Supreme Court that the income tax was unconstitutional, he expressed the opinion that it was a grand decision, evidencing a high respect for private property, but in the next breath came the question, "How are you ever to manage continuing the payment of those enormous pensions of yours?"

It is not, I think, difficult to explain why Stubbs and Gardiner are more precious possessions for students than Lecky. Gardiner devoted his life to the seventeenth century. If we may reckon the previous preparation and the ceaseless revision, Stubbs devoted a good part of his life to the constitutional history from the beginnings of it to Henry VII. Lecky's eight volumes on the eighteenth century were published in thirteen years. A mastery of such an amount of original material as Stubbs and Gardiner mastered was impossible within that time. Lecky had the

faculty of historic divination which compensated to some
extent for the lack of a more thorough study of the sources.
Genius stood in the place of painstaking engrossment in a
single task.

The last important work of Lecky, "Democracy and
Liberty," was a brave undertaking. Many years ago he
wrote: "When I was deeply immersed in the 'History of
England in the Eighteenth Century,' I remember being
struck by the saying of an old and illustrious friend that he
could not understand the state of mind of a man who, when
so many questions of burning and absorbing interest were
rising around him, could devote the best years of his life to
the study of a vanished past." Hence the book which considered present issues of practical politics and party con-
troversies, and a result that satisfied no party and hardly
any faction. It is an interesting question who chose the
better part, — he or Stubbs and Gardiner — they who devoted themselves entirely to the past or he who made a
conscientious endeavor to bring to bear his study of history
upon the questions of the present.

SIR SPENCER WALPOLE

A paper read before the Massachusetts Historical Society at the November meeting of 1907.

SIR SPENCER WALPOLE

SIR SPENCER WALPOLE was an excellent historian and industrious writer. His first important work, entitled "The History of England from 1815," was published at intervals from 1878 to 1886; the first installment appeared when he was thirty-nine years old. This in six volumes carried the history to 1858 in an interesting, accurate, and impartial narrative. Four of the five chapters of the first volume are entitled "The Material Condition of England in 1815," "Society in England," "Opinion in 1815," "The Last of the Ebb Tide," and they are masterly in their description and relation. During the Napoleonic wars business was good. The development of English manufactures, due largely to the introduction of steam as a motive power, was marked. "Twenty years of war," he wrote, "had concentrated the trade of the world in the British Empire." Wheat was dear; in consequence the country gentlemen received high rents. The clergy, being largely dependent on tithes, — the tenth of the produce, — found their incomes increased as the price of corn advanced. But the laboring classes, both those engaged in manufactures and agriculture, did not share in the general prosperity. Either their wages did not rise at all or did not advance commensurately with the increase of the cost of living and the decline in the value of the currency. Walpole's detailed and thorough treatment of this subject is historic work of high value.

In the third volume I was much impressed with his account of the Reform Act of 1832. We all have read that wonderful story over and over again, but I doubt whether its

salient points have been better combined and presented
than in Walpole's chapter. I had not remembered the
reason of the selection of Lord John Russell to present the
bill in the House of Commons when he was only Paymaster
of the Forces, without a seat in the Cabinet. It will, of
course, be recalled that Lord Grey, the Prime Minister, was
in the House of Lords, and, not so readily I think, that
Althorp was Chancellor of the Exchequer and the leader of
the House of Commons. On Althorp, under ordinary circumstances, it would have been incumbent to take charge
of this highly important measure, which had been agreed
upon by the Cabinet after counsel with the King. Russell
was the youngest son of the Duke of Bedford; and the
Duke was one of the large territorial magnates and a pro-
prietor of rotten boroughs. "A bill recommended by his
son's authority," wrote Walpole, "was likely to reassure
timid or wavering politicians." "Russell," Walpole continued, "told his tale in the plainest language. But the
tale which he had to tell required no extraordinary language
to adorn it. The Radicals had not dared to expect, the
Tories, in their wildest fears, had not apprehended, so complete a measure. Enthusiasm was visible on one side of
the House; consternation and dismay on the other. At
last, when Russell read the list of boroughs which were
doomed to extinction, the Tories hoped that the complete-
ness of the measure would insure its defeat. Forgetting
their fears, they began to be amused and burst into peals of
derisive laughter" (III, 208).

Walpole's next book was the "Life of Lord John Russell,"
two volumes published in 1889. This was undertaken at
the request of Lady Russell, who placed at his disposal a
mass of private and official papers and "diaries and letters
of a much more private nature." She also acceded to his

request that she was not to see the biography until it was ready for publication, so that the whole responsibility of it would be Walpole's alone. The Queen gave him access to three bound volumes of Russell's letters to herself, and sanctioned the publication of certain letters of King William IV. Walpole wrote the biography in about two years and a half; and this, considering that at the time he held an active office, displayed unusual industry. If I may judge the work by a careful study of the chapter on "The American Civil War," it is a valuable contribution to political history.

Passing over three minor publications, we come to Walpole's "History of Twenty-five Years," two volumes of which were published in 1904. A brief extract from his preface is noteworthy, written as it is by a man of keen intelligence, with great power of investigation and continuous labor, and possessed of a sound judgment. After a reference to his "History of England from 1815," he said: "The time has consequently arrived when it ought to be as possible to write the History of England from 1857 to 1880, as it was twenty years ago to bring down the narrative of that History to 1856 or 1857. . . . So far as I am able to judge, most of the material which is likely to be available for British history in the period with which these two volumes are concerned [1856–1870] is already accessible. It is not probable that much which is wholly new remains unavailable." I read carefully these two volumes when they first appeared, and found them exceedingly fascinating. Palmerston and Russell, Gladstone and Disraeli, are made so real that we follow their contests as if we ourselves had a hand in them. A half dozen or more years ago an Englishman told me that Palmerston and Russell were no longer considered of account in England. But I do not believe one can rise from reading these volumes without being glad of a knowledge of these two men whose patriotism was of a high order. Walpole's several characterizations, in a summing up of Palmerston, display his knowledge of men. "Men pronounced Lord Melbourne indifferent," he wrote, "Sir Robert Peel cold, Lord John Russell uncertain, Lord Aberdeen weak, Lord Derby haughty, Mr. Gladstone subtle, Lord Beaconsfield unscrupulous. But they had no such epithet for Lord Palmerston. He was as earnest as Lord Melbourne was indifferent, as strong as Lord Aberdeen was weak, as honest as Lord Beaconsfield was unscrupulous. Sir Robert Peel repelled men by his temper; Lord John Russell, by his coldness; Lord Derby offended them by his pride; Mr. Gladstone distracted them by his subtlety. But Lord Palmerston drew both friends and foes together by the warmth of his manners and the excellence of his heart" (I, 525).

Walpole's knowledge of continental politics was apparently thorough. At all events, any one who desires two entrancing tales, should read the chapter on "The Union of Italy," of which Cavour and Napoleon III are the heroes; and the two chapters entitled "The Growth of Prussia and the Decline of France" and "The Fall of the Second Empire." In these two chapters Napoleon III again appears, but Bismarck is the hero. Walpole's chapter on "The American Civil War" is the writing of a broad-minded, intelligent man, who could look on two sides.

Of Walpole's last book, "Studies in Biography," published in 1907, I have left myself no time to speak. Those who are interested in it should read the review of it in the *Nation* early this year, which awards it high and unusual commendation.

The readers of Walpole's histories may easily detect in them a treatment not possible from a mere closet student of books and manuscripts. A knowledge of the science of government and of practical politics is there. For Walpole was of a political family. He was of the same house as the great Whig Prime Minister, Sir Robert; and his father was Home Secretary in the Lord Derby ministry of 1858, and again in 1866, when he had to deal with the famous Hyde Park meeting of July 23. On his mother's side he was a grandson of Spencer Perceval, the Prime Minister who in 1812 was assassinated in the lobby of the House of Commons. Walpole's earliest publication was a biography of Perceval.

And Spencer Walpole himself was a man of affairs. A clerk in the War Office in 1858, private secretary to his father in 1866, next year Inspector of Fisheries, later Lieutenant-Governor of the Isle of Man, and from 1893 to 1899 Secretary to the Post-office. In spite of all this administrative work his books show that he was a wide, general reader, apart from his special historical studies. He wrote in an agreeable literary style, with Macaulay undoubtedly as his model, although he was by no means a slavish imitator. His "History of Twenty-five Years" seems to me to be written with a freer hand than the earlier history. He is here animated by the spirit rather than the letter of Macaulay. I no longer noticed certain tricks of expression which one catches so easily in a study of the great historian, and which seem so well to suit Macaulay's own work, but nobody else's.

An article by Walpole on my first four volumes, in the *Edinburgh Review* of January, 1901, led to a correspondence which resulted in my receiving an invitation last May to pass Sunday with him at Hartfield Grove, his Sussex country place. We were to meet at Victoria station and take an early morning train. Seeing Mr. Frederic Harrison the day previous, I asked for a personal description of his friend Walpole in order that I might easily recognize him. "Well," says Harrison, "perhaps I can guide you. A while ago I sat next to a lady during a dinner who took me for Walpole and never discovered her mistake until, when she addressed me as Sir Spencer, I undeceived her just as the ladies were retiring from the table. Now I am the elder by eight years and I don't think I look like Walpole, but that good lady had another opinion." Walpole and Harrison met that Saturday evening at the Academy dinner, and Walpole obtained a personal description of myself. This caution on both our parts was unnecessary. We were the only historians traveling down on the train and could not possibly have missed one another. I found him a thoroughly genial man, and after fifteen minutes in the railway carriage we were well acquainted. The preface to his "History of Twenty-five Years" told that the two volumes were the work of five years. I asked him how he was getting on with the succeeding volumes. He replied that he had done a good deal of work on them, and now that he was no longer in an administrative position he could concentrate his efforts, and he expected to have the work finished before long. I inquired if the prominence of his family in politics hampered him at all in writing so nearly contemporary history, and he said, "Not a bit." An hour of the railroad and a half-hour's drive brought us to his home. It was not an ancestral place, but a purchase not many years back. An old house had been remodeled with modern improvements, and comfort and ease were the predominant aspects. Sir Spencer proposed a "turn" before luncheon, which meant a short walk, and after luncheon we had a real walk. I am aware that the English mile and our own are alike 5280 feet, but I am always impressed with the fact that the English mile seems longer, and so I was on this Sunday. For after a good two hours' exertion over hills and meadows my host told me that we had gone only five miles. Only by direct question did I elicit the fact that had he been alone he would have done seven miles in the same time.

There were no other guests, and Lady Walpole, Sir Spencer, and I had all of the conversation at luncheon and dinner and during the evening. We talked about history and literature, English and American politics, and public men. He was singularly well informed about our country, although he had only made one brief visit and then in an official capacity. English expressions of friendship are now so common that I will not quote even one of the many scattered through his volumes, but he displayed everywhere a candid appreciation of our good traits and creditable doings. I was struck with his knowledge and love of lyric poetry. Byron, Shelley, Keats, Tennyson, Longfellow, and Lowell were thoroughly familiar to him. He would repeat some favorite passage of Keats, and at once turn to a discussion of the administrative details of his work in the post-office. Of course the day and evening passed very quickly, — it was one of the days to be marked with a white stone, — and when I bade Walpole good-by on the Monday morning I felt as if I were parting from a warm friend. I found him broad-minded, intelligent, sympathetic, affable, and he seemed as strong physically as he was sound intellectually. His death on Sunday, July 7, of cerebral hemorrhage was alike a shock and a grief.

JOHN RICHARD GREEN

Address at a gathering of historians on June 5, 1909, to mark the placing of a tablet in the inner quadrangle of Jesus College, Oxford, to the memory of John Richard Green.

JOHN RICHARD GREEN

I WISH indeed that I had the tongues of men and of angels
to express the admiration of the reading public of America
for the History of John Richard Green.   I suppose that he
has had more readers in our country than any other historian
except Macaulay, and he has shaped the opinions of men who
read, more than any writers of history except those whom
John Morley called the great born men of letters, — Gibbon,
Macaulay, and Carlyle.

I think it is the earlier volumes rather than the last volume
of his more extended work which have taken hold of us.   Of
course we thrill at his tribute to Washington, where he has
summed up our reverence, trust, and faith in him in one
single sentence which shows true appreciation and deep
feeling; and it flatters our national vanity, of which we
have a goodly stock, to read in his fourth volume that the
creation of the United States was one of the turning points
in the history of the world.

No saying is more trite, at any rate to an educated American audience, than that the development of the English
nation is one of the most wonderful things, if not the most
wonderful thing, which history records.   That history before James I is our own, and, to our general readers, it has
never been so well presented as in Green's first two volumes.
The victories of war are our own.   It was our ancestors
who preserved liberty, maintained order, set the train moving toward religious toleration, and wrought out that language and literature which we are proud of, as well
as you.

For my own part, I should not have liked to miss reading and re-reading the five chapters on Elizabeth in the second volume. What eloquence in simply the title of the last, — The England of Shakespeare! And in fact my conception of Elizabeth, derived from Shakespeare, is confirmed by Green. As I think how much was at stake in the last half of the sixteenth century, and how well the troubles were met by that great monarch and the wise statesman whom she called to her aid, I feel that we could not be what we are, had a weak, irresolute sovereign been at the head of the state.

With the power of a master Green manifests what was accomplished. At the accession of Elizabeth — "Never" so he wrote — "had the fortunes of England sunk to a lower ebb. The loss of Calais gave France the mastery of the Channel. The French King in fact 'bestrode the realm, having one foot in Calais, and the other in Scotland.' "

And at the death of Elizabeth, thus Green tells the story: "The danger which had hitherto threatened our national existence and our national unity had disappeared: France clung to the friendship of England, Spain trembled beneath its blows."

With the wide range of years of his subject, with a grasp of an extended period akin to Gibbon's, complete accuracy was, of course, not attainable, but Samuel R. Gardiner once told me that Green, although sometimes inaccurate in details, gave a general impression that was justifiable and correct; and that is in substance the published opinion of Stubbs.

Goethe said that in reading Molière you perceive that he possessed the charm of an amiable nature in habitual contact with good society. So we, who had not the advantage of personal intercourse, divined was the case of Green; and when the volume of Letters appeared, we saw that we had guessed correctly. But not until then did we know of his devotion to his work, and his heroic struggle, which renders the story of his short and brilliant career a touching and fascinating biography of a historian who made his mark upon his time.

EDWARD L. PIERCE

A paper read before the Massachusetts Historical Society at the
October meeting of 1897.

EDWARD L. PIERCE

I SHALL first speak of Mr. Pierce as an author. His Life of Sumner it seems to me is an excellent biography, and the third and fourth volumes of it are an important contribution to the history of our country. Any one who has gone through the original material of the period he embraces must be struck not only with the picture of Sumner, but with the skill of the biographer in the use of his data to present a general historical view. The injunction of Cicero, "Choose with discretion out of the plenty that lies before you," Mr. Pierce observed. To those who know how extensive was his reading of books, letters, newspaper files, how much he had conversed with the actors in those stirring scenes — and who will take into account the mass of memories that crowd upon the mind of one who has lived through such an era — this biography will seem not too long but rather admirable in its relative brevity. In a talk that I had with Mr. Pierce I referred to the notice in an English literary weekly of his third and fourth volumes which maintained that the biography was twice too long, and I took occasion to say that in comparison with other American works of the kind the criticism seemed unjust. "Moreover," I went on, "I think you showed restraint in not making use of much of your valuable material, — of the interesting and even important unprinted letters of Cobden, the Duke of Argyll, and of John Bright." "Yes," replied Mr. Pierce, with a twinkle in his eye, "I can say with Lord Clive, 'Great Heavens, at this moment I stand astonished at my own moderation.'"

Any one who has studied public sentiment in this country for any period knows how easy it is to generalize from a few facts, and yet, if the subject be more thoroughly investigated, it becomes apparent how unsatisfactory such generalizations are apt to be; not that they are essentially untrue, but rather because they express only a part of the truth. If a student should ask me in what one book he would find the best statement of popular opinion at the North during the Civil War, I should say, Read Sumner's letters as cited in Mr. Pierce's biography with the author's comments. The speeches of Sumner may smell too much of the lamp to be admirable, but the off-hand letters written to his English and to a few American friends during our great struggle are worthy of the highest esteem. From his conversations with the President, the Cabinet ministers, his fellow-senators and congressmen, his newspaper reading, — in short, from the many impressions that go to make up the daily life of an influential public man, — there has resulted an accurate statement of the popular feeling from day to day. In spite of his intense desire to have Englishmen of power and position espouse the right side, he would not misrepresent anything by the suppression of facts, any more than he would make a misleading statement. In the selection of these letters Mr. Pierce has shown a nice discrimination.

Sumner, whom I take to have been one of the most truthful of men, was fortunate in having one of the most honest of biographers. Mr. Pierce would not, I think, have wittingly suppressed anything that told against him. I love to think of one citation which would never have been made by an idolizing biographer, so sharply did it bring out the folly of the opinion expressed. Sumner wrote, May 3, 1863: "There is no doubt here about Hooker. He told Judge Bates . . . that he 'did not mean to drive the enemy but to bag him.' It is thought he is now doing it." The biographer's comment is brief, "The letter was written on the day of Hooker's defeat at Chancellorsville."

It seems to me that Mr. Pierce was as impartial in his writing as is possible for a man who has taken an active part in political affairs, who is thoroughly in earnest, and who has a positive manner of expression. It is not so difficult as some imagine for a student of history whose work is done in the library to be impartial, provided he has inherited or acquired the desire to be fair and honest, and provided he has the diligence and patience to go through the mass of evidence. His historical material will show him that to every question there are two sides. But what of the man who has been in the heat of the conflict, and who, when the fight was on, believed with Sumner that there was no other side? If such a man displays candor, how much greater his merit than the impartiality of the scholar who shuns political activity and has given himself up to a life of speculation!

I had the good fortune to have three long conversations with the Hon. Robert C. Winthrop, the last of which occurred shortly after the publication of the third and fourth volumes of the Life of Sumner. "What," said Mr. Winthrop to me, "do you think of the chapter on the Annexation of Texas and the Mexican War?" "I think," was my reply, "that Mr. Pierce has treated a delicate subject like a gentleman." "From what I have heard of it," responded Mr. Winthrop, earnestly, "and from so much as I have read of it, that is also my own opinion." Such a private conversation I could, of course, repeat, and, somewhat later the occasion presenting itself, I did so to Mr. Pierce. "That is more grateful to me," he said, almost with tears in his eyes, "than all the praise I have received for these volumes."

Mr. Pierce had, I think, the historic sense. I consulted

him several times on the treatment of historical matters,
taking care not to trench on questions where, so different
was our point of view, we could not possibly agree, and I
always received from him advice that was suggestive, even
if I did not always follow it to the letter. I sent to him,
while he was in London, my account of Secretary Cameron's
report proposing to arm the slaves and of his removal from
office by President Lincoln. Mr. Pierce thought my inferences were far-fetched, and wrote: "I prefer the natural
explanation. Horace says we must not introduce a god
into a play unless it is necessary."

As a friend, he was warm-hearted and true. He brought
cheer and animation into your house. His talk was fresh;
his zeal for whatever was uppermost in his mind was con-
tagious, and he inspired you with enthusiasm. He was not
good at conversation, in the French sense of the term, for
he was given to monologue; but he was never dull. His
artlessness was charming. He gave you confidences that
you would have shrunk from hearing out of the mouth of any
other man, in the fear that you intruded on a privacy where
you had no right; but this openness of mind was so natural
in Mr. Pierce that you listened with concern and sympathized warmly. He took interest in everything; he had in-
finite resources, and until his health began to fail, enjoyed
life thoroughly. He loved society, conversation, travel;
and while he had no passion for books, he listened to you
attentively while you gave an abstract or criticism of some
book that was attracting attention. In all intercourse with
him you felt that you were in a healthy moral atmosphere.
I never knew a man who went out of his way oftener to do
good works in which there was absolutely no reward, and
at a great sacrifice of his time — to him a most precious
commodity. He was in the true sense of the word a philan-

thropist, and yet no one would have approved more heartily than he this remark of Emerson: "The professed philanthropists are an altogether odious set of people, whom one would shun as the worst of bores and canters."

His interest in this Society the published Proceedings will show in some measure, but they cannot reflect the tone of devotion in which he spoke of it in conversation, or exhibit his loyalty to it as set forth in the personal letter. It was a real privation that his legislative duties prevented his attending these meetings last winter.

Of Mr. Pierce as a citizen most of you, gentlemen, can speak better than I, but it does appear to me an instance of rare civic virtue that a man of his age, political experience, ability, and mental resources could take pride and pleasure in his service in the House of Representatives of his Commonwealth. He was sixty-eight years old, suffering from disease, yet in his service last winter he did not miss one legislative session nor a day meeting of his committee. His love for his town was a mark of local attachment both praiseworthy and useful. "I would rather be moderator of the Milton town-meeting," he said, "than hold any other office in the United States."

JACOB D. COX

A paper read before the Massachusetts Historical Society at the
October meeting of 1900.

JACOB D. COX

A useful member of the legislature of his state, a general in the army during the Civil War, governor of his state, Secretary of the Interior in President Grant's Cabinet, a member of Congress, the president of a large railroad, a writer of books, dean and teacher in a law school, and a reviewer of books in the *Nation*, — such were the varied activities of General Cox. All this work was done with credit. He bore a prominent part in the battle of Antietam, where Ropes speaks of his "brilliant success"; he was the second in command at the battle of Franklin, and bore the brunt of the battle. "Brigadier-General J. D. Cox," wrote Schofield, the commanding general, in his report, "deserves a very large share of credit for the brilliant victory at Franklin."

The governor of the state of Ohio did not then have a great opportunity of impressing himself upon the minds of the people of his state, but Cox made his mark in the canvass for that office. We must call to mind that in the year 1865, when he was the Republican candidate for governor, President Johnson had initiated his policy of reconstruction, but had not yet made a formal break with his party. Negro suffrage, which only a few had favored during the last year of the war, was now advocated by the radical Republicans, and the popular sentiment of the party was tending in that direction. Cox had been a strong antislavery man before the war, a supporter of President Lincoln in his emancipation measures, but soon after his nomination for governor he wrote a letter to his radical friends at Oberlin in opposition to negro suffrage. "You assume," he said, "that the extension of the right of suffrage to the blacks, leaving them intermixed with the whites, will cure all the trouble. I believe it would rather be like the decision in that outer darkness of which Milton speaks where

> "'chaos umpire sits,
> And by decision more embroils the fray.'"

While governor, he said in a private conversation that he had come to the conclusion "that so large bodies of black men and white as were in presence in the Southern States never could share political power, and that the insistence upon it on the part of the colored people would lead to their ruin."

President Grant appointed General Cox Secretary of the Interior, and he remained for nearly two years in the Cabinet. James Russell Lowell, on a visit to Washington in 1870, gave expression to the feeling among independent Republicans. "Judge Hoar," he wrote, "and Mr. Cox struck me as the only really strong men in the Cabinet." This was long before the Civil Service Reform Act had passed Congress, but Secretary Cox put the Interior Department on a merit basis, and he was ever afterwards an advocate of civil service reform by word of mouth and with his pen. Differences with the President, in which I feel pretty sure that the Secretary was in the right, caused him to resign the office.

Elected to Congress in 1876, he was a useful member for one term. He has always been known to men in public life, and when President McKinley offered him the position of Minister to Spain something over three years ago, it was felt that a well-known and capable man had been selected. For various reasons he did not accept the appointment, but if he had done so, no one could doubt that he would have shown tact and judgment in the difficult position.

As president of the Wabash Railroad, one of the large railroads in the West, he gained a name among business men, and five or six years ago was offered the place of Railroad Commissioner in New York City. This was practically the position of arbitrator between the trunk lines, but he was then Dean of the Cincinnati Law School and interested in a work which he did not care to relinquish.

Besides a controversial monograph, he wrote three books on military campaigns: "Atlanta"; "The March to the Sea; Franklin and Nashville"; "The Battle of Franklin"; and he wrote four excellent chapters for Force's "Life of General Sherman." In these he showed qualities of a military historian of a high order. Before his death he had finished his Reminiscences, which will be brought out by the Scribners this autumn.

His differences with President Grant while in his Cabinet left a wound, and in private conversation he was quite severe in his strictures of many of the President's acts, but he never let this feeling influence him in the slightest degree in the consideration of Grant the General. He had a very high idea of Grant's military talents, which he has in many ways emphatically stated.

Since 1874 he had been a constant contributor to the literary department of the *Nation*. In his book reviews he showed a fine critical faculty and large general information, and some of his obituary notices — especially those of Generals Buell, Grant, Sherman, Joseph E. Johnston, and Jefferson Davis — showed that power of impartial characterization which is so great a merit in a historian. He was an omnivorous reader of serious books. It was difficult to name any noteworthy work of history or biography or any popular book on natural science with which he was not acquainted.

As I saw him two years ago, when he was seventy years old, he was in the best of health and vigor, which seemed to promise many years of life. He was tall, erect, with a frame denoting great physical strength, and he had distinctively a military bearing. He was an agreeable companion, an excellent talker, a scrupulously honest and truthful man, and a gentleman.

EDWARD GAYLORD BOURNE

A paper read before the Massachusetts Historical Society at the
March meeting of 1908.

EDWARD GAYLORD BOURNE

When an associate dies who was not yet forty-eight years old, whom most of us knew as a strong enduring man, who was capable of an immense amount of intellectual work, it is a real calamity, — a calamity which in this case History mourns, as Edward Gaylord Bourne was an excellent teacher and a thorough historical scholar. The physical details of any illness are apt to be repulsive, but the malady in Bourne's case was somehow so bound up in his life that an inquiry into it comes from no morbid curiosity. When ten years old he was attacked with tubercular disease of the hip, and for some weeks his life was despaired of; but he was saved by the loving care of his parents, receiving particular devotion from his father, who was a Congregational minister in charge of a parish in Connecticut. As the left leg had outgrown the other, Bourne was obliged to use crutches for three years, when his father took him to a specialist in Boston, and the result was that he was able to abandon crutches and in the end to get about by an appliance to adjust the lengths of the different legs, such as his friends were familiar with. Despite this disability he developed great physical strength, especially in the chest and arms, but his lameness prevented his accompanying his college companions on long tramps, so that the bicycle was for him a most welcome invention. He became expert in the use of it, riding on it down Pike's Peak at the time of his visit to Colorado; and he performed a similar feat of endurance on another occasion when stopping with me at Jefferson in the White Mountains. Starting early in the morning, he traveled by rail to the terminus of the mountain railroad, went up Mount Washington on the railroad, and rode down the carriage road on his wheel to the Glen House, which ought to have been enough of fatigue and exertion for one day, but he then had about ten miles to make on his bicycle over a somewhat rough mountain road to reach Jefferson. Jefferson he did make, but not until after midnight.

During an acquaintance of over nineteen years with Bourne, I was always impressed with his physical strength and endurance; and I was therefore much surprised to learn, in a letter received from him last winter while I was in Rome, that his youthful malady had attacked him, that he was again on crutches and had been obliged to give up his work at Yale. In truth ever since the autumn of 1906 he has had a painful, hopeless struggle. He has had the benefit of all the resources of medicine and surgery, and he and his wife were buoyed up by hope until the last; but as the sequel of one of a series of operations death came to his relief on February 24.

Only less remarkable than his struggle for life and physical strength was his energy in acquiring an education. The sacrifices that parents in New England and the rest of the country make in order to send their boys to school and college is a common enough circumstance, but not always is the return so satisfactory as it was in the case of Edward Bourne, and his brother. Edward went to the Norwich Academy, where his studious disposition and diligent purpose gained him the favor of the principal. Thence to Yale, where he attracted the attention of Professor William G. Sumner, who became to him a guide and a friend. Until his senior year at Yale his favorite studies were Latin and Greek; and his brother, who was in his class, informs me that ever since his preparatory school days, it was his custom to read the whole of any author in hand as well as the part set for the class. During recitations he recalls seeing him again and again reading ahead in additional books of the author, keeping at the same time "a finger on the page where the class was translating, in order not to be caught off his guard." In his senior year at Yale, under the influence of Professor Sumner, he became interested in economics and won the Cobden medal. After graduation he wrote his first historical book, "The History of the Surplus Revenue of 1837," published in 1885 in Putnam's "Questions of the Day" series. For this and his other graduate work his university later conferred upon him the degree of Ph.D. Since I have learned the story of his boyhood and youth, it is with peculiar appreciation that I read the dedication of this first book: "To my Father and Mother." I may add in this connection that while pursuing his indefatigable labors for the support of his large family, his father's sickness and death overtaxed his strength, and the breakdown followed.

At Yale during his graduate work he won the Foote scholarship; he was instructor in history there from 1886 to 1888, then took a similar position at Adelbert College, Cleveland, becoming Professor of History in 1890. This post he held until 1895, when he was called to Yale University as Professor of History, a position that he held at the time of his death.

Besides the doctor's thesis, Bourne published two books, the first of which was "Essays in Historical Criticism," one of the Yale bicentennial publications, the most notable essay in which is that on Marcus Whitman. A paper read at the Ann Arbor session of the American Historical meeting in Detroit and later published in the *American Historical Review* is here amplified into a long and exhaustive treatment of the subject. The original paper gained Bourne some celebrity and subjected him to some harsh criticism, both of which, I think, he thoroughly enjoyed. Feeling sure of his facts and ground, he delighted in his final word to support the contention which he had read with emphasis and pleasure to an attentive audience in one of the halls of the University of Michigan. The final paragraph sums up what he set out to prove with undoubted success:

That Marcus Whitman was a devoted and heroic missionary who braved every hardship and imperilled his life for the cause of Christian missions and Christian civilization in the far Northwest and finally died at his post, a sacrifice to the cause, will not be gainsaid. That he deserves grateful commemoration in Oregon and Washington is beyond dispute. But that he is a national figure in American history, or that he "saved" Oregon, must be rejected as a fiction [p. 100].

Bourne had a good knowledge of American history, and he specialized on the Discoveries period, to which he gave close and continuous attention. He was indebted to Professor Hart's ambitious and excellent coöperative history, "The American Nation," for the opportunity to obtain a hearing on his favorite subject. His "Spain in America," his third published book, is the book of a scholar. While the conditions of his narrative allowed only forty-six pages to the story of Columbus, he had undoubtedly material enough well arranged and digested to fill the volume on this topic alone. I desire to quote a signal example of compression:

It was November, 1504, when Columbus arrived in Seville, a broken man, something over twelve years from the time he first set sail from Palos. Each successive voyage since his first had left him at a lower point. On his return from the second he was on the defensive; after his third he was deprived of his viceroyalty; on his fourth he was shipwrecked. . . . The last blow, the death of his patron Isabella, soon followed. It was months before he was able to attend court. His strength gradually failed, he sank from public view, and on the eve of Ascension Day, May 20, 1506, he passed away in obscurity [p. 81].

And I am very fond of this final characterization:

Columbus . . . has revealed himself in his writings as few men of action have been revealed. His hopes, his illusions, his vanity, and love of money, his devotion to by-gone ideals, his keen and sensitive observation of the natural world, his credulity and utter lack of critical power in dealing with literary evidence, his practical abilities as a navigator, his tenacity of purpose and boldness of execution, his lack of fidelity as a husband and a lover, . . . all stand out in clear relief. . . . Of all the self-made men that America has produced, none has had a more dazzling success, a more pathetic sinking to obscurity, or achieved a more universal celebrity [p. 82].

His chapter on Magellan is thoroughly interesting. The treatment of Columbus and Magellan shows what Bourne might have achieved in historical work if he could have had leisure to select his own subjects and elaborate them at will.

Before "Spain in America" appeared, he wrote a scholarly introduction to the vast work on the "Philippine Islands" published by the Arthur H. Clark Company, of Cleveland, of which fifty-one volumes are already out. The study of this subject gave Bourne a chance for the exhibition of his dry wit at one of the gatherings of the American Historical Association. It was asserted that in the acquisition of the Philippine Islands our country had violated the spirit of the Monroe Doctrine, which properly confined our indulgence of the land hunger that is preying upon the world to the Western hemisphere. Bourne took issue with this statement. He said that it might well be a question whether the Philippine Islands did not belong to the Western hemisphere and that —

for the first three centuries of their recorded history, they were in a sense a dependency of America. As a dependency of New Spain

they constituted the extreme western verge of the Spanish dominions and were commonly known as the Western Islands.
When the sun rose in Madrid it was still early afternoon of the
preceding day in Manila.   Down to the end of the year 1844 the
Manilan calendar was reckoned after that of Spain, that is, Manila
time was about sixteen hours slower than Madrid time.

Bourne undertook to write the Life of Motley for
Houghton, Mifflin and Company's American Men of Letters
series, and he had done considerable work in the investigation of material.   He was editor of a number of publications,
one of which was John Fiske's posthumous volume, "New
France and New England," and he wrote critical notices
for the *Nation, New York Tribune,* and the *New York
Times.*   As I have said, he had a large family to support,
and he sought work of the potboiling order; but in this
necessary labor he never sacrificed his ideal of thorough-
ness.   A remark that he made to me some while ago has
come back with pathetic interest.   After telling me what he
was doing, how much time his teaching left for outside work,
why he did this and that because it brought him money, he
said: "I can get along all right.   I can support my family,
educate my children, and get a little needed recreation, if
only my health does not break down."

Bourne took great interest in the American Historical
Association, and rarely if ever missed an annual meeting.
He frequently read papers, which were carefully prepared,
and a number of them are printed in the volume of Essays
to which I have referred.   He was the efficient chairman of
the programme committee at the meeting in New Haven in
1898; and as chairman of an important committee, or as
member of the Council, he attended the November dinners
and meetings in New York, so that he came to be looked
upon as one of the chief supporters of the Association.

Interested also in the *American Historical Review,* he was a frequent contributor of critical book notices.

My acquaintance with Bourne began in 1888, the year in which I commenced the composition of my history. We were both living in Cleveland, and, as it was his custom to dine with me once or twice a month, acquaintance grew into friendship, and I came to have a great respect for his training and knowledge as a historical scholar. The vastness of historical inquiry impressed me, as it has all writers of history. Recognizing in Bourne a kindred spirit, it occurred to me whether I could not hasten my work if he would employ part of his summer vacation in collecting material. I imparted the idea to Bourne, who received it favorably, and he spent a month of the summer of 1889 at work for me in the Boston Athenæum on my general specifications, laboring with industry and discrimination over the newspapers of the early '50's to which we had agreed to confine his work. His task completed, he made me a visit of a few days at Bar Harbor, affording an opportunity for us to discuss the period and his material. I was so impressed with the value of his assistance that, when the manuscript of my first two volumes was completed in 1891, I asked him to spend a month with me and work jointly on its revision. We used to devote four or five hours a day to this labor, and in 1894, when I had finished my third volume, we had a similar collaboration.[1] I have never known a better test of general knowledge and intellectual temper.

Bourne was a slow thinker and worker, but he was sure, and, when he knew a thing, his exposition was clear and pointed. The chance of reflection over night and the

---

[1] Bourne also revised the manuscript of my fourth volume, but the conditions did not admit of our being together more than two days, and the revision was not so satisfactory to either of us as that of the first three volumes.

occasional discussion at meal times, outside of our set hours, gave him the opportunity to recall all his knowledge bearing on the subject in hand, to digest and classify it thoroughly, so that, when he tackled a question, he talked, so to speak, like a book. Two chapters especially attracted him, — the one on Slavery in my first volume, and the one on general financial and social conditions at the beginning of the third; and I think that I may say that not only every paragraph and sentence, but every important word in these two chapters was discussed and weighed. Bourne was a good critic, and, to set him entirely at ease, as he was twelve years younger, I told him to lay aside any respect on account of age, and to speak out frankly, no matter how hard it hit, adding that I had better hear disagreeable things from him than to have them said by critics after the volumes were printed.

The intelligent note on page 51 of my third volume was written by Bourne, as I state in the note itself, but I did not speak of the large amount of study he gave to it. I never knew a man take keener interest in anything, and as we had all the necessary authorities at hand, he worked over them for two days, coming down on the morning of the third day with the triumphant air of one who had wrestled successfully with a mathematical problem all night. He sat down and, as I remember it, wrote the note substantially as it now stands in the volume. He was very strong on all economic and sociological questions, displaying in a marked degree the intellectual stimulus he had derived from his association with Professor Sumner. He was a born controversialist and liked to argue. "The appetite comes in eating" is a French saying, and with Bourne his knowledge seemed to be best evolved by the actual joint working and collision with another mind.

I remember one felicitous suggestion of Bourne's which after much working over we incorporated into a paragraph to our common satisfaction; and this paragraph received commendation in some critical notice. Showing this to Bourne, I said: "That is the way of the world. You did the thinking, I got the credit." Bourne had, however, forgotten his part in the paragraph. His mind was really so full of knowledge, when one could get at it, that he did not remember giving off any part of it. In addition to his quality of close concentration, he acquired a good deal of knowledge in a desultory way. In my library when conversation lagged he would go to the shelves and take down book after book, reading a little here or there, lighting especially upon any books that had been acquired since his previous visit, and with reading he would comment. This love of browsing in a library he acquired when a boy, so his brother informs me, and when at Yale it was said that he knew the library as well as the librarian himself.

It will be remembered that last spring our accomplished editor, Mr. Smith, decided that he could no longer bear the burden of this highly important work; and the question of a fit successor came up at once in the mind of our President. Writing to me while I was in Europe, he expressed the desire of consulting with me on the subject as soon as I returned. I was unfortunately unable to get back in time for the June meeting of the Society; and afterwards when I reached Boston the President had gone West, and when he got home I was at Seal Harbor. To spare me the trip to Boston and Lincoln, he courteously offered to come to see me at Seal Harbor, where we had the opportunity to discuss the subject in all its bearings. It will be quite evident from this narrative that my choice for editor would be no other than Professor Bourne, and I was much gratified to learn that the President from his own observation and reflection had determined on the same man. Mr. Adams had been accustomed to see Bourne at meetings of the American Historical Association and at dinners of their Council; but, so he informed me, he was not specially impressed by him until he read the essay on Marcus Whitman, which gave him a high idea of Bourne's power of working over material, and his faculty of trenchant criticism. We arrived readily at the conclusion that Bourne would be an ideal editor and that the position would suit him perfectly. Relieved of the drudgery of teaching, he could give full swing to his love of books and to his desire of running down through all the authorities some fact or reference bearing upon the subject in hand. The work would be a labor of love on which he could bring to bear his knowledge, conscientious endeavor, and historical training. It would have been a case of mutual benefit. He would be fortunate in securing such a position, and the Society might be congratulated on being able to get a man so peculiarly qualified for editorial work. But there was the question of Bourne's health. We both knew that he had been failing, but we were not aware that his case was hopeless. The President did not wish to present his recommendation to the Council until there was a reasonable chance of his recovery, and I undertook from time to time to get information from a common friend in New Haven of his progress. But there was no good news. While Bourne, with the help of his devoted wife, made an energetic fight for life, it was unavailing. In his death Yale lost an excellent teacher of history and this Society a candidate who, if he had been chosen, would have made an accomplished editor.

THE PRESIDENTIAL OFFICE

Printed in *Scribner's Magazine*, of February, 1903.

THE PRESIDENTIAL OFFICE

THE English Constitution, as it existed between 1760 and 1787, was the model of the American, but parts of it were inapplicable to the conditions in which the thirteen Colonies found themselves, and where the model failed the Convention struck out anew. The sagacity of the American statesmen in this creative work may well fill Englishmen, so Sir Henry Maine wrote, "with wonder and envy." Mr. Bryce's classification of constitutions as flexible and rigid is apt: of our Constitution it may be said that in the main it is rigid in those matters which should not be submitted to the decision of a legislature or to a popular vote without checks which secure reflection and a chance for the sober second thought, and that it has proved flexible in its adaptation to the growth of the country and to the development of the nineteenth century. Sometimes, though, it is flexible to the extent of lacking precision. An instance of this is the proviso for the counting of the electoral vote. "The votes shall then be counted" are the words. Thus, when in 1876 it was doubtful whether Tilden or Hayes had been chosen President, a fierce controversy arose as to who should count the votes, the President of the Senate or Congress. While many regretted the absence of an incontrovertible provision, it was fortunate for the country that the Constitution did not provide that the vote should be counted by the President of the Senate, who, the Vice President having died in office, was in 1877 a creature of the partisan majority. It is doubtful, too, if the decision of such an officer would have been acquiesced in by the mass of Democrats, who thought that they had fairly elected their candidate. There being no express declaration of the Constitution, it devolved upon Congress to settle the dispute; the ability and patriotism of that body was equal to the crisis. By a well-devised plan of arbitration, Congress relieved the strain and provided for a peaceful settlement of a difficulty which in most countries would have led to civil war.

In the provisions conferring the powers and defining the duties of the executive the flexible character of the Constitution is shown in another way. Everything is clearly stated, but the statements go not beyond the elementary. The Convention knew what it wanted to say, and Gouverneur Morris, who in the end drew up the document, wrote this part of it, as indeed all other parts, in clear and effective words. It is due to him, wrote Laboulaye, that the Constitution has a "distinctness entirely French, in happy contrast to the complicated language of the English laws." Yet on account of the elementary character of the article of the Constitution on the powers of the President, there is room for inference, a chance for development, and an opportunity for a strong man to imprint his character upon the office. The Convention, writes Mr. Bryce, made its executive a George III "shorn of a part of his prerogative," his influence and dignity diminished by a reduction of the term of office to four years. The English writer was thoroughly familiar with the *Federalist*, and appreciated Hamilton's politic efforts to demonstrate that the executive of the Constitution was modeled after the governors of the states, and not after the British monarch; but "an enlarged copy of the state governor," Mr. Bryce asserts, is one and the same thing as "a reduced and improved copy of the English king." But, on the other hand, Bagehot did not believe that the Americans comprehended the English

Constitution. "Living across the Atlantic," he wrote, "and misled by accepted doctrines, the acute framers of the Federal Constitution, even after the keenest attention, did not perceive the Prime Minister to be the principal executive of the British Constitution, and the sovereign a cog in the mechanism;" and he seems to think that if this had been understood the executive power would have been differently constituted.

It is a pertinent suggestion of Mr. Bryce's that the members of the Convention must have been thinking of their presiding officer, George Washington, as the first man who would exercise the powers of the executive office they were creating. So it turned out. Never did a country begin a new enterprise with so wise a ruler. An admirable polity had been adopted, but much depended upon getting it to work, and the man who was selected to start the government was the man of all men for the task. Histories many and from different points of view have been written of Washington's administration; all are interesting, and the subject seems to ennoble the writers. Statesmen meeting with students to discuss the character and political acts of Washington marvel at his wisdom in great things and his patience in small things, at the dignity and good sense with which he established the etiquette of his office, at the tact which retained in his service two such irreconcilable men as Jefferson and Hamilton. The importance of a good start for an infant government is well understood. But for our little state of four million people such a start was difficult to secure. The contentions which grew out of the ratification of the Constitution in the different states had left bitter feelings behind them, and these domestic troubles were heightened by our intimate relations with foreign countries. We touched England, France, and Spain at delicate points, and the infancy of our nation was passed during the turmoil of the French Revolution and the Reign of Terror. In our midst there was an English and a French party. Moreover, in the judgment of the world the experiment of the new government was foredoomed to failure. Wrote Sir Henry Maine, "It is not at all easy to bring home to the men of the present day how low the credit of republics had sunk before the establishment of the United States." Hardly were success to be won had we fallen upon quiet times; but with free governments discredited, and the word "liberty" made a reproach by the course of the French Revolution, it would seem impossible.

Washington's prescience is remarkable. Recognizing, in October, 1789, that France had "gone triumphantly through the first paroxysm," he felt that she must encounter others, that more blood must be shed, that she might run from one extreme to another, and that "a higher-toned despotism" might replace "the one which existed before." Mentally prepared as he was, he met with skill the difficulties as they arose, so that the conduct of our foreign relations during the eight years of his administration was marked by discretion and furnished a good pattern to follow. During his foreign negotiations he determined a constitutional question of importance. When the Senate had ratified and Washington, after some delay, had signed the Jay treaty, the House of Representatives, standing for the popular clamor against it, asked the President for all the papers relating to the negotiation, on the ground that the House of Representatives must give its concurrence. This demand he resisted, maintaining that it struck at "the fundamental principles of the Constitution," which conferred upon the President and the Senate the power of making treaties, and provided that these treaties when made and ratified were the supreme law of the land. In domestic affairs he showed discernment in selecting as his confidential adviser, Alexander Hamilton, a man who had great constructive talent; and he gave a demonstration of the physical strength of the government by putting down the whisky rebellion in Pennsylvania. During his eight years he construed the powers conferred upon the executive by the Constitution with wisdom, and exercised them with firmness and vigor. Washington was a man of exquisite manners and his conduct of the office gave it a dignity and prestige which, with the exception of a part of one term, it has never lost.

Four of the five Presidents who followed Washington were men of education and ability, and all of them had large political training and experience; they reached their position by the process of a natural selection in politics, being entitled fitly to the places for which they were chosen. The three first fell upon stormy times and did their work during periods of intense partisan excitement; they were also subject to personal detraction, but the result in the aggregate of their administrations was good, inasmuch as they either maintained the power of the executive or increased its influence. Despite their many mistakes they somehow overcame the great difficulties. Each one did something of merit and the country made a distinct gain from John Adams to Monroe. Any one of them suffers by comparison with Washington: the "era of good feeling" was due to Congress and the people as well as to the executive. Nevertheless, the three turbulent administrations and the two quiet ones which succeeded Washington's may at this distance from them be contemplated with a feeling of gratulation. The Presidents surrounded themselves for the most part with men of ability, experience, and refinement, who carried on the government with dignity and a sense of proportion, building well upon the foundations which Washington had laid.

A contrast between France and the United States leads to curious reflections. The one has a past rich in art, literature, and architecture, which the other almost entirely lacks. But politically the older country has broken with the past, while we have political traditions peculiar to ourselves of the highest value. For the man American-born they may be summed up in Washington, the rest of the "Fathers," and the Constitution; and those who leave England, Scotland, Ireland, Wales, Germany, and Scandinavia to make their home in America soon come to share in these possessions. While the immigrants from southern Europe do not comprehend the Constitution, they know Washington. An object lesson may be had almost any pleasant Sunday or holiday in the public garden in Boston from the group of Italians who gather about the statue of Washington, showing, by their mobile faces and animated talk, that they revere him who is the father of their adopted country.

During these five administrations, at least two important extensions or assertions of executive power were made. In 1803 Jefferson bought Louisiana, doing, he said, "an act beyond the Constitution." He was a strict constructionist, and was deeply concerned at the variance between his constitutional principles and a desire for the material advantage of his country. In an effort to preserve his consistency he suggested to his Cabinet and political friends an amendment to the Constitution approving and confirming the cession of this territory, but they, deeming such an amendment entirely unnecessary, received his suggestion coldly. In the debate on the Louisiana treaty in the Senate and the House, all speakers of both parties agreed that "the United

States government had the power to acquire new territory either by conquest or by treaty." [1] Louisiana, "without its consent and against its will," was annexed to the United States, and Jefferson "made himself monarch of the new territory, and wielded over it, against its protests, the powers of its old kings." [2]

The assertion by the President in 1823 of the Monroe Doctrine (which Mr. Worthington C. Ford has shown to be the John Quincy Adams doctrine) is an important circumstance in the development of the executive power.

President John Quincy Adams was succeeded by Andrew Jackson, a man of entirely different character from those who had preceded him in the office, and he represented different aims. Adams deserved another term. His sturdy Americanism, tempered by the cautiousness in procedure which was due to his rare training, made him an excellent public servant, and the country erred in not availing itself of his further service. The change from the *régime* of the first six Presidents to that of Jackson was probably inevitable. A high-toned democracy, based on a qualified suffrage, believing in the value of training for public life and administrative office, setting a value on refinement and good manners, was in the end sure to give way to a pure democracy based on universal suffrage whenever it could find a leader to give it force and direction. Jackson was such a leader. His followers felt: "He is one of us. He is not proud and does not care for style." [3] The era of vulgarity in national politics was ushered in by Jackson, who as President introduced the custom of rewarding political workers with offices, an innovation entirely indefensible; he ought to have continued the practice of his six predecessors. The interaction between government and politics on the one hand

[1] Henry Adams, II, 113.   [2] *Ibid.*, 130.   [3] Sumner's Jackson, 138.

and the life of the people on the other is persistent, and it may be doubted whether the United States would have seemed as it did to Dickens had not Jackson played such an important part in the vulgarization of politics. Yet it was a happy country, as the pages of Tocqueville bear witness.

Jackson was a strong executive and placed in his Cabinet men who would do his will, and who, from his own point of view, were good advisers, since they counseled him to pursue the course he had marked out for himself. Comparing his Cabinet officers to those of the Presidents preceding him, one realizes that another plan of governing was set on foot, based on the theory that any American citizen is fit for any position to which he is called. It was an era when special training for administrative work began to be slighted, when education beyond the rudiments was considered unnecessary except in the three professions, when the practical man was apotheosized and the bookish man despised. Jackson, uneducated and with little experience in civil life, showed what power might be exercised by an arbitrary, unreasonable man who had the people at his back. The brilliant three — Webster, Clay, and Calhoun — were unable to prevail against his power.

Jackson's financial policy may be defended; yet had it not been for his course during the nullification trouble, his declaration, "Our Federal Union: It must be preserved," and his consistent and vigorous action in accordance with that sentiment it would be difficult to affirm that the influence of his two terms of office was good. It cannot be said that he increased permanently the power of the executive, but he showed its capabilities. It is somewhat curious, however, that Tocqueville, whose observations were made under Jackson, should have written: "The President possesses almost royal prerogatives, which he never has an opportunity of using. . . . The laws permit him to be strong; circumstances keep him weak."

The eight Presidents from Jackson to Lincoln did not raise the character of the presidential office. Van Buren was the heir of Jackson. Of the others, five owed their nominations to their availability. The evil which Jackson did lived after him; indeed, only a man as powerful for the good as he had been for the bad could have restored the civil service to the merit system which had prevailed before he occupied the White House. The offices were at stake in every election, and the scramble for them after the determination of the result was great and pressing. The chief business of a President for many months after his inauguration was the dealing out of the offices to his followers and henchmen. It was a bad scheme, from the political point of view, for every President except him who inaugurated it. Richelieu is reported to have said, on making an appointment, "I have made a hundred enemies and one ingrate." So might have said many times the Presidents who succeeded Jackson.

The Whig, a very respectable party, having in its ranks the majority of the men of wealth and education, fell a victim to the doctrine of availability when it nominated Harrison on account of his military reputation. He lived only one month after his inauguration, and Tyler, the Vice President, who succeeded him, reverted to his old political principles, which were Democratic, and broke with the Whigs. By an adroit and steady use of the executive power he effected the annexation of Texas, but the master spirit in this enterprise was Calhoun, his Secretary of State. Polk, his Democratic successor, coveted California and New Mexico, tried to purchase them, and not being able to do this, determined on war. In fact, he had decided to send in a war message to Congress before the news came that the Mexicans, goaded to it by the action of General Taylor, under direct orders of the President, had attacked an American force and killed sixteen of our dragoons. This gave a different complexion to his message, and enabled him to get a strong backing from Congress for his war policy. The actions of Tyler and of Polk illustrate the power inherent in the executive office. It might seem that the exercise of this authority, securing for us at small material cost the magnificent domains of Texas, California, and New Mexico, would have given these Presidents a fame somewhat like that which Jefferson won by the purchase of Louisiana. But such has not been the case. The main reason is that the extension of slavery was involved in both enterprises, and the histories of these times, which have molded historical sentiment, have been written from the anti-slavery point of view. It seems hardly probable that this sentiment will be changed in any time that we can forecast, but there is an undoubted tendency in the younger historical students to look upon the expansion of the country as the important consideration, and the slavery question as incidental. Professor von Holst thought this changing historical sentiment entirely natural, but he felt sure that in the end men would come round to the antislavery view, of which he was so powerful an advocate.

From Taylor to Lincoln slavery dominated all other questions. Taylor was a Southern man and a slaveholder, and by his course on the Compromise measures attracted the favor of antislavery men; while Fillmore of New York, who succeeded this second President to die in office, and who exerted the power of the Administration to secure the passage of Clay's Compromise and signed the Fugitive

Slave Law, had but a small political following at the North. Pierce and Buchanan were weak, the more positive men in their Cabinets and in the Senate swayed them. For a part of both of their terms the House of Representatives was controlled by the opposition, the Senate remaining Democratic. These circumstances are evidence both of the length of time required to change the political complexion of the Senate and of the increasing power of the North, which was dominant in the popular House. For the decade before the Civil War we should study the Senate, the House of Representatives, the Supreme Court, the action of the states, and popular sentiment. The executive is still powerful, but he is powerful because he is the representative of a party or faction which dictates the use that shall be made of his constitutional powers. The presidential office loses interest: irresolute men are in the White House, strong men everywhere else.

Lincoln is inaugurated President; the Civil War ensues, and with it an extraordinary development of the executive power. It is an interesting fact that the ruler of a republic which sprang from a resistance to the English king and Parliament should exercise more arbitrary power than any Englishman since Oliver Cromwell, and that many of his acts should be worthy of a Tudor. Lincoln was a good lawyer who reverenced the Constitution and the laws, and only through necessity assumed and exercised extra-legal powers, trying at the same time to give to these actions the color of legality. Hence his theory of the war power of the Constitution, which may be construed to permit everything necessary to carry on the war. Yet his dictatorship was different from Cæsar's and different from the absolute authority of Napoleon. He acted under the restraints imposed by his own legal conscience and patriotic soul, whose influence was revealed in his confidential letters and talks. We know furthermore that he often took counsel of his Cabinet officers before deciding matters of moment. Certain it is that in arbitrary arrests Seward and Stanton were disposed to go further than Lincoln. The spirit of arbitrary power was in the air, and unwise and unjust acts were done by subordinates, which, although Lincoln would not have done them himself, he deemed it better to ratify than to undo. This was notably the case in the arrest of Vallandigham. Again, Congress did not always do what Lincoln wished, and certain men of his own party in Congress were strong enough to influence his actions in various ways. But, after all, he was himself a strong man exercising comprehensive authority; and it is an example of the flexibility of the Constitution that, while it surely did not authorize certain of Lincoln's acts, it did not expressly forbid them. It was, for example, an open question whether the Constitution authorized Congress or the President to suspend the writ of *habeas corpus*.

It seems to be pretty well settled by the common sense of mankind that when a nation is fighting for its existence it cannot be fettered by all the legal technicalities which obtain in the time of peace. Happy the country whose dictatorship, if dictator there must be, falls into wise and honest hands! The honesty, magnanimity, and wisdom of Lincoln guided him aright, and no harm has come to the great principles of liberty from the arbitrary acts which he did or suffered to be done. On the other hand he has so impressed himself upon the Commonwealth that he has made a precedent for future rulers in a time of national peril, and what he excused and defended will be assumed as a matter of course because it will be according to the Constitution as interpreted by Abraham Lincoln. This the

Supreme Court foresaw when it rendered its judgment in the Milligan case, saying: "Wicked men ambitious of power, with hatred of liberty and contempt of law, may fill the place once occupied by Washington and Lincoln, and if this right is conceded [that of a commander in a time of war to declare martial law within the lines of his military district and subject citizens as well as soldiers to the rule of his will] and the calamities of war again befall us, the dangers to human liberty are frightful to contemplate." No one can deny that a danger here exists, but it is not so great as the solemn words of the Supreme Court might lead one to believe. For Lincoln could not have persisted in his arbitrary acts had a majority of Congress definitely opposed them, and his real strength lay in the fact that he had the people at his back. This may be said of the period from the first call of troops in April, 1861, until the summer of 1862. McClellan's failure on the Peninsula, Pope's disaster at the second battle of Bull Run, the defeats at Fredericksburg and Chancellorsville lost Lincoln the confidence of many; and while the emancipation proclamation of September, 1862, intensified the support of others, it nevertheless alienated some Republicans and gave to the opposition of the Democrats a new vigor. But after Gettysburg and Vicksburg in July, 1863, Lincoln had the support of the mass of the Northern people. Whatever he did the people believed was right because he had done it. The trust each placed in the other is one of the inspiring examples of free government and democracy. Lincoln did not betray their confidence: they did not falter save possibly for brief moments during the gloomy summer of 1864. The people who gave their unreserved support to Lincoln were endued with intelligence and common sense; not attracted by any personal magnetism of the man, they had, by a process of homely reasoning, attained their convictions and from these they were not to be shaken. This is the safety of a dictatorship as long as the same intelligence obtains among the voters as now; for the people will not support a ruler in the exercise of extra-legal powers unless he be honest and patriotic. The danger may come in a time of trouble from either an irresolute or an unduly obstinate executive. The irresolute man would baffle the best intentions of the voters; the obstinate man might quarrel with Congress and the people. Either event in time of war would be serious and might be disastrous. But the chances are against another Buchanan or Johnson in the presidential office.

If the Civil War showed the flexibility of the Constitution in that the executive by the general agreement of Congress and the people was able to assume unwarranted powers, the course of affairs under Johnson demonstrated the strength that Congress derived from the organic act. The story is told in a sentence by Blaine: "Two thirds of each House united and stimulated to one end can practically neutralize the executive power of the government and lay down its policy in defiance of the efforts and opposition of the President." [1] What a contrast between the two administrations! Under Lincoln Congress, for the most part, simply registered the will of the President; under Johnson the President became a mere executive clerk of Congress. In the one case the people supported the President, in the other they sustained Congress. Nothing could better illustrate the flexibility of the Constitution than the contrast between these administrations; but it needs no argument to show that to pass from one such extreme to another is not healthy for the body politic. The violent antagonisms aroused during Johnson's administration, when the difficult

[1] Twenty Years of Congress, II, 185.

questions to be settled needed the best statesmanship of
the country, and when the President and Congress should
have coöperated wisely and sympathetically, did incal-
culable harm. Johnson, by habits, manners, mind, and
character, was unfit for the presidential office, and whatever
may have been the merit of his policy, a policy devised by
angels could never have been carried on by such an advocate. The American people love order and decency; they
have a high regard for the presidential office, and they desire
to see its occupant conduct himself with dignity. Jackson
and Lincoln lacked many of the external graces of a gentleman, but both had native qualities which enabled them to
bear themselves with dignity on public occasions. Johnson
degraded the office, and he is the only one of our Presidents
of whom this can be said. Bagehot, writing in 1872, drew
an illustration from one of the darkest periods of our republic to show the superiority of the English Constitution. If
we have a Prime Minister who does not suit Parliament and
the people, he argued, we remove him by a simple vote of
the House of Commons. The United States can only get
rid of its undesirable executive by a cumbrous and tedious
process which can only be brought to bear during a period
of revolutionary excitement; and even this failed because
a legal case was not made against the President. The criticism was pregnant, but the remedy was not Cabinet responsibility. Whatever may be the merits or demerits of
our polity, it has grown as has the English; it has fitted
itself to the people, and cabinet government cannot be had
without a complete change of the organic act, which is
neither possible nor desirable. The lesson was that the
national conventions should exercise more care in naming
their vice-presidential candidates; and these bodies have
heeded it. When Grant, popular throughout the country,

nominated by the unanimous vote of the Republican convention, became President, Congress restored to the executive a large portion of the powers of which it had been shorn during Johnson's administration. Grant had splendid opportunities which he did not improve, and he left no especial impression on the office. In the opinion of one of his warm friends and supporters he made "a pretty poor President." An able opposition to him developed in his own party; and as he was a sensitive man he felt keenly their attacks. Colonel John Hay told me that, when on a visit to Washington during Grant's administration, he had arrived at the Arlington Hotel at an early hour and started out for a walk; in front of the White House he was surprised to meet the President, who was out for the same purpose. The two walked together to the Capitol and back, Grant showing himself to be anything but a silent man. Manifesting a keen sensitiveness to the attacks upon him, he talked all of the time in a voluble manner, and the burden of his talk was a defense of his administrative acts. It is impossible in our minds to dissociate Grant the President from Grant the General, and for this reason American historical criticism will deal kindly with him. The brilliant victor of Donelson, the bold strategist of Vicksburg, the compeller of men at Chattanooga, the vanquisher of Robert E. Lee in March and April, 1865, the magnanimous conqueror at Appomattox, will be treated with charity by those who write about his presidential terms, because he meant well although he did not know how to do well. Moreover, the good which Grant did is of that salient kind which will not be forgotten. The victorious general, with two trusted military subordinates in the prime of life and a personnel for a strong navy, persisted, under the guidance of his wise Secretary of State, Hamilton Fish, in negotiating a treaty which provided for arbitration and preserved the peace with Great Britain; although, in the opinion of the majority, the country had a just cause of war in the escape of the Florida and the Alabama. After the panic of 1873, when financiers and capitalists lost their heads, and Congress with the approval of public sentiment passed an act increasing the amount of United States notes in circulation, Grant, by a manly and bold veto, prevented this inflation of the currency. The wisdom of the framers of the Constitution in giving the President the veto power was exemplified. Congress did not pass the act over the veto, and Grant has been justified by the later judgment of the nation. His action demonstrated what a President may do in resisting by his constitutional authority some transitory wave of popular opinion, and it has proved a precedent of no mean value. Johnson's vetoes became ridiculous. Grant's veto compensates for many of his mistakes.

Said Chancellor Kent in 1826: "If ever the tranquillity of this nation is to be disturbed and its liberties endangered by a struggle for power, it will be upon this very subject of the choice of a President. This is the question that is eventually to test the goodness and try the strength of the Constitution, and if we shall be able for half a century hereafter to continue to elect the chief magistrate of the Union with discretion, moderation, and integrity we shall undoubtedly stamp the highest value on our national character." Just fifty years later came a more dangerous test than Kent could have imagined. Somewhat more than half of the country believed that the states of Florida and Louisiana should be counted for Tilden, and that he was therefore elected. On the other hand, nearly one half of the voters were of the opinion that those electoral votes should be given to Hayes, which would elect him by the majority of one electoral vote. Each of the parties had apparently a good case, and after an angry controversy became only the more firmly and sincerely convinced that its own point of view was unassailable. The Senate was Republican, the House Democratic. The great Civil War had been ended only eleven years before, and the country was full of fighting men. The Southern people were embittered against the dominant party for the reason that Reconstruction had gone otherwise than they had expected in 1865 when they laid down their arms. The country was on the verge of a civil war over the disputed Presidency — a war that might have begun with an armed encounter on the floor of the Senate or the House. This was averted by a carefully prepared congressional act, which in effect left the dispute to a board of arbitration. To the statesmen of both parties who devised this plan and who coöperated in carrying the measure through Congress; to the members of the Electoral Commission, who in the bitterest strife conducted themselves with dignity; to the Democratic Speaker of the House and the Democrats who followed his lead, the eternal gratitude of the country is due. "He that ruleth his spirit is better than he that taketh a city." The victories of Manila and Santiago are as nothing compared with the victorious restraint of the American people in 1876 and 1877 and the acquiescence of one half of the country in what they believed to be an unrighteous decision. Hayes was inaugurated peacefully, but had to conduct his administration in the view of 4,300,000 voters who believed that, whatever might be his legal claim, he had no moral right to the place he occupied. The Democrats controlled the House of Representatives during the whole of his term, and the Senate for a part of it, and at the outset he encountered the opposition of the stalwart faction of his own party. Nevertheless,

he made a successful President, and under him the office
gained in force and dignity. Hayes was not a man of brilliant parts or wide intelligence, but he had common sense
and decision of character. Surrounding himself with a
strong Cabinet, three members of which were really remarkable for their ability, he entered upon a distinct policy from
which flowed good results. He withdrew the Federal troops
from the states of South Carolina and Louisiana, inaugu-
rating in these states an era of comparative peace and tranquillity. Something was done in the interest of Civil
Service Reform. In opposition to the view of his Secretary
of the Treasury and confidential friend, John Sherman, he
vetoed the act of 1878 for the remonetization of silver by
the coinage of a certain amount of silver dollars — the first
of those measures which almost brought us to the monetary
basis of silver. His guiding principle was embodied in a
remark he made in his inaugural address, "He serves his
party best who serves the country best." He and his accomplished wife had a social and moral influence in Washington of no mean value. The Civil War had been followed
by a period of corruption, profligacy, and personal immorality. In politics, if a man were sound on the main question,
which meant if he were a thorough-going Republican, all
else was forgiven. Under Hayes account was again taken
of character and fitness. The standard of political administration was high. While Mrs. Hayes undoubtedly carried
her total abstinence principles to an extreme not warranted
by the usage of good society, the moral atmosphere of the
White House was that of most American homes. Mr. and
Mrs. Hayes belonged to that large class who are neither rich
nor poor, neither learned nor ignorant, but who are led both
by their native common sense and by their upbringing to
have a high respect for learning, a belief in education,

morality, and religion, and a lofty ideal for their own personal conduct.

The salient feature of Garfield's few months of administration was a quarrel between him and the senators from New York State about an important appointment. Into this discussion, which ended in a tragedy, entered so many factors that it is impossible to determine exactly the influence on the power of the President and the growing power of the Senate. One important result of it shall be mentioned. The Civil Service Reform Bill, introduced into the Senate by a Democrat, was enacted during Arthur's administration by a large and non-partisan majority. It provided for a non-partisan civil service commission, and established open competitive examinations for applicants for certain offices, making a commencement by law of the merit system, which before had depended entirely upon executive favor. It was a victory for reformers who had been advocating legislation of such a character from a period shortly after the close of the Civil War; for it was at that time that a few began the work of educating public sentiment, which had acquiesced in the rotation of offices as an American principle well worthy of maintenance. Consequences far-reaching and wholesome followed the passage of this important act. Grant had attempted and Hayes had accomplished a measure of reform, but to really fix the merit system in the civil service a law was needed.

Regarded by the lovers of good government as a machine politician, Arthur happily disappointed them by breaking loose from his old associations and pursuing a manly course. He gave the country a dignified administration; but, even had he been a man to impress his character upon the office, conditions were against him. His party was torn by internal dissensions and suffered many defeats, of which the most notable was in his own state of New York, where his Secretary of the Treasury and personal friend was overwhelmingly defeated for governor by Grover Cleveland.

The unprecedented majority which Cleveland received in this election and his excellent administration as Governor of New York secured for him the Democratic nomination for President in 1884. New York State decided the election, but the vote was so close that for some days the result was in doubt and the country was nervous lest there should be another disputed Presidency; in the end it was determined that Cleveland had carried that state by a plurality of 1149. Cleveland was the first Democratic President elected since 1856; the Democrats had been out of office for twenty-four years, and it had galled them to think that their historic party had so long been deprived of power and patronage. While many of their leaders had a good record on the question of Civil Service Reform, the rank and file believed in the Jacksonian doctrine of rewarding party workers with the offices, or, as most of them would have put it, "To the victors belong the spoils." With this principle so fixed in the minds of his supporters, it became an interesting question how Cleveland would meet it. No one could doubt that he would enforce fairly the statute, but would he content himself with this and use the offices not covered by the act to reward his followers in the old Democratic fashion? An avowed civil service reformer, and warmly supported by independents and some former Republicans on that account, he justified the confidence which they had reposed in him and refused "to make a clean sweep." In resisting this very powerful pressure from his party he accomplished much toward the establishment of the merit system in the civil service. It is true that he made political changes gradually, but his insistence on a rule

which gained him time for reflection in making appointments was of marked importance. It would be idle to
assert that in his two terms he lived wholly up to the ideal
of the reformers; undoubtedly a long list of backslidings
might be made up, but in striking a fair balance it is not too
much to say that in this respect his administration made
for righteousness. All the more credit is due him in that he
not only resisted personal pressure, but, aspiring to be a
party leader for the carrying out of a cherished policy on
finance and the tariff, he made more difficult the accomplishment of these ends by refusing to be a mere partisan
in the question of the offices. In his second term it is
alleged, probably with truth, that he made a skillful use of
his patronage to secure the passage by the Senate of the
repeal of the Silver Act of 1890, which repeal had gone easily
through the House. It seemed to him and to many financiers that unless this large purchase of silver bullion should
be stopped the country would be forced on to a silver basis,
the existing financial panic would be grievously intensified,
and the road back to the sound money basis of the rest of
the civilized world would be long and arduous. His course
is defended as doing a little wrong in order to bring about
a great right; and the sequence of events has justified that
defense. Harm was done to the cause of Civil Service
Reform, but probably no permanent injury. The repeal of
the Silver Act of 1890 was the first important step in
the direction of insuring a permanent gold standard, and
Grover Cleveland is the hero of it.

The presidential office gained in strength during Cleveland's two terms. As we look back upon them, the President is the central figure round which revolves each policy
and its success or failure. At the same time, it is his party
more than he that is to be blamed for the failures. He

made a distinct move toward a reduction of the tariff, and while this failed, leaving us with the reactionary result of higher duties than ever before, it is not impossible that the words, actions, and sacrifices of Cleveland will be the foundation of a new tariff-reform party. Allusion has been made to his soundness on finance. His course in this respect was unvarying. Capitalists and financiers can take care of themselves, no matter what are the changes in the currency; but men and women of fixed incomes, professors of colleges, teachers in schools, clergymen and ministers, accountants and clerks in receipt of salaries, and farmers and laborers have had their comfort increased and their anxieties lessened by the adoption of the gold standard; and to Cleveland, as one of the pioneers in this movement for stability, their thanks are due.

In the railroad riots of 1894 Cleveland, under the advice of his able Attorney-General, made a precedent in the way of interference for the supremacy of law and the maintenance of order. The Governor of Illinois would not preserve order, and the President determined that at all hazards riotous acts must be suppressed and law must resume its sway. In ordering United States troops to the scene of the disturbance without an application of the Legislature or Governor of Illinois he accomplished a fresh extension of executive power without an infraction of the Constitution.

In his most important diplomatic action Cleveland was not so happy as in his domestic policy. There are able men experienced in diplomacy who defend his message of December 17, 1895, to Congress in regard to Venezuela, and the wisdom of that action is still a mooted question. Yet two facts placed in juxtaposition would seem to indicate that the message was a mistake. It contained a veiled threat of war if England would not arbitrate her difference with

Venezuela, the implication being that the stronger power was trying to browbeat the weaker one. Later an arbitration took place, the award of which was a compromise, England gaining more than Venezuela, and the award demonstrated that England had not been as extreme and unjust in her claim as had been Venezuela. It is even probable that England might have accepted, as the result of negotiation, the line decided on by the arbitrators. But, to the credit of Mr. Cleveland and his Secretary of State, Mr. Olney, it must be remembered that they later negotiated a treaty "for the arbitration of all matters in difference between the United States and Great Britain," which unfortunately failed of ratification by the Senate.

It is a fair charge against Cleveland as a partisan leader that, while he led a strong following to victory in 1892, he left his party disorganized in 1897. But it fell to him to decide between principle and party, and he chose principle. He served his country at the expense of his party. From the point of view of Democrats it was grievous that the only man under whom they had secured victory since the Civil War should leave them in a shattered condition, and it may be a question whether a ruler of more tact could not have secured his ends without so great a schism. Those, however, to whom this party consideration does not appeal have no difficulty in approving Cleveland's course. It is undeniable that his character is stamped on the presidential office, and his occupancy of it is a distinct mark in the history of executive power.

Harrison occupied the presidential office between the two terms of Cleveland, and although a positive man, left no particular impress upon the office. He was noted for his excellent judicial appointments, and he had undoubtedly a high standard of official conduct which he endeavored to live up to. Cold in his personal bearing he did not attract friends, and he was not popular with the prominent men in his own party. While Cleveland and McKinley were denounced by their opponents, Harrison was ridiculed; but the universal respect in which he was held after he retired to private life is evidence that the great office lost no dignity while he held it. During his term Congress overshadowed the executive and the House was more conspicuous than the Senate. Thomas B. Reed was speaker and developed the power of that office to an extraordinary extent. McKinley was the leader of the House and from long service in that body had become an efficient leader. The election of Harrison was interpreted to mean that the country needed a higher tariff, and McKinley carried through the House the bill which is known by his name. Among the other Representatives Mr. Lodge was prominent. It was not an uncommon saying at that time that the House was a better arena for the rising politician than the Senate. In addition to the higher tariff the country apparently wanted more silver and a determined struggle was made for the free coinage of silver which nearly won in Congress. In the end, however, a compromise was effected by Senator Sherman which averted free silver but committed the country to the purchase annually of an enormous amount of silver bullion against which Treasury notes redeemable in coin were issued. This was the Act of 1890 which, as I have mentioned, was repealed under Cleveland in 1893. It is entirely clear from the sequence of events that the Republican party as a party should have opposed the purchase of more silver. It could not have been beaten worse than it was in 1892, but it could have preserved a consistency in principle which, when the tide turned, would have been of political value. The party which has stuck to the right principle has in the long run generally been rewarded with power, and as the Republicans, in spite of certain defections, had been the party of sound money since the Civil War, they should now have fought cheap money under the guise of unlimited silver as they had before under the guise of unlimited greenbacks. But the leaders thought differently, and from their own point of view their course was natural. The country desired more silver. Business was largely extended, overtrading was the rule. Farmers and business men were straitened for money. Economists, statesmen, and politicians had told them that, as their trouble had come largely from the demonetization of silver, their relief lay in bimetallism. It was easy to argue that the best form of bimetallism was the free coinage of gold and silver, and after the panic of 1893 this delusion grew, but the strength of it was hardly appreciated by optimistic men in the East until the Democrats made it the chief plank in the platform on which they fought the presidential campaign of 1896. Nominating an orator who had an effective manner of presenting his arguments to hard-working farmers whose farms were mortgaged, to business men who were under a continued strain to meet their obligations, and to laborers out of employment, it seemed for two or three months as if the party of silver and discontent might carry the day. After some hesitation the Republicans grappled with the question boldly, took ground against free silver, and with some modification declared their approval of the gold standard. On this issue they fought the campaign. Their able and adroit manager was quick to see, after the issue was joined, the force of the principle of sound money and started a remarkable campaign of education by issuing speeches and articles by the millions in a number of different languages, in providing excellent arguments for the country press, and in convincing those who would listen only to arguments of sententious brevity by a well-devised circulation of "nuggets" of financial wisdom. McKinley had also the support of the greater part of the Independent and Democratic press. While financial magnates and the bankers of the country were alarmed at the strength of the Bryan party, and felt that its defeat was necessary to financial surety, the strength of the Republican canvass lay in the fact that the speakers and writers who made it believed sincerely that the gold standard would conduce to the greatest good of the greatest number. It was an inspiring canvass. The honest advocacy of sound principle won.

Under McKinley the Democratic tariff bill was superseded by the Dingley act, which on dutiable articles is, I believe, the highest tariff the country has known. The Republican party believes sincerely in the policy of protection, and the country undoubtedly has faith in it. It is attractive to those who allow immediate returns to obscure prospective advantage, and if a majority decides whether or not a political and economic doctrine is sound, it has a powerful backing, for every large country in the civilized world, I think, except England, adheres to protection; and some of them have returned to it after trying a measure of commercial freedom. McKinley and the majority of Congress were in full sympathy, and the Dingley act had the approval of the administration. But the change in business conditions which, though long in operation, became signally apparent after 1893, wrought in McKinley, during his four and a half years of office, a change of opinion. Under improved processes and economies in all branches of manufactures the United States began to make many articles cheaper than any other country, and sought foreign markets for its surplus, disputing successfully certain open marts with England and Germany. In McKinley's earlier utterances the home market is the dominating feature; in his later ones, trade with foreign countries. In his last speech at Buffalo he gave mature expression to his views, which for one who had been a leader of protectionists showed him to have taken advanced ground. "We find our long-time principles echoed," declared the *Nation*. McKinley's manner of developing foreign trade was not that of the tariff reformers, for he proposed to bring this about by a variety of reciprocity treaties; but it was important that he recognized the sound economic principle that if we are to sell to foreign countries we must buy from them also. That McKinley had a strong hold on the country is indisputable from the unanimous renomination by his party and his triumphant reëlection, and it was a step toward commercial freedom that he who more than all other men had the ear of the country and who had been an arch-protectionist should advocate the exchange of commodities with foreign lands. Economists do not educate the mass of voters, but men like McKinley do, and these sentences of his were read and pondered by millions: "A system which provides a mutual exchange of commodities is manifestly essential to the continued and healthful growth of our export trade. We must not repose in fancied security that we can forever sell everything and buy little or nothing. If such a thing were possible it would not be best for us or for those with whom we deal." It is useless to speculate on what would have been the result had McKinley lived. Those who considered him a weak President aver that when he encountered opposition in Congress from interests which were seemingly menaced, he would have yielded and abandoned reciprocity. Others believe that he understood the question thoroughly and that his arguments would in the end have prevailed with Congress; yielding, perhaps, in points of detail he would have secured the adoption of the essential part of his policy.

After his election McKinley became a believer in the gold standard and urged proper legislation upon Congress. It is to his credit and to that of Congress that on March 14, 1900, a bill became a law which establishes the gold standard and puts it out of the power of any President to place the country upon a silver basis by a simple direction to his Secretary of the Treasury, which could have been done in 1897. As it has turned out, it was fortunate that there was no undue haste in this financial legislation. A better act was obtained than would have been possible in the first two years of McKinley's administration. The reaction from the crisis following the panic of 1893 had arrived, made sure by the result of the election of 1896; and the prosperity had become a telling argument in favor of the gold standard with the people and with Congress.

McKinley was essentially adapted for a peace minister, but under him came war. Opinions of him will differ, not only according to one's sentiments on war and imperialism, but according to one's ideal of what a President should be. Let us make a comparison which shall not include Washington, for the reason that under him the country had not become the pure democracy it is at the present day. Of such a democracy it seems to me that Lincoln is the ideal President, in that he led public sentiment, represented it, and followed it. "I claim not to have controlled events," he said, "but confess plainly that events have controlled me." During his term of office he was one day called "very weak," and the next "a tyrant"; but when his whole work was done, a careful survey of it could bring one only to the conclusion that he knew when to follow and when to lead. He was in complete touch with popular sentiment, and divined with nicety when he could take a step in advance. He made an effort to keep on good terms with Congress, and he differed with that body reluctantly, although, when the necessity came, decisively. While he had consideration for those who did not agree with him, and while he acted always with a regard to proportion, he was nevertheless a strong and self-confident executive. Now Cleveland did not comprehend popular opinion as did Lincoln. In him the desire to lead was paramount, to the exclusion at times of a proper consideration for Congress and the people. It has been said by one of his political friends that he used the same energy and force in deciding a small matter as a great one, and he alienated senators, congressmen, and other supporters by an unyielding disposition when no principle was involved. He did not possess the gracious quality of Lincoln, who yielded in small things that he might prevail in great ones. Yet for this quality of sturdy insistence on his own idea Cleveland has won admiration from a vast number of independent thinkers. Temperaments such as these are not in sympathy with McKinley, who represents another phase of Lincoln's genius. The controlling idea of McKinley probably was that as he was elected by the people he should represent them. He did not believe that, if a matter were fully and fairly presented, the people would go wrong. At times he felt he should wait for their sober, second thought, but if, after due consideration, the people spoke, it was his duty to carry out their will. Unquestionably if the Cleveland and McKinley qualities can be happily combined as they were in Lincoln, the nearest possible approach to the ideal ruler is the result. One Lincoln, though, in a century, is all that any country can expect: and there is a place in our polity for either the Cleveland or the McKinley type of executive. So it seemed to the makers of the Constitution. "The republican principle," wrote Hamilton in the *Federalist*, "demands that the deliberate sense of the community should govern the conduct of those to whom they intrust the management of their affairs." "But," he said in the same essay, "however inclined we might be to insist upon an unbounded complaisance in the executive to the inclinations of the people, we can with no propriety contend for a like complaisance to the humors of the legislature. . . . The executive should be in a situation to dare to act his own opinion with vigor and decision." It is frequently remarked that no President since Lincoln had so thorough a comprehension of public sentiment as McKinley. This knowledge and his theory of action, if I have divined it aright, are an explanation of his course in regard to the Spanish War and the taking of the Philippines. It does not fall to me to discuss in this article these two questions, nor do I feel certain that all the documents necessary to a fair judgment are accessible to the public, but I can show what was McKinley's attitude toward them by reporting a confidential conversation he had on May 2, 1899, with Mr. Henry S. Pritchett, president of the Massachusetts Institute of Technology, who made a record of it the day afterward. The President, Mr. Pritchett relates, spoke of the "war and of his own responsibility, and the way in which he has gradually come to have his present position with respect to the Philippines. The talk was started by my reminding him of the fact that just a year ago that morning, on May 2, 1898, I had come into his room with a map of Manila and Cavité on a large scale — the first time he had seen such a map — and from this he drifted into a most serious and interesting talk of his own place in the history of the past twelve months. He described his efforts to avert the war, how he had carried the effort to the point of rupture with his party, then came the Maine incident, and, finally, a declaration of war over all efforts to stem the tide. Then he spoke of Cuba and Porto Rico and the Philippines, related at some length the correspondence he had had with the Paris Commission, how he had been gradually made to feel in his struggling for the right ground that first Luzon and finally all the Philippines must be kept. He then went on to indicate his belief that Providence had led in all this matter, that to him the march of events had been so irresistible that nothing could turn them aside. Nobody, he said, could have tried harder than he to be rid of the burden of the Philippines, and yet the trend of events had been such that it seemed impossible to escape this duty. He finally came to speak with more emotion than I have ever seen him exhibit, and no one could doubt the sincerity of the man."

Of McKinley's achievements in the field of diplomacy Secretary Hay in his memorial address spoke with knowledge and in words of high praise. Sometimes the expression of a careful foreign observer anticipates the judgment of posterity, and with that view the words of the *Spectator*,[1] in an article on the presidential election of 1900, are worth quoting: "We believe that Mr. McKinley and the wise statesman who is his Secretary of State, Colonel Hay, are administrators of a high order. They have learnt their business thoroughly, hold all the strings of policy in their hands."

Opinions will differ as to the impress McKinley has left on the presidential office. It is the judgment of two men of large knowledge of American history and present affairs that no President since Jefferson has been so successful in getting Congress to adopt the positive measures he desired.

Of the administration of Theodore Roosevelt it would be

[1] July 14, 1900.

neither proper nor wise for me to speak in other terms than those of expectation and prophecy. But of Mr. Roosevelt himself something may be said. His birth, breeding, education, and social advantages have been of the best. He has led an industrious and useful life. As an American citizen we are all proud of him, and when he reached the presidential office by a tragedy that nobody deplored more than he, every one wished him success. His transparent honesty and sincerity are winning qualities, and in the opinion of Burke especially important in him who is the ruler of a nation. "Plain good intention," he wrote, "which is as easily discovered at the first view as fraud is surely detected at last, is, let me say, of no mean force in the government of mankind." To these qualities, and to a physical and moral courage that can never be questioned, Mr. Roosevelt adds a large intelligence and, as his books show, a power of combination of ideas and cohesive thought. Moreover, he has had a good political training, and he has the faculty of writing his political papers in a pregnant and forcible literary style. He is fit for what Mr. Bryce calls "the greatest office in the world, unless we except the Papacy." His ideals are Washington and Lincoln. "I like to see in my mind's eye," he said, "the gaunt form of Lincoln stalking through these halls." "To gratify the hopes, secure the reverence, and sustain the dignity of the nation," said Justice Story, "the presidential office should always be occupied by a man of elevated talents, of ripe virtues, of incorruptible integrity, and of tried patriotism; one who shall forget his own interests and remember that he represents not a party but the whole nation." These qualities Theodore Roosevelt has. Whether he shall in action carry out the other requirements of Justice Story may only be judged after he shall have retired to private life.

Mr. Roosevelt merits the encouragement and sympathy of all lovers of good government, and he is entitled, as indeed is every President, to considerate and forbearing criticism. For, ardently desired as the office is, it is a hard place to fill. Through the kindness of President Roosevelt, I have been enabled to observe the daily routine of his work, and I am free to say that from the business point of view, no man better earns his pay than does he. Mr. Bryce remarks that a good deal of the President's work is like that of the manager of a railway. So far as concerns the consultation with heads of departments, prompt decisions, and the disposition of daily matters, the comparison is apt, if a great American railway and a manager like Thomas A. Scott are borne in mind. But the railway manager's labor is done in comparative privacy, he can be free from interruption and dispose of his own time in a systematic manner. That is impossible for the President during the session of Congress. Office-seekers themselves do not trouble the President so much as in former days; they may be referred to the heads of the departments; and, moreover, the introduction of competitive examinations and the merit system has operated as a relief to the President and his Cabinet officers. But hearing the recommendations by senators and congressmen of their friends for offices consumes a large amount of time. There are, as Senator Lodge has kindly informed me, 4818 presidential offices exclusive of 4000 presidential post offices; in addition there are army and naval officers to be appointed. The proper selection in four years of the number of men these figures imply is in itself no small labor; it would by a railway manager be considered an onerous and exacting business. But the railway manager may hear the claims of applicants in his own proper way, and to prevent encroachments on his time may give the candidates or their friends a curt dismissal. The President may not treat senators and representatives in that manner, nor would he desire to do so, for the intercourse between them and the executive is of great value. "The President," wrote John Sherman, "should 'touch elbows' with Congress." There are important legislative measures to be discussed in a frank interchange of opinion. Senators and representatives are a guide to the President in their estimates of public sentiment; often they exert an influence over him, and he is dependent on them for the carrying out of any policy he may have at heart. While the encroachments on the President's time are great, I am convinced that no plan should be adopted which should curtail the unconventional and frank interchange of views between the President and members of the National Legislature. The relief lies with the public. Much of the President's time is taken up with receptions of the friends of senators and representatives, of members of conventions and learned bodies meeting in Washington, of deputations of school-teachers and the like who have gone to the capital for a holiday: all desire to pay their respects to the Chief Magistrate. Undoubtedly, if he could have a quiet talk with most of these people, it would be of value, but the conventional shaking of hands and the "I am glad to see you" is not a satisfaction great enough to the recipients to pay for what it costs the President in time and the expenditure of nervous force. He should have time for deliberation. The railway manager can closet himself when he likes: that should be the privilege of the President; yet on a certain day last April, when he wished to have a long confidential talk with his Secretary of War, this was only to be contrived by the two taking a long horseback ride in the country. It is difficult for the President to refuse to see these good, patriotic, and learned people; and senators and representatives like to gratify their constituents. The remedy lies with the public in denying themselves this pleasant feature of a visit to Washington. One does not call on the president of the Pennsylvania Railroad or the president of the New York Central Railroad in business hours unless for business purposes; and this should be the rule observed by citizens of the United States toward the President. The weekly public receptions are no longer held. All these other receptions and calls simply for shaking hands and wishing him God-speed should no longer be asked for. For the President has larger and more serious work than the railway manager and should have at least as much time for thought and deliberation.

Moreover, the work of the railway manager is done in secret. Fiercer by far than the light which beats upon the throne is that which beats upon the White House. The people are eager to know the President's thoughts and plans, and an insistent press endeavors to satisfy them. Considering the conditions under which the President does his work, the wonder is not that he makes so many mistakes, but that he makes so few. There is no railway or business manager or college president who has not more time to himself for the reflection necessary to the maturing of large and correct policies. I chanced to be in the President's room when he dictated the rough draft of his famous dispatch to General Chaffee respecting torture in the Philippines. While he was dictating, two or three cards were brought in, also some books with a request for the President's autograph, and there were some other interruptions. While the dispatch as it went out in its revised form could not be improved, a President cannot expect to be always so happy in dictating dispatches in the midst of distractions. Office work of far-reaching importance should be done in the closet. Certainly no monarch or minister in Europe does administrative work under such unfavorable conditions; indeed, this public which exacts so much of the President's time should in all fairness be considerate in its criticism.

No one, I think, would care to have abated the fearless political criticism which has in this country and in England attained to the highest point ever reached. From the nature of things the press must comment promptly and without the full knowledge of conditions that might alter its judgments. But on account of the necessary haste of its expressions, the writers should avoid extravagant language and the too ready imputation of bad motives to the public servants. "It is strange that men cannot allow others to differ with them without charging corruption as the cause of the difference," are the plaintive words of Grant during a confidential conversation with his Secretary of State.

The contrast between the savage criticism of Cleveland and Harrison while each occupied the presidential chair and the respect each enjoyed from political opponents after retiring to private life is an effective illustration of the lesson I should like to teach. At the time of Harrison's death people spoke from their hearts and said, "Well done, good and faithful servant." A fine example of political criticism in a time of great excitement were two articles by Mr. Carl Schurz in *Harper's Weekly* during the Venezuela crisis. Mr. Schurz was a supporter and political friend of Cleveland, but condemned his Venezuela message. In the articles to which I refer he was charitable in feeling and moderate in tone, and though at the time I heard the term "wishy-washy" applied to one of them, I suspect that Mr. Schurz now looks back with satisfaction to his reserve; and those of us who used more forcible language in regard to the same incident may well wish that we had emulated his moderation.

The presidential office differs from all other political offices in the world, and has justified the hopes of its creators. It has not realized their fears, one of which was expressed by Hamilton in the *Federalist*. "A man raised from the station of a private citizen to the rank of Chief Magistrate," he wrote, "possessed of a moderate or slender fortune, and looking forward to a period not very remote, when he may probably be obliged to return to the station from which he was taken, might sometimes be under temptations to sacrifice his duty to his interest, which it would require superlative virtue to withstand. An avaricious man might be tempted to betray the interests of the state to the acquisition of wealth. An ambitious man might make his own aggrandizement, by the aid of a foreign power, the price of his treachery to his constituents." [1] From dangers of this sort the political virtue which we inherited from our English ancestors has preserved us. We may fairly maintain that the creation and administration of our presidential office have added something to political history, and when we contrast in character and ability the men who have filled it with the monarchs of England and of France, we may have a feeling of just pride. Mr. Bryce makes a suggestive comparison in ability of our Presidents to the prime ministers of England, awarding the palm to the Englishmen,[2] and from his large knowledge of both countries and impartial judgment we may readily accept his conclusion. It is, however, a merit of our Constitution that as great ability is not required for its chief executive office as is demanded in England. The prime minister must have

[1] See also the *Federalist* (Lodge's edition), 452. Bryce, Studies in History and Jurisprudence, 308.   [2] American Commonwealth, I, 80.

a talent for both administration and debate, which is a rare combination of powers, and if he be chosen from the House of Commons, it may happen that too much stress will be laid upon oratory, or the power of making ready replies to the attacks of the opposition. It is impossible to conceive of Washington defending his policy in the House or the Senate from a fire of questions and cross-questions. Lincoln might have developed this quality of a prime minister, but his replies and sallies of wit to put to confusion his opponents would have lacked the dignity his state papers and confidential letters possess. Hayes and Cleveland were excellent administrators, but neither could have reached his high position had the debating ability of a prime minister been required. On the other hand, Garfield, Harrison, and McKinley would have been effective speakers in either the House or the Senate.

An American may judge his own country best from European soil, impregnated as he there is with European ideas. Twice have I been in Europe during Cleveland's administration, twice during McKinley's, once during Roosevelt's. During the natural process of comparison, when one must recognize in many things the distinct superiority of England, Germany, and France, I have never had a feeling other than high respect for each one of these Presidents; and taking it by and large, in the endeavor to consider fairly the hits and misses of all, I have never had any reason to feel that the conduct of our national government has been inferior to that of any one of these highly civilized powers.

A REVIEW OF PRESIDENT HAYES'S ADMINIS-TRATION

Address delivered at the annual meeting of the Graduate School of
Arts and Sciences, and the Graduate Schools of Applied Science
and Business Administration, Harvard University, on October 8,
1908; printed in the *Century Magazine* for October, 1909.

A REVIEW OF PRESIDENT HAYES'S ADMINIS-
TRATION

MANY of our Presidents have been inaugurated under
curious and trying circumstances, but no one of them except Hayes has taken the oath of office when there was a
cloud on his title. Every man who had voted for Tilden, —
whose popular vote exceeded that of Hayes by 264,000, —
believed that Hayes had reached his high place by means of
fraud. Indeed, some of the Hayes voters shared this belief,
and stigmatized as monstrous the action of the Louisiana
returning board in awarding the electoral vote of Louisiana
to Hayes. The four men, three of them dishonest and the
fourth incompetent, who constituted this returning board,
rejected, on the ground of intimidation of negro voters,
eleven thousand votes that had been cast in due form for
Tilden. In the seventh volume of my history I have told
the story of the compromise in the form of the Electoral
Commission which passed on the conflicting claims and ad-
judged the votes of the disputed states, notably Florida
and Louisiana, to Hayes, giving him a majority of one in
the electoral college, thus making him President. When
the count was completed and the usual declaration made,
Hayes had no choice but to abide by the decision. Duty
to his country and to his party, the Republican, required
his acceptance of the office, and there is no reason for thinking that he had any doubts regarding his proper course.
His legal title was perfect, but his moral title was unsound,
and it added to the difficulty of his situation that the opposition, the Democrats, had a majority in the House of Rep-

resentatives.   None but a determined optimist could have predicted anything but failure for an administration beginning under such conditions.

Hayes was an Ohio man, and we in Ohio now watched his successive steps with keen interest.   We knew him as a man of high character, with a fine sense of honor, but we placed no great faith in his ability.   He had added to his reputation by the political campaign that he had made for governor, in 1875, against the Democrats under William Allen, who demanded an inflation of the greenback currency. He took an uncompromising stand for sound money, although that cause was unpopular in Ohio, and he spoke from the stump unremittingly and fearlessly, although overshadowed by the greater ability and power of expression of Senator Sherman and of Carl Schurz, who did yeoman's service for the Republicans in this campaign.   Senator Sherman had suggested Hayes as candidate for President, and the nomination by the Republican national convention had come to him in June, 1876.   While his letter of acceptance may not have surprised his intimate friends, it was a revelation to most of us from its outspoken and commonsense advocacy of civil service reform, and it gave us the first glimmering that in Rutherford B. Hayes the Republicans had for standard bearer a man of more than respectable ability.

His inaugural address confirmed this impression.   He spoke with dignity and sympathy of the disputed Presidency, promised a liberal policy toward the Southern states, and declared that a reform in our civil service was a "paramount necessity."   He chose for his Cabinet men in sympathy with his high ideals.   William M. Evarts, the Secretary of State, was one of the ablest lawyers in the country.   He had been one of the leading counsel in the defense of President Johnson in the impeachment trial, and had managed the Republican cause before the Electoral Commission with adroitness and zeal.   John Sherman, the Secretary of the Treasury, was the most capable financier in public life.   Carl Schurz, the Secretary of the Interior, was an aggressive and uncompromising reformer, who had served the Republican party well in the campaigns of 1875 and 1876.   If these three men could work together under Hayes, the United States need envy the governors of no other country.   They were in the brilliant but solid class, were abreast of the best thought of their time, had a solemn sense of duty, and believed in righteous government. Devens, the Attorney-General, had served with credit in the army and had held the honorable position of Justice of the Supreme Judicial Court of Massachusetts.   Thompson of Indiana, Secretary of the Navy, was a political appointment due to the influence of Senator Morton, but, all things considered, it was not a bad choice.   McCrary of Iowa, as Secretary of War, had been a useful member of the House of Representatives.   The Postmaster-General was Key of Tennessee, who had served in the Confederate army and voted for Tilden.   This appointment was not so genuine a recognition of the South as would have been made if Hayes could have carried out his first intention, which was the appointment of General Joseph E. Johnston as Secretary of War.   Considering that Johnston had surrendered the second great army of the Confederacy only twelve years before, the thought was possible only to a magnanimous nature, and in the inner circle of Hayes's counselors obvious and grave objections were urged.   General Sherman doubted the wisdom of the proposed appointment, although he said that as General of the army he would be entirely content to receive the President's orders through his old antagonist.   Although the appointment of Johnston would have added strength, the Cabinet as finally made up was strong, and the selection of such advisers created a favorable impression upon the intelligent sentiment of the country; it was spoken of as the ablest Cabinet since Washington's.

A wise inaugural address and an able Cabinet made a good beginning, but before the harmonious coöperation of these extraordinary men could be developed a weighty question, which brooked no delay, had to be settled. The Stevens-Sumner plan of the reconstruction of the South on the basis of universal negro suffrage and military support of the governments thus constituted had failed. One by one in various ways the Southern states had recovered home rule until, on the inauguration of Hayes, carpet-bag negro governments existed in only two states, South Carolina and Louisiana. In both of these the Democrats maintained that their candidates for governor had been lawfully elected. The case of South Carolina presented no serious difficulty. Hayes electors had been rightfully chosen, and so had the Democratic governor, Hampton. But Chamberlain, the Republican candidate, had a claim based on the exclusion of the votes of two counties by the board of state canvassers. After conferences between each of the claimants and the President, the question was settled in favor of the Democrat, which was the meaning of the withdrawal of the United States troops from the State House in Columbia.

The case of Louisiana was much more troublesome. Packard, the Republican candidate for governor, had received as many votes as Hayes, and logic seemed to require that, if Hayes be President, Packard should be governor. While the question was pending, Blaine said in the Senate: "You discredit Packard, and you discredit Hayes. You hold that Packard is not the legal governor of Louisiana, and President Hayes has no title." And the other leaders of the Republican party, for the most part, held this view. To these and their followers Blaine applied the name "Stalwarts," stiff partisans, who did not believe in surrendering the hold of the Republicans on the Southern states.

Between the policies of a continuance of the support of the Republican party in Louisiana or its withdrawal, a weak man would have allowed things to drift, while a strong man of the Conkling and Chandler type would have sustained the Packard government with the whole force at his command. Hayes acted slowly and cautiously, asked for and received much good counsel, and in the end determined to withdraw the United States troops from the immediate vicinity of the State House in Louisiana. The Packard government fell, and the Democrats took possession. The lawyers could furnish cogent reasons why Packard was not entitled to the governorship, although the electoral vote of Louisiana had been counted for Hayes; but the Stalwarts maintained that no legal quibble could varnish over so glaring an inconsistency. Indeed, it was one of those illogical acts, so numerous in English and American history, that resolve difficulties, when a rigid adherence to logic would tend to foment trouble.

The inaugural address and the distinctively reform Cabinet did not suit the party workers, and when the President declined to sustain the Packard government in Louisiana, disapproval was succeeded by rage. In six weeks after his inauguration Hayes was without a party; that is to say, the men who carried on the organization were bitterly opposed to his policy, and they made much more noise than the independent thinking voters who believed that a man had arisen after their own hearts. Except from the Southern wing, he received little sympathy from the Democratic party. In their parlance, fraud was written on his brow. He had the honor and perquisites of office which were rightfully theirs.

Once the troops were withdrawn from South Carolina and Louisiana, no backward step was possible, and although Hayes would have liked congressional support and sympathy for his act, this was not necessary. The next most important question of his administration related to finance. He and his Secretary of the Treasury would have been gratified by an obedient majority in Congress at their back. Presidents before and after Hayes have made a greater or less employment of their patronage to secure the passage of their favorite measures, but Hayes immediately relinquished that power by taking a decided position for a civil service based on merit. In a little over a month after the withdrawal of the troops from the immediate vicinity of the State House in Louisiana, he announced his policy in a letter to his Secretary of the Treasury. "It is my wish," he wrote, "that the collection of the revenues should be free from partisan control, and organized on a strictly business basis, with the same guaranties for efficiency and fidelity in the selection of the chief and subordinate officers that would be required by a prudent merchant. Party leaders should have no more influence in appointments than other equally respectable citizens. No assessments for political purposes on officers or subordinates should be allowed. No useless officer or employee should be retained. No officer should be required or permitted to take part in the management of political organizations, caucuses, conventions, or election campaigns." The mandatory parts of this letter he incorporated in an order to Federal office-holders, adding: "This rule is applicable to every department of the civil service. It should be understood by every officer of the general government that he is expected to conform his conduct to its requirements."

It must be a source of gratification to the alumni and faculty of Harvard College that its president and governing boards were, in June, 1877, in the judicious minority, and recognized their appreciation of Hayes by conferring upon him its highest honorary degree.   Schurz, who had received his LL.D. the year before, accompanied Hayes to Cambridge, and, in his Harvard speech at Commencement, gave his forcible and sympathetic approval of the "famous order of the President," as it had now come to be called.

A liberal and just Southern policy, the beginning of a genuine reform in the civil service and the resumption of specie payments, are measures which distinguish and glorify President Hayes's administration, but in July, 1877, public attention was diverted from all these by a movement which partook of the nature of a social uprising.   The depression following the panic of 1873 had been widespread and severe. The slight revival of business resulting from the Centennial Exposition of 1876 and the consequent large passenger traffic had been succeeded by a reaction in 1877 that brought business men to the verge of despair.   Failures of merchants and manufacturers, stoppage of factories, diminished traffic on the railroads, railroad bankruptcies and receiverships, threw a multitude of laborers out of employment; and those fortunate enough to retain their jobs were less steadily employed, and were subject to reductions in wages.

The state of railroad transportation was deplorable. The competition of the trunk lines, as the railroads running from Chicago to the seaboard were called, was sharp, and, as there was not business enough for all, the cutting of through freight rates caused such business to be done at an actual loss, while the through passenger transportation afforded little profit. Any freight agent knew the remedy: an increase of freight rates by agreement or through a system of pooling earnings. Agreements were made, but not honestly kept, and, after a breach of faith, the fight was renewed with increased fury. As the railroad managers thought that they could not increase their gross earnings, they resolved on decreasing their expenses, and somewhat hastily and jauntily they announced a reduction of ten per cent in the wages of their employees.

This was resisted. Trouble first began on the Baltimore and Ohio Railroad, where the men not only struck against the reduction, but prevented other men from taking their places, and stopped by force the running of trains. The militia of West Virginia was inadequate to cope with the situation, and the governor of that state called on the President for troops, which were sent with a beneficial effect. But the trouble spread to Maryland, and a conflict in Baltimore between the militia and rioters in sympathy with the strikers resulted in a number of killed and wounded. The next day, Saturday, July 21, a riot in Pittsburg caused the most profound sensation in the country since the draft riots of the Civil War. The men on the Pennsylvania and the Pittsburg, Fort Wayne and Chicago railroads, had struck, and all freight traffic was arrested. On this day six hundred and fifty men of the first division of the Pennsylvania national guard at Philadelphia arrived in Pittsburg, and, in the attempt to clear the Twenty-eighth Street crossing, they replied to the missiles thrown at them by the mob with volleys of musketry, killing instantly sixteen of the rioters and wounding many.

Here was cause for exasperation, and a furious mob, composed of strikers, idle factory hands, and miners, tramps, communists, and outcasts, began its work of vengeance and plunder. Possessed of firearms, through breaking into a number of gun shops, they attacked the Philadelphia soldiers, who had withdrawn to the railroad roundhouse, and a fierce battle ensued. Unable to dislodge the soldiers by assault, the rioters attempted to roast them out by setting fire to cars of coke saturated with petroleum and pushing these down the track against the roundhouse. This eventually forced the soldiers to leave the building, but, though pursued by the rioters, they made a good retreat across the Allegheny River. The mob, completely beyond control, began the destruction of railroad property. The torch was applied to two roundhouses, to railroad sheds, shops and offices, cars and locomotives. Barrels of spirits, taken from the freight cars, and opened and drunk, made demons of the men, and the work of plunder and destruction of goods in transit went on with renewed fury.

That Saturday night Pittsburg witnessed a reign of terror. On Sunday the rioting and pillage were continued, and in the afternoon the Union Depot and Railroad Hotel and an elevator near by were burned. Then as the rioters were satiated and too drunk to be longer dangerous, the riot died out: it was not checked. On Monday, through the action of the authorities, armed companies of law-abiding citizens, and some faithful companies of the militia, order was restored. But meanwhile the strike had spread to a large number of other railroads between the seaboard and Chicago and St. Louis. Freight traffic was entirely suspended, and passenger trains were run only on sufferance of the strikers. Business was paralyzed, and the condition of disorganization and unrest continued throughout the month of July. The governors of West Virginia, Maryland, Pennsylvania, and Illinois called upon the President for United States troops, which were promptly sent, and in

Indiana and Missouri they were employed on the demand of the United States marshals. Where the regular soldiers appeared order was at once restored without bloodshed, and it was said that the rioters feared one Federal bayonet more than a whole company of militia. The gravity of the situation is attested by three proclamations of warning from President Hayes.

Strikes had been common in our country, and, while serious enough in certain localities, had aroused no general concern, but the action of the mob in Baltimore, Pittsburg, and Chicago seemed like an attack on society itself, and it came like a thunderbolt out of a clear sky, startling Americans, who had hugged the delusion that such social uprisings belonged to Europe, and had no reason of being in a great, free republic where all men had an equal chance. The railroad managers had no idea that they were letting loose a slumbering giant when their edict of a ten per cent reduction went forth. It was due to the prompt and efficient action of the President that order was ultimately restored. In the profound and earnest thinking and discussion that went on during the rest of the year, whenever thoughtful men gathered together, many a grateful word was said of the quiet, unassuming man in the White House who saw clearly his duty and never faltered in pursuing it. It was seen that the Federal government, with a resolute President at its head, was a tower of strength in the event of a social uprising.

In the reform of the civil service Hayes proceeded from words to action. He reappointed Thomas L. James as postmaster of New York City, who had conducted his office on a thorough business basis, and gave him sympathetic support. The New York Custom-house had long been a political machine in which the interests of politicians had been more considered than those of the public it was supposed to serve. The President began an investigation of it through an impartial commission, and he and Sherman came to the conclusion that the renovation desired, in line with his letter to the Secretary of the Treasury and his order to the Federal officers, could not be effected so long as the present collector, Chester A. Arthur, and the naval officer, A. B. Cornell, remained in office. Courteous intimations were sent to them that their resignations were desired on the ground that new officers could better carry out the reform which the President had at heart. Arthur and Cornell, under the influence of Senator Conkling, refused to resign, and a plain issue was made between the President and the New York senator. At the special session of Congress, in October, 1877, he sent to the Senate nominations of new men for these places, but the power of Conkling, working through the "courtesy of the Senate," was sufficient to procure their rejection; and this was also the result when the same nominations were made in December.

In July, 1878, after the adjournment of Congress, Hayes removed Arthur and Cornell, and appointed Merritt and Burt in their places. During the following December these appointments came before the Senate for confirmation. Sherman decided to resign if they were rejected, and he made a strong personal appeal to Senators Allison, Windom, and Morrill that they should not permit "the insane hate of Conkling" to override the good of the service and the party. A seven hours' struggle ensued in the Senate, but Merritt and Burt were confirmed by a decisive majority. After the confirmation, Hayes wrote to Merritt: "My desire is that the office be conducted on strictly business principles and according to the rules for the civil service which were recommended by the Civil Service Commission in the administration of General Grant."

In three of his annual messages, Hayes presented strong arguments for a reform in the civil service, and he begged Congress, without avail, to make appropriations to sustain the Civil Service Commission. He sympathized with and supported Schurz in his introduction into the Interior Department of competitive examinations for appointments and promotions, and he himself extended that system to the custom-houses and post-offices of the larger cities.

All that was accomplished in this direction was due to his efforts and those of his Cabinet. He received neither sympathy nor help from Congress; indeed, he met with great opposition from his own party. A picture not without humor is Hayes reading, as his justification, to the Republican remonstrants against his policy of appointments the strong declaration for a civil service based on merit in the Republican platform, on which he had stood as candidate for President. Though his preaching did not secure the needed legislation from Congress, it produced a marked effect on public sentiment.

The organization of civil service reform associations began under Hayes. The New York association was begun in 1877, reorganized three years later, and soon had a large national membership, which induced the formation of other state associations; and although the national civil service reform league was not formed until after his term of office expired, the origin of the society may be safely referred to his influence. In the melioration of the public service which has been so conspicuously in operation since 1877, Hayes must be rated the pioneer President. Some of Grant's efforts in this direction were well meant, but he had no fundamental appreciation of the importance of the question or enthusiasm for the work, and, in a general way, it may be said that he left the civil service in a demoralized condition. How pregnant was Hayes's remark in his last annual message, and what a text it has been for many homilies! "My views," he wrote, "concerning the dangers of patronage or appointments for personal or partisan considerations have been strengthened by my observation and experience in the executive office, and I believe these dangers threaten the stability of the government."

The brightest page in the history of the Republican party since the Civil War tells of its work in the cause of sound finance, and no administration is more noteworthy than that of Hayes. Here again the work was done by the President and his Cabinet in the face of a determined opposition in Congress. During the first two years of his administration, the Democrats had a majority in the House, and during the last two a majority in both the House and the Senate. The Republican party was sounder than the Democratic on the resumption of specie payments and in the advocacy of a correct money standard, but Hayes had by no means all of his own party at his back. Enough Republicans, however, were of his way of thinking to prevent an irremediable inflation of either greenbacks or silver.

The credit for what was accomplished in finance belongs in the main to John Sherman, a great financier and consummate statesman; but he had the constant sympathy and support of the President. It was their custom to take long drives together every Sunday afternoon and discuss systematically and thoroughly the affairs of the Treasury and the official functions of the President. No President ever had a better counselor than Sherman, no Secretary of the Treasury more sympathetic and earnest support than was given by Hayes. Sherman refunded 845 millions of the public debt at a lower rate of interest, showing in his negotiations with bankers a remarkable combination of business and political ability. Cool, watchful, and confident, he grasped the point of view of New York and London financial syndicates, and to that interested and somewhat narrow vision he joined the intelligence and foresight of a statesman. Sherman brought about the resumption of specie payments on the 1st of January, 1879, the date fixed in the bill of which he was the chief author and which, four years before, he had carried through the Senate. It was once the fashion of his opponents to discredit his work, and, emphasizing the large crop of 1878 and the European demand for our breadstuffs, to declare that resumption was brought about by Providence and not by John Sherman. No historian of American finance can fail to see how important is the part often played by bountiful nature, but it is to the lasting merit of Sherman and Hayes that, in the dark years of 1877 and 1878, with cool heads and unshaken faith, they kept the country in the path of financial safety and honor despite bitter opposition and clamorous abuse.

These two years formed a part of my own business career, and I can add my vivid recollection to my present study of the period. As values steadily declined and losses rather than profits in business became the rule, the depression and even despair of business men and manufacturers can hardly be exaggerated. The daily list of failures and bankruptcies was appalling. How often one heard that iron and coal and land were worth too little and money too much, that only the bondholder could be happy, for his interest was sure and the purchasing power of his money great! In August, 1878, when John Sherman went to Toledo to speak to a gathering three thousand strong, he was greeted with such cries as, "You are responsible for all the failures in the country"; "You work to the interest of the capitalist"; "Capitalists own you, John Sherman, and you rob the poor widows and orphans to make them rich."

By many the resumption of specie payments was deemed impossible. The most charitable of Sherman's opponents looked upon him as an honest but visionary enthusiast who would fail in his policy and be "the deadest man politically" in the country. Others deemed resumption possible only by driving to the wall a majority of active business men. It was this sentiment which gave strength to the majority in the House of Representatives, which was opposed to any contraction of the greenback currency and in favor of the free coinage of silver, and of making it likewise a full legal tender. Most of these members of Congress were sincere, and thought that they were asking no more than justice for the trader, the manufacturer, and the laborer. The "Ohio idea" was originally associated with an inflation of the paper currency, but by extension it came to mean an abundance of cheap money, whether paper or silver. Proposed legislation, with this as its aim, was very popular in Ohio, but, despite the intense feeling against the President's and Secretary's policy in their own state and generally throughout the West, Hayes and Sherman maintained it consistently, and finally brought about the resumption of specie payments.

In their way of meeting the insistent demand for the remonetization of silver Hayes and Sherman differed. In November, 1877, the House of Representatives, under a suspension of the rules, passed by a vote of 163 to 34 a bill for the free coinage of the $412\frac{1}{2}$ grain silver dollar, making that dollar likewise a legal tender for all debts and dues. The Senate was still Republican, but the Republican senators were by no means unanimous for the gold standard. Sherman became convinced that, although the free-silver bill could not pass the Senate, something must nevertheless be done for silver, and, in coöperation with Senator Allison, he was instrumental in the adoption of the compromise which finally became law. This remonetized silver, providing for the purchase of not less than two million dollars' worth of silver bullion per month, nor more than four millions, and for its coinage into 412½ grain silver dollars. Hayes vetoed this bill, sending a sound and manly message to the House of Representatives; but Congress passed it over his veto by a decided majority.

The regard for John Sherman's ability in Ohio was unbounded, and it was generally supposed that in all financial affairs, as well as in many others, he dominated Hayes. I shared that opinion until I learned indirectly from John Hay, who was first assistant Secretary of State and intimate in inner administration circles, that this was not true; that Hayes had decided opinions of his own and did not hesitate to differ with his Secretary of the Treasury. Nevertheless, not until John Sherman's "'Recollections'" were published was it generally known, I believe, that Sherman had a share in the Allison compromise, and did not approve of the President's veto of the bill remonetizing silver.

The Federal control of congressional and presidential elections, being a part of the Reconstruction legislation, was obnoxious to the Democrats, and they attempted to abrogate it by "riders" attached to several appropriation bills, especially that providing for the army. While the Senate remained Republican, there was chance for an accommodation between the President and the Senate on one side and the House on the other. Two useful compromises were made, the Democrats yielding in one case, the Republicans in the other. But in 1879, when both the House and the Senate were Democratic, a sharp contest began between

Congress and the executive, the history of which is written in seven veto messages. For lack of appropriations to carry on the government, the President called an extra session of Congress in the first year of his administration and another in 1879, which was a remarkable record of extra sessions in a time of peace. The Democratic House passed a resolution for the appointment of a committee to investigate Hayes's title and aroused some alarm lest an effort might be made "to oust President Hayes and inaugurate Tilden." Although this alarm was stilled less than a month later by a decisive vote of the House, the action and investigation were somewhat disquieting.

Thus Hayes encountered sharp opposition from the Democrats, who frequently pointed their arguments by declaring that he held his place by means of fraud. He received sympathy from hardly any of the leaders of his own party in Congress, and met with open condemnation from the Stalwarts; yet he pursued his course with steadiness and equanimity, and was happy in his office. His serene amiability and hopefulness, especially in regard to affairs in the Southern states, were a source of irritation to the Stalwarts; but it was the serenity of a man who felt himself fully equal to his responsibilities.

In his inaugural address, Hayes contributed an addition to our political idiom, "He serves his party best who serves the country best." His administration was a striking illustration of this maxim. When he became President, the Republican party was in a demoralized condition, but, despite the factional criticism to which he was subject, he gained in the first few months of his Presidency the approval of men of intelligence and independent thought, and, as success attended his different policies, he received the support of the masses. The signal Republican triumph in the presidential election of 1880 was due to the improvement in business conditions and to the clean and efficient administration of Hayes.

In recalling his predecessor in office, we think more gladly of the Grant of Donelson, Vicksburg, and Appomattox than of Grant the President, for during his two administrations corruption was rife and bad government to the fore. Financial scandals were so frequent that despairing patriots cried out, "Is there no longer honesty in public life?" Our country then reached the high-water mark of corruption in national affairs. A striking improvement began under Hayes, who infused into the public service his own high ideals of honesty and efficiency. Hayes was much assisted in his social duties by his wife, a woman of character and intelligence, who carried herself with grace and dignity. One sometimes heard the remark that as Hayes was ruled in political matters by John Sherman, so in social affairs he was ruled by his wife. The sole foundation for this lay in his deference to her total abstinence principles, which she held so strongly as to exclude wine from the White House table except, I believe, at one official dinner, that to the Russian Grand Dukes.

Hayes's able Cabinet was likewise a harmonious one. Its members were accustomed to dine together at regular intervals (fortnightly, I think), when affairs of state and other subjects were discussed, and the geniality of these occasions was enhanced by a temperate circulation of the wine bottle. There must have been very good talk at these social meetings. Evarts and Schurz were citizens of the world. Evarts was a man of keen intelligence and wide information, and possessed a genial as well as a caustic wit. Schurz could discuss present politics and past history. He was well versed in European history of the eighteenth century and the Napoleonic wars, and could talk about the power of Voltaire in literature and the influence of Lessing on Goethe. From appreciative discourse on the Wagner opera and the French drama, he could, if the conversation turned to the Civil War, give a lively account of the battles of Chancellorsville or Gettysburg, in both of which he had borne an honorable part. Sherman was not a cosmopolitan like his two colleagues, but he loved dining out. His manners were those of the old-school gentleman; he could listen with genial appreciation, and he could talk of events in American history of which he had been a contemporaneous observer; as, for example, of the impressive oratory of Daniel Webster at a dinner in Plymouth; or the difference between the national conventions of his early political life and the huge ones of the present, illustrating his comparison with an account of the Whig convention of 1852, to which he went as a delegate.

Differing in many respects, Hayes and Grover Cleveland were alike in the possession of executive ability and the lack of oratorical. We all know that it is a purely academic question which is the better form of government, the English or our own, as both have grown up to adapt themselves to peculiar conditions. But when I hear an enthusiast for Cabinet government and ministerial responsibility, I like to point out that men like Hayes and Cleveland, who made excellent Presidents, could never have been prime ministers. One cannot conceive of either in an office equivalent to that of First Lord of the Treasury, being heckled by members on the front opposition bench and holding his own or getting the better of his opponents.

I have brought Hayes and Cleveland into juxtaposition, as each had a high personal regard for the other. Hayes died on January 17, 1893. Cleveland, the President-elect, was to be inaugurated on the following fourth of March. Despite remonstrance and criticism from bitter partisans of his own party, who deprecated any honor paid to one whom all good Democrats deemed a fraudulent President, Cleveland traveled from New York to Fremont, Ohio, to attend the funeral. He could only think of Hayes as an ex-President and a man whom he highly esteemed.

EDWIN LAWRENCE GODKIN

Lecture read at Harvard University, April 13, 1908; printed in the
Atlantic Monthly for September, 1908.

EDWIN LAWRENCE GODKIN

OUR two great journalists of the nineteenth century were Greeley and Godkin. Though differing in very many respects, they were alike in possessing a definite moral purpose. The most glorious and influential portion of Greeley's career lay between the passage of the Kansas-Nebraska Act in 1854 and the election of Lincoln in 1860, when the press played an important part in the upbuilding of a political party which formulated in a practical manner the antislavery sentiment of the country. Foremost among newspapers was the *New York Tribune;* foremost among editors was Horace Greeley. Of Greeley in his best days Godkin wrote: "He has an enthusiasm which never flags, and a faith in principles which nothing can shake, and an English style which, for vigor, terseness, clearness, and simplicity, has never been surpassed, except perhaps by Cobbett." [1]

Greeley and Godkin were alike in furnishing their readers with telling arguments. In northern New York and the Western Reserve of Ohio the *Weekly Tribune* was a political Bible. "Why do you look so gloomy?" said a traveler, riding along the highway in the Western Reserve during the old antislavery days, to a farmer who was sitting moodily on a fence. "Because," replied the farmer, "my Democratic friend next door got the best of me in an argument last night. But when I get my *Weekly Tribune* tomorrow I'll knock the foundations all out from under him." [2]

Premising that Godkin is as closely identified with *The*

---

[1] R. Ogden's Life and Letters of E. L. Godkin, I, 255.
[2] Rhodes's History of the United States, II, 72 (C. M. Depew).

Nation and the *Evening Post* as Greeley with the *Tribune*, I shall refer to a personal experience. Passing a part of the winter of 1886 in a hotel at Thomasville, Georgia, it chanced that among the hundred or more guests there were eight or ten of us who regularly received *The Nation* by post. Ordinarily it arrived on the Friday noon train from Savannah, and when we came from our mid-day dinner into the hotel office, there, in our respective boxes, easily seen, and from their peculiar form recognized by every one, were our copies of *The Nation*. Occasionally the papers missed connection at Savannah, and our *Nations* did not arrive until after supper. It used to be said by certain scoffers that if a discussion of political questions came up in the afternoon of one of those days of disappointment, we readers were mum; but in the late evening, after having digested our political pabulum, we were ready to join issue with any antagonist. Indeed, each of us might have used the words of James Russell Lowell, written while he was traveling on the Continent and visiting many places where *The Nation* could not be bought: "All the time I was without it, my mind was chaos and I didn't feel that I had a safe opinion to swear by." [1]

While the farmer of the Western Reserve and Lowell are extreme types of clientèle, each represents fairly well the peculiar following of Greeley and of Godkin, which differed as much as did the personal traits of the two journalists. Godkin speaks of Greeley's "odd attire, shambling gait, simple, good-natured and hopelessly peaceable face, and long yellow locks." [2] His "old white hat and white coat," which in New York were regarded as an affectation, counted with his following west of the Hudson River as a winning eccentricity. When he came out upon the

[1] Ogden, II, 88.   [2] *Ibid.*, I, 257.

lecture platform with crumpled shirt, cravat awry, and wrinkled coat looking as if he had traveled for a number of nights and days, such disorder appeared to many of his Western audiences as nothing worse than the mark of a very busy man, who had paid them the compliment of leaving his editorial rooms to speak to them in person, and who had their full sympathy as he thus opened his discourse, "You mustn't, my friends, expect fine words from a rough busy man like me." [1]

The people who read the *Tribune* did not expect fine words; they were used to the coarse, abusive language in which Greeley repelled attacks, and to his giving the lie with heartiness and vehemence. They enjoyed reading that "another lie was nailed to the counter," and that an antagonist "was a liar, knowing himself to be a liar, and lying with naked intent to deceive." [2]

On the contrary, the dress, the face, and the personal bearing of Godkin proclaimed at once the gentleman and cultivated man of the world. You felt that he was a man whom you would like to meet at dinner, accompany on a long walk, or cross the Atlantic with, were you an acquaintance or friend.

An incident related by Godkin himself shows that at least one distinguished gentleman did not enjoy sitting at meat with Greeley. During the spring of 1864 Godkin met Greeley at breakfast at the house of Mr. John A. C. Gray. William Cullen Bryant, at that time editor of the New York *Evening Post*, was one of the guests, and, when Greeley entered the room, was standing near the fireplace conversing with his host. On observing that Bryant did not speak to Greeley, Gray asked him in a whisper, "Don't you know

---

[1] Parton's Greeley, 331, 576; my own recollections; Ogden, I, 255.
[2] Godkin, Random Recollections, *Evening Post*, December 30, 1899.

Mr. Greeley?" In a loud whisper Bryant replied, "No, I don't; he's a blackguard — he's a blackguard." [1]

In the numbers of people whom he influenced, Greeley had the advantage over Godkin. In February, 1855, the circulation of the *Tribune* was 172,000, and its own estimate of its readers half a million, which was certainly not excessive. It is not a consideration beyond bounds to infer that the readers of the *Tribune* in 1860 furnished a goodly part of the 1,886,000 votes which were received by Lincoln.

At different times, while Godkin was editor, *The Nation* stated its exact circulation, which, as I remember it, was about 10,000, and it probably had 50,000 readers. As many of its readers were in the class of Lowell, its indirect influence was immense. Emerson said that *The Nation* had "breadth, variety, self-sustainment, and an admirable style of thought and expression." — "I owe much to *The Nation*," wrote Francis Parkman. "I regard it as the most valuable of American journals, and feel that the best interests of the country are doubly involved in its success." — "What an influence you have!" said George William Curtis to Godkin. "What a sanitary element in our affairs *The Nation* is!" — "To my generation," wrote William James, "Godkin's was certainly the towering influence in all thought concerning public affairs, and indirectly his influence has certainly been more pervasive than that of any other writer of the generation, for he influenced other writers who never quoted him, and determined the whole current of discussion." — "When the work of this century is summed up," wrote Charles Eliot Norton to Godkin, "what you have done for the good old cause of civilization, the cause which is always defeated, but always after defeat taking more advanced position than before — what you have done for this cause will

[1] Ogden, I, 168.

count for much." — "I am conscious," wrote President
Eliot to Godkin, "that *The Nation* has had a decided effect
on my opinions and my action for nearly forty years; and
I believe it has had like effect on thousands of educated
Americans." [1]

A string of quotations, as is well known, becomes wearisome; but the importance of the point that I am trying to
make will probably justify one more. "I find myself so
thoroughly agreeing with *The Nation* always," wrote Lowell,
"that I am half persuaded that I edit it myself!" [2]   Truly
Lowell had a good company: Emerson, Parkman, Curtis,
Norton, James, Eliot, — all teachers in various ways.
Through their lectures, books, and speeches, they influenced
college students at an impressible age; they appealed to
young and to middle-aged men; and they furnished comfort
and entertainment for the old.   It would have been difficult to find anywhere in the country an educated man whose
thought was not affected by some one of these seven; and
their influence on editorial writers for newspapers was remarkable.   These seven were all taught by Godkin.

"Every Friday morning when *The Nation* comes," wrote
Lowell to Godkin, "I fill my pipe, and read it from beginning
to end.   Do you do it all yourself?   Or are there really so
many clever men in the country?" [3]   Lowell's experience,
with or without tobacco, was undoubtedly that of hundreds,
perhaps of thousands, of educated men, and the query he
raised was not an uncommon one.   At one time, Godkin, I
believe, wrote most of "The Week," which was made up
of brief and pungent comments on events, as well as the principal editorial articles.   The power of iteration, which the
journalist possesses, is great, and, when that power is wielded

[1] Ogden, I, 221, 249, 251, 252; II, 222, 231.
[2] Letters of J. R. Lowell, II, 76.   [3] *Ibid.*, I, 368.

by a man of keen intelligence and wide information, possessing a knowledge of the world, a sense of humor, and an effective literary style, it becomes tremendous. The only escape from Godkin's iteration was one frequently tried, and that was, to stop *The Nation*.

Although Godkin published three volumes of Essays, the honors he received during his lifetime were due to his work as editor of *The Nation* and the *Evening Post;* and this is his chief title of fame. The education, early experience, and aspiration of such a journalist are naturally matter of interest. Born in 1831, in the County of Wicklow in the southeastern part of Ireland, the son of a Presbyterian minister, he was able to say when referring to Goldwin Smith, "I am an Irishman, but I am as English in blood as he is." [1] Receiving his higher education at Queen's College, Belfast, he took a lively interest in present politics, his college friends being Liberals. John Stuart Mill was their prophet, Grote and Bentham their daily companions, and America was their promised land. "To the scoffs of the Tories that our schemes were impracticable," he has written of these days, "our answer was that in America, barring slavery, they were actually at work. There, the chief of the state and the legislators were freely elected by the people. There, the offices were open to everybody who had the capacity to fill them. There was no army or navy, two great curses of humanity in all ages. There was to be no war except war in self-defense. . . . In fact, we did not doubt that in America at last the triumph of humanity over its own weaknesses and superstitions was being achieved, and the dream of Christendom was at last being realized." [2]

As a correspondent of the London *Daily News* he went to the Crimea. The scenes at Malakoff gave him a disgust for

---

[1] Ogden, I, 1.   [2] *Evening Post*, December 30, 1899; Odgen, I, 11.

war which thenceforth he never failed to express upon every opportunity. When a man of sixty-eight, reckoning its cost in blood and treasure, he deemed the Crimean War entirely unnecessary and very deplorable.[1] Godkin arrived in America in November, 1856, and soon afterwards, with Olmsted's "Journey in the Seaboard Slave States," the "Back Country," and "Texas," as guidebooks, took a horseback journey through the South. Following closely Olmsted's trail, and speaking therefore with knowledge, he has paid him one of the highest compliments one traveler ever paid another. "Olmsted's work," he wrote, "in vividness of description and in photographic minuteness far surpasses Arthur Young's."[2] During this journey he wrote letters to the London *Daily News*, and these were continued after his return to New York City. For the last three years of our Civil War, he was its regular correspondent, and, as no one denies that he was a powerful advocate when his heart was enlisted, he rendered efficient service to the cause of the North. The *News* was strongly pro-Northern, and Godkin furnished the facts which rendered its leaders sound and instructive as well as sympathetic. All this while he was seeing socially the best people in New York City, and making useful and desirable acquaintances in Boston and Cambridge.

The interesting story of the foundation of *The Nation* has been told a number of times, and it will suffice for our purpose to say that there were forty stockholders who contributed a capital of one hundred thousand dollars, one half of which was raised in Boston, and one quarter each in Philadelphia and New York. Godkin was the editor, and next to him the chief promoters were James M. McKim of Philadelphia and Charles Eliot Norton. The first number

---

[1] *Evening Post*, December 30, 1899.   [2] *Ibid.*; Ogden, I, 113.

of this "weekly journal of politics, literature, science, and art" appeared on July 6, 1865. Financial embarrassment and disagreements among the stockholders marked the first year of its existence, at the end of which Godkin, McKim, and Frederick Law Olmsted took over the property, and continued the publication under the proprietorship of E. L. Godkin & Co. "*The Nation* owed its continued existence to Charles Eliot Norton," wrote Godkin in 1899. "It was his calm and confidence amid the shrieks of combatants . . . which enabled me to do my work even with decency." [1]

Sixteen years after *The Nation* was started, in 1881, Godkin sold it out to the *Evening Post*, becoming associate editor of that journal, with Carl Schurz as his chief. *The Nation* was thereafter published as the weekly edition of the *Evening Post*. In 1883 Schurz retired and Godkin was made editor-in-chief, having the aid and support of one of the owners, Horace White. On January 1, 1900, on account of ill health, he withdrew from the editorship of the *Evening Post*,[2] thus retiring from active journalism.

For thirty-five years he had devoted himself to his work with extraordinary ability and singleness of purpose. Marked appreciation came to him: invitations to deliver courses of lectures from both Harvard and Yale, the degree of A.M. from Harvard, and the degree of D.C.L. from Oxford. What might have been a turning point in his career was the offer in 1870 of the professorship of history at Harvard. He was strongly tempted to accept it, but, before coming to a decision, he took counsel of a number of friends; and few men, I think, have ever received such wise and disinterested advice as did Godkin when he was thus hesitating in what way he should apply his teaching.

[1] *Evening Post*, December 30, 1899; Ogden, I, *passim; The Nation*, June 25, 1885, May 23, 1902.   [2] Ogden, II, Chap. XVII.

The burden of the advice was not to take the professorship, if he had to give up *The Nation*.

Frederick Law Olmsted wrote to him: "If you can't write fully half of 'The Week' and half the leaders, and control the drift and tone of the whole while living at Cambridge, give up the professorship, for *The Nation* is worth many professorships. It is a question of loyalty over a question of comfort." Lowell wrote to him in the same strain: "*Stay* if the two things are incompatible. We may find another professor by and by . . . but we can't find another editor for *The Nation*." From Germany, John Bigelow sent a characteristic message: "Tell the University to require each student to take a copy of *The Nation*. Do not profess history for them in any other way. I dare say your lectures would be good, but why limit your pupils to hundreds which are now counted by thousands?" [1]

As is well known, Godkin relinquished the idea of the college connection and stuck to his job, although the quiet and serenity of a professor's life in Cambridge contrasted with his own turbulent days appealed to him powerfully. "Ten years hence," he wrote to Norton, "if things go on as they are now I shall be the most odious man in America. Not that I shall not have plenty of friends, but my enemies will be far more numerous and active." Six years after he had founded *The Nation*, and one year after he had declined the Harvard professorship, when he was yet but forty years old, he gave this humorously exaggerated account of his physical failings due to his nervous strain: "I began *The Nation* young, handsome, and fascinating, and am now withered and somewhat broken, rheumatism gaining on me rapidly, my complexion ruined, as also my figure, for I am growing stout." [2]

[1] Ogden, II, Chap. XI.   [2] *Ibid.*, II, 51.

But his choice between the Harvard professorship and *The Nation* was a wise one. He was a born writer of paragraphs and editorials. The files of *The Nation* are his monument. A crown of his laborious days is the tribute of James Bryce: "*The Nation* was the best weekly not only in America but in the world." [1]

Thirty-five years of journalism, in which Godkin was accustomed to give hard blows, did not, as he himself foreshadowed, call forth a unanimous chorus of praise; and the objections of intelligent and high-minded men are well worth taking into account. The most common one is that his criticism was always destructive; that he had an eye for the weak side of causes and men that he did not favor, and these he set forth with unremitting vigor without regard for palliating circumstances; that he erected a high and impossible ideal and judged all men by it; hence, if a public man was right eight times out of ten, he would seize upon the two failures and so parade them with his withering sarcasm that the reader could get no other idea than that the man was either weak or wicked. An editor of very positive opinions, he was apt to convey the idea that if any one differed from him on a vital question, like the tariff or finance or civil service reform, he was necessarily a bad man. He made no allowances for the weaknesses of human nature, and had no idea that he himself ever could be mistaken. Though a powerful critic, he did not realize the highest criticism, which discerns and brings out the good as well as the evil. He won his reputation by dealing out censure, which has a rare attraction for a certain class of minds, as Tacitus observed in his "History." "People," he wrote, "lend a ready ear to detraction and spite," for "malignity wears the imposing appearance of independence." [2]

---

[1] Studies in Contemporary Biography, 372.   [2] Tacitus, History, I, 1.

The influence of *The Nation*, therefore, — so these objectors to Godkin aver, — was especially unfortunate on the intelligent youth of the country. It was in 1870 that John Bigelow, whom I have just quoted, advised Harvard University to include *The Nation* among its requirements; and it is true that at that time, and for a good while afterwards, *The Nation* was favorite reading for serious Harvard students. The same practice undoubtedly prevailed at most other colleges. Now I have been told that the effect of reading *The Nation* was to prevent these young men from understanding their own country; that, as Godkin himself did not comprehend America, he was an unsound teacher and made his youthful readers see her through a false medium. And I am further informed that in mature life it cost an effort, a mental wrench, so to speak, to get rid of this influence and see things as they really were, which was necessary for usefulness in lives cast in America. The United States was our country; she was entitled to our love and service; and yet such a frame of mind was impossible, so this objection runs, if we read and believed the writing of *The Nation*. A man of character and ability, who had filled a number of public offices with credit, told me that the influence of *The Nation* had been potent in keeping college graduates out of public life; that things in the United States were painted so black both relatively and absolutely that the young men naturally reasoned, "Why shall we concern ourselves about a country which is surely going to destruction?" Far better, they may have said, to pattern after Plato's philosopher who kept out of politics, being "like one who retires under the shelter of a wall in the storm of dust and sleet which the driving wind hurries along." [1]

Such considerations undoubtedly lost *The Nation* valuable

[1] Republic.

subscribers. I have been struck with three circumstances in juxtaposition. At the time of Judge Hoar's forced resignation from Grant's Cabinet in 1870, *The Nation* said, "In peace as in war 'that is best blood which hath most iron in't;' and much is to be excused to the man [that is, Judge Hoar] who has for the first time in many years of Washington history given a back-handed blow to many an impudent and arrogant dispenser of patronage. He may well be proud of most of the enmity that he won while in office, and may go back contented to Massachusetts to be her most honored citizen." [1] Two months later Lowell wrote to Godkin, "The bound volumes of *The Nation* standing on Judge Hoar's library table, as I saw them the other day, were a sign of the estimation in which it is held by solid people and it is they who in the long run decide the fortunes of such a journal." [2] But *The Nation* lost Judge Hoar's support. When I called upon him in 1893 he was no longer taking or reading it.

It is the sum of individual experiences that makes up the influence of a journal like *The Nation*, and one may therefore be pardoned the egotism necessarily arising from a relation of one's own contact with it. In 1866, while a student at the University of Chicago, I remember well that, in a desultory talk in the English Literature class, Professor William Matthews spoke of *The Nation* and advised the students to read it each week as a political education of high value. This was the first knowledge I had of it, but I was at that time, along with many other young men, devoted to the *Round Table*, an "Independent weekly review of Politics, Finance, Literature, Society, and Art," which flourished between the years 1864 and 1868. We asked the professor, "Do you consider *The Nation* superior to the

[1] June 23, Rhodes, VI, 382.   [2] Ogden, II, 66.

Round Table ?" — "Decidedly," was his reply. "The editors of the *Round Table* seem to write for the sake of writing, while the men who are expressing themselves in *The Nation* do so because their hearts and minds are full of their matter." This was a just estimate of the difference between the two journals. The *Round Table*, modeled after the *Saturday Review*, was a feeble imitation of the London weekly, then in its palmy days, while *The Nation*, which was patterned after the *Spectator*, did not suffer by the side of its model. On this hint from Professor Matthews, I began taking and reading *The Nation*, and with the exception of one year in Europe during my student days, I have read it ever since.

Before I touch on certain specifications I must premise that the influence of this journal on a Westerner, who read it in a receptive spirit, was probably more potent than on one living in the East. The arrogance of a higher civilization in New York, Boston, and Philadelphia than elsewhere in the United States, the term "wild and woolly West," applied to the region west of the Alleghany Mountains, is somewhat irritating to a Westerner. Yet it remains none the less true that, other things being equal, a man living in the environment of Boston or New York would have arrived more easily and more quickly at certain sound political views I shall proceed to specify than he would while living in Cleveland or Chicago. The gospel which Godkin preached was needed much more in the West than in the East; and his disciples in the western country had for him a high degree of reverence. In the biography of Godkin, allusion is made to the small pecuniary return for his work, but in thinking of him we never considered the money question. We supposed that he made a living; we knew from his articles that he was a gentleman, and saw much of good society, and there was not one of us who would not rather have been in his shoes than in those of the richest man in New York. We placed such trust in him — which his life shows to have been abundantly justified — that we should have lost all confidence in human nature had he ever been tempted by place or profit. And his influence was abiding. Presidents, statesmen, senators, congressmen rose and fell; political administrations changed; good, bad, and weak public men passed away; but Godkin preached to us every week a timely and cogent sermon.

To return now to my personal experience. I owe wholly to *The Nation* my conviction in favor of civil service reform; in fact, it was from these columns that I first came to understand the question. The arguments advanced were sane and strong, and especially intelligible to men in business, who, in the main, chose their employees on the ground of fitness, and who made it a rule to retain and advance competent and honest men in their employ. I think that on this subject the indirect influence of *The Nation* was very great, in furnishing arguments to men like myself, who never lost an opportunity to restate them, and to editorial writers for the Western newspapers, who generally read *The Nation* and who were apt to reproduce its line of reasoning. When I look back to 1869, the year in which I became a voter, and recall the strenuous opposition to civil service reform on the part of the politicians of both parties, and the indifference of the public, I confess that I am amazed at the progress which has been made. Such a reform is of course effected only by a number of contributing causes and some favoring circumstances, but I feel certain that it was accelerated by the constant and vigorous support of *The Nation*.

I owe to *The Nation* more than to any other agency my correct ideas on finance in two crises. The first was the "greenback craze" from 1869 to 1875. It was easy to be a hard-money man in Boston or New York, where one might imbibe the correct doctrine as one everywhere takes in the fundamental principles of civilization and morality. But it was not so in Ohio, Indiana, and Illinois, where the severe money stringency before and during the panic of 1873, and the depression after it, caused many good and representative men to join in the cry for a larger issue of greenbacks by the government. It required no moral courage for the average citizen to resist what in 1875 seemed to be the popular move, but it did require the correct knowledge and the forcible arguments put forward weekly by *The Nation*. I do not forget my indebtedness to John Sherman, Carl Schurz, and Senator Thurman, but Sherman and Thurman were not always consistent on this question, and Schurz's voice was only occasionally heard; but every seven days came *The Nation* with its unremitting iteration, and it was an iteration varied enough to be always interesting and worthy of study. As one looks back over nearly forty years of politics one likes to recall the occasions when one has done the thing one's mature judgment fully approves; and I like to think that in 1875 I refused to vote for my party's candidate for governor, the Democratic William Allen, whose platform was "that the volume of currency be made and kept equal to the wants of trade."

A severer ordeal was the silver question of 1878, because the argument for silver was more weighty than that for irredeemable paper, and was believed to be sound by business men of both parties. I remember that many representative business men of Cleveland used to assemble around the large luncheon table of the Union Club and discuss the pending silver-coinage bill, which received the votes of both of the senators from Ohio and of all her representatives except Garfield. The gold men were in a minority also at the luncheon table, but, fortified by *The Nation,* we thought that we held our own in this daily discussion.

In my conversion from a belief in a protective tariff to the advocacy of one for revenue only, I recognize an obligation to Godkin, but his was only one of many influences. I owe *The Nation* much for its accurate knowledge of foreign affairs, especially of English politics, in which its readers were enlightened by one of the most capable of living men, Albert V. Dicey. I am indebted to it for sound ideas on municipal government, and for its advocacy of many minor measures, such for instance as the International Copyright Bill. I owe it something for its later attitude on Reconstruction, and its condemnation of the negro carpet-bag governments in the South. In a word, *The Nation* was on the side of civilization and good political morals.

Confessing thus my great political indebtedness to Godkin, it is with some reluctance that I present a certain phase of his thought which was regretted by many of his best friends, and which undoubtedly limited his influence in the later years of his life. A knowledge of this shortcoming is, however, essential to a thorough comprehension of the man. It is frequently said that Godkin rarely, if ever, made a retraction or a rectification of personal charges shown to be incorrect. A thorough search of *The Nation's* columns would be necessary fully to substantiate this statement, but my own impression, covering as it does thirty-three years' reading of the paper under Godkin's control, inclines me to believe in its truth, as I do not remember an instance of the kind.

A grave fault of omission occurs to me as showing a regrettable bias in a leader of intelligent opinion. On January 5, 1897, General Francis A. Walker died. He had served with credit as an officer during our Civil War, and in two thought-ful books had made a valuable contribution to its military history. He was superintendent of the United States Census of 1870, and did work that statisticians and historians refer to with gratitude and praise. For sixteen years he served with honor the Massachusetts Institute of Technology as its president. He was a celebrated political economist, his books being (I think) as well known in England as in this country. Yale, Amherst, Harvard, Columbia, St. Andrews, and Dublin conferred upon him the degree of LL.D. Withal he served his city with public spirit. Trinity Church, "crowded and silent" in celebrating its last service over the dead body of Walker, witnessed one of the three most impressive funerals which Boston has seen for at least sixteen years — a funeral conspicuous for the attendance of a large number of delegates from colleges and learned societies.

Walker was distinctly of the intellectual élite of the country. But *The Nation* made not the slightest reference to his death. In the issue of January 7, appearing two days later, I looked for an allusion in "The Week," and subsequently for one of those remarkable and discriminating eulogies, which in smaller type follow the editorials, and for which *The Nation* is justly celebrated; but there was not one word. You might search the 1897 volume of *The Nation* and, but for a brief reference in the April "Notes" to Walker's annual report posthumously published, you would not learn that a great intellectual leader had passed away. I wrote to a valued contributor of *The Nation*, a friend of Walker, of Godkin, and of Wendell P. Garrison (the literary editor), inquiring if he knew the reason for the omission, and in answer he could only tell me that his amazement had been as great as mine. He at first looked eagerly, and, when the last number came in which a eulogy could possibly appear, he turned over the pages of *The Nation* with sorrowful regret, hardly believing his eyes that the article he sought was not there.

Now I suspect that the reason of this extraordinary omission was due to the irreconcilable opinions of Walker and Godkin on a question of finance. It was a period when the contest between the advocates of a single gold standard and the bimetallists raged fiercely, and the contest had not been fully settled by the election of McKinley in 1896. Godkin was emphatically for gold, Walker equally emphatic for a double standard. And they clashed. It is a notable example of the peculiarity of Godkin, to allow at the portal of death the one point of political policy on which he and Walker disagreed to overweigh the nine points in which they were at one.

Most readers of *The Nation* noticed distinctly that, from 1895 on, its tone became more pessimistic and its criticism was marked by greater acerbity. Mr. Rollo Ogden in his biography shows that Godkin's feeling of disappointment over the progress of the democratic experiment in America, and his hopelessness of our future, began at an earlier date.

During his first years in the United States, he had no desire to return to his mother country. When the financial fortune of *The Nation* was doubtful, he wrote to Norton that he should not go back to England except as a "last extremity. It would be going back into an atmosphere that I detest, and a social system that I have hated since I was fourteen years old." [1] In 1889, after an absence of twenty-seven years, he went to England. The best intellectual society of London and Oxford opened its doors to him and

[1] Ogden, II, 140.

he fell under its charm as would any American who was the recipient of marked attentions from people of such distinction. He began to draw contrasts which were not favorable to his adopted country. "I took a walk along the wonderful Thames embankment," he wrote, "a splendid work, and I sighed to think how impossible it would be to get such a thing done in New York. The differences in government and political manners are in fact awful, and for me very depressing. Henry James [with whom he stopped in London] and I talk over them sometimes 'des larmes dans la voix.'" In 1894, however, Godkin wrote in the *Forum*: "There is probably no government in the world to-day as stable as that of the United States. The chief advantage of democratic government is, in a country like this, the enormous force it can command in an emergency."[1] But next year his pessimism is clearly apparent. On January 12, 1895, he wrote to Norton: "You see I am not sanguine about the future of democracy. I think we shall have a long period of decline like that which followed (?) the fall of the Roman Empire, and then a recrudescence under some other form of society."[2]

A number of things had combined to affect him profoundly. An admirer of Grover Cleveland and three times a warm supporter of his candidacy for the Presidency, he saw with regret the loss of his hold on his party, which was drifting into the hands of the advocates of free silver. Then in December, 1895, Godkin lost faith in his idol. "I was thunderstruck by Cleveland's message" on the Venezuela question, he wrote to Norton. His submission to the Jingoes "is a terrible shock."[3] Later, in a calm review of passing events, he called the message a "sudden declaration of

[1] Problems of Modern Democracy, 209.
[2] Ogden, II, 199.   [3] *Ibid.*, II, 202.

war without notice against Great Britain." [1] The danger
of such a proceeding he had pointed out to Norton: Our
"immense democracy, mostly ignorant . . . is constantly
on the brink of some frightful catastrophe like that which
overtook France in 1870." [2] In 1896 he was deeply dis-
tressed at the country having to choose for President between the arch-protectionist McKinley and the free-silver
advocate Bryan, for he had spent a good part of his life
combating a protective tariff and advocating sound money.
Though the *Evening Post* contributed powerfully to the election of McKinley, from the fact that its catechism, teaching
financial truths in a popular form, was distributed throughout the West in immense quantities by the chairman of the
Republican National Committee, Godkin himself refused to
vote for McKinley and put in his ballot for Palmer, the gold
Democrat. [3]

The Spanish-American war seems to have destroyed any
lingering hope that he had left for the future of American
democracy. He spoke of it as "a perfectly avoidable war
forced on by a band of unscrupulous politicians" who had
behind them "a roaring mob." [4] The taking of the Philippines and the subsequent war in these islands confirmed
him in his despair. In a private letter written from Paris,
he said, "American ideals were the intellectual food of my
youth, and to see America converted into a senseless, Old-
World conqueror, embitters my age." [5] To another he
wrote that his former "high and fond ideals about America
were now all shattered." [6] "Sometimes he seemed to feel,"
said his intimate friend, James Bryce, "as though he had
labored in vain for forty years." [7]

---

[1] Random Recollections, *Evening Post*, December 30, 1899.
[2] Ogden, II, 202.   [3] *Ibid.*, II, 214.   [4] *Ibid.*, II, 238.
    Ibid., II, 219.   [6] *Ibid.*, II, 237.   [7] Biographical Studies, 378.

Such regrets expressed by an honest and sincere man with a high ideal must command our respectful attention. Though due in part to old age and enfeebled health, they are still more attributable to his disappointment that the country had not developed in the way that he had marked out for her. For with men of Godkin's positive convictions, there is only one way to salvation. Sometimes such men are true prophets; at other times, while they see clearly certain aspects of a case, their narrowness of vision prevents them from taking in the whole range of possibilities, especially when the enthusiasm of manhood is gone.

Godkin took a broader view in 1868, which he forcibly expressed in a letter to the London *Daily News*. "There is no careful and intelligent observer," he wrote, "whether he be a friend to democracy or not, who can help admiring the unbroken power with which the popular common sense — that shrewdness, or intelligence, or instinct of self-preservation, I care not what you call it, which so often makes the American farmer a far better politician than nine tenths of the best read European political philosophers — works under all this tumult and confusion of tongues. The newspapers and politicians fret and fume and shout and denounce; but the great mass, the nineteen or twenty millions, work away in the fields and workshops, saying little, thinking much, hardy, earnest, self-reliant, very tolerant, very indulgent, very shrewd, but ready whenever the government needs it, with musket, or purse, or vote, as the case may be, laughing and cheering occasionally at public meetings, but when you meet them individually on the highroad or in their own houses, very cool, then, sensible men, filled with no delusions, carried away by no frenzies, believing firmly in the future greatness and glory of the republic, but holding to no other article of faith as essential to political salvation."

Before continuing the quotation I wish to call attention to the fact that Godkin's illustration was more effective in 1868 than now: then there was a solemn and vital meaning to the prayers offered up for persons going to sea that they might be preserved from the dangers of the deep. "Every now and then," he went on to say, "as one watches the political storms in the United States, one is reminded of one's feelings as one lies in bed on a stormy night in an ocean steamer in a head wind. Each blow of the sea shakes the ship from stem to stern, and every now and then a tremendous one seems to paralyze her. The machinery seems to stop work; there is a dead pause, and you think for a moment the end has come; but the throbbing begins once more, and if you go up on deck and look down in the hold, you see the firemen and engineers at their posts, apparently unconscious of anything but their work, and as sure of getting into port as if there was not a ripple on the water."

This letter of Godkin's was written on January 8, 1868, when Congress was engaged in the reconstruction of the South on the basis of negro suffrage, when the quarrel between Congress and President Johnson was acute and his impeachment not two months off. At about this time Godkin set down Evarts's opinion that "we are witnessing the decline of public morality which usually presages revolution," and reported that Howells was talking "despondently like everybody else about the condition of morals and manners."[1] Of like tenor was the opinion of an arch-conservative, George Ticknor, written in 1869, which bears a resemblance to the lamentation of Godkin's later years. "The civil war of '61," wrote Ticknor, "has made a great gulf between what happened before it in our century and what has happened

[1] Ogden, I, 301, 307.

since, or what is likely to happen hereafter. It does not seem to me as if I were living in the country in which I was born, or in which I received whatever I ever got of political education or principles. Webster seems to have been the last of the Romans." [1]

In 1868 Godkin was an optimist, having a cogent answer to all gloomy predictions; from 1895 to 1902 he was a pessimist; yet reasons just as strong may be adduced for considering the future of the country secure in the later as were urged in the earlier period. But as Godkin grew older, he became a moral censor, and it is characteristic of censors to exaggerate both the evil of the present and the good of the past. Thus in 1899 he wrote of the years 1857–1860: "The air was full of the real Americanism. The American gospel was on people's lips and was growing with fervor. Force was worshiped, but it was moral force: it was the force of reason, of humanity, of human equality, of a good example. The abolitionist gospel seemed to be permeating the views of the American people, and overturning and destroying the last remaining traditions of the old-world public morality. It was really what might be called the golden age of America." [2] These were the days of slavery. James Buchanan was President. The internal policy of the party in power was expressed in the Dred Scott decision and the attempt to force slavery on Kansas; the foreign policy, in the Ostend Manifesto, which declared that if Spain would not sell Cuba, the United States would take it by force. The rule in the civil service was, "to the victors belong the spoils." And New York City, where Godkin resided, had for its mayor Fernando Wood.

In this somewhat rambling paper I have subjected Godkin

---

[1] Life and Letters, II, 485.
[2] Random Recollections, *Evening Post*, December 30, 1899.

to a severe test by a contrast of his public and private utterances covering many years, not however with the intention of accusing him of inconsistency. Ferrero writes that historians of our day find it easy to expose the contradictions of Cicero, but they forget that probably as much could be said of his contemporaries, if we possessed also their private correspondence. Similarly, it is a pertinent question how many journalists and how many public men would stand as well as Godkin in this matter of consistency if we possessed the same abundant records of their activity?

The more careful the study of Godkin's utterances, the less will be the irritation felt by men who love and believe in their country. It is evident that he was a born critic, and his private correspondence is full of expressions showing that if he had been conducting a journal in England, his criticism of certain phases of English policy would have been as severe as those which he indulged in weekly at the expense of this country. "How Ireland sits heavy on your soul!" he wrote to James Bryce. "Salisbury was an utterly discredited Foreign Secretary when you brought up Home Rule. Now he is one of the wisest of men. Balfour and Chamberlain have all been lifted into eminence by opposition to Home Rule simply." To Professor Norton: "Chamberlain is a capital specimen of the rise of an unscrupulous politician." Again: "The fall of England into the hands of a creature like Chamberlain recalls the capture of Rome by Alaric." To another friend: "I do not like to talk about the Boer War, it is too painful. . . . When I do speak of the war my language becomes unfit for publication." On seeing the Queen and the Prince of Wales driving through the gardens at Windsor, his comment was "Fat, useless royalty;" and in 1897 he wrote from England to Arthur Sedgwick, "There are many things here which reconcile me to America." [1]

In truth, much of his criticism of America is only an elaboration of his criticism of democracy. In common with many Europeans born at about the same time, who began their political life as radicals, he shows his keen disappointment that democracy has not regenerated mankind. "There is not a country in the world, living under parliamentary government," he wrote, "which has not begun to complain of the decline in the quality of its legislators. More and more, it is said, the work of government is falling into the hands of men to whom even small pay is important, and who are suspected of adding to their income by corruption. The withdrawal of the more intelligent class from legislative duties is more and more lamented, and the complaint is somewhat justified by the mass of crude, hasty, incoherent, and unnecessary laws which are poured on the world at every session." [2]

I have thus far spoken only of the political influence of *The Nation*, but its literary department was equally important. Associated with Godkin from the beginning was Wendell P. Garrison, who became literary editor of the journal, and, who, Godkin wrote in 1871, "has really toiled for six years with the fidelity of a Christian martyr and upon the pay of an oysterman." [3] I have often heard the literary criticism of *The Nation* called destructive like the political, but, it appears to me, with less reason. Books for review were sent to experts in different parts of the country, and the list of contributors included many professors from various colleges. While the editor, I believe,

[1] Ogden, II, 30, 136, 213, 214, 247, 253.
[2] Unforeseen Tendencies of Democracy, 117.
[3] Ogden, II, 51.

retained, and sometimes exercised, the right to omit parts of the review and make some additions, yet writers drawn from so many sources must have preserved their own individuality. I have heard it said that *The Nation* gave you the impression of having been entirely written by one man; but whatever there is more than fanciful in that impression must have arisen from the general agreement between the editor and the contributors. Paul Leicester Ford once told me that, when he wrote a criticism for *The Nation*, he unconsciously took on *The Nation's* style, but he could write in that way for no other journal, nor did he ever fall into it in his books. Garrison was much more tolerant than is sometimes supposed. I know of his sending many books to two men, one of whom differed from him radically on the negro question and the other on socialism.

It is only after hearing much detraction of the literary department of *The Nation*, and after considerable reflection, that I have arrived at the conviction that it came somewhat near to realizing criticism as defined by Matthew Arnold, thus: "A disinterested endeavor to learn and propagate the best that is known and thought in the world." [1] I am well aware that it was not always equal, and I remember two harsh reviews which ought not to have been printed; but this simply proves that the editor was human and *The Nation* was not perfect. I feel safe, however, in saying that if the best critical reviews of *The Nation* were collected and printed in book form, they would show an aspiration after the standard erected by Sainte-Beuve and Matthew Arnold.

Again I must appeal to my individual experience. The man who lived in the middle West for the twenty-five years between 1865 and 1890 needed the literary department of *The Nation* more than one who lived in Boston or New York.

[1] Essays, 38.

Most of the books written in America were by New England, New York, and Philadelphia authors, and in those communities literary criticism was evolved by social contact in clubs and other gatherings. We had nothing of the sort in Cleveland, where a writer of books walking down Euclid Avenue would have been stared at as a somewhat remarkable personage. The literary columns of *The Nation* were therefore our most important link between our practical life and the literary world. I used to copy into my *Index Rerum* long extracts from important reviews, in which the writers appeared to have a thorough grasp of their subjects; and these I read and re-read as I would a significant passage in a favorite book. In the days when many of us were profoundly influenced by Herbert Spencer's "Sociology," I was somewhat astonished to read one week in *The Nation,* in a review of Pollock's "Introduction to the Science of Politics," these words: "Herbert Spencer's contributions to political and historical science seem to us mere commonplaces, sometimes false, sometimes true, but in both cases trying to disguise their essential flatness and commonness in a garb of dogmatic formalism." [1] Such an opinion, evidencing a conflict between two intellectual guides, staggered me, and it was with some curiosity that I looked subsequently, when the *Index to Periodicals* came out, to see who had the temerity thus to belittle Spencer—the greatest political philosopher, so some of his disciples thought, since Aristotle. I ascertained that the writer of the review was James Bryce, and whatever else might be thought, it could not be denied that the controversy was one between giants. I can, I think, date the beginning of my emancipation from Spencer from that review in 1891.

In the same year I read a discriminating eulogy of George

[1] Vol. 52, p. 267.

Bancroft, ending with an intelligent criticism of his history, which produced on me a marked impression. The reviewer wrote: Bancroft falls into "that error so common with the graphic school of historians — the exaggerated estimate of manuscripts or fragmentary material at the expense of what is printed and permanent. . . . But a fault far more serious than this is one which Mr. Bancroft shared with his historical contemporaries, but in which he far exceeded any of them — an utter ignoring of the very meaning and significance of a quotation mark." [1] Sound and scientific doctrine is this; and the whole article exhibited a thorough knowledge of our colonial and revolutionary history which inspired confidence in the conclusions of the writer, who, I later ascertained, was Thomas Wentworth Higginson.

These two examples could be multiplied at length. There were many reviewers from Harvard and Yale; and undoubtedly other Eastern colleges were well represented. The University of Wisconsin furnished at least one contributor, as probably did the University of Michigan and other Western colleges. Men in Washington, New York, and Boston, not in academic life, were drawn upon; a soldier of the Civil War, living in Cincinnati, a man of affairs, sent many reviews. James Bryce was an occasional contributor, and at least three notable reviews came from the pen of Albert V. Dicey. In 1885, Godkin, in speaking of *The Nation's* department of Literature and Art, wrote that "the list of those who have contributed to the columns of the paper from the first issue to the present day contains a large number of the most eminent names in American literature, science, art, philosophy, and law." [2] With men so gifted, and chosen from all parts of the country, uniformly destructive criticism could not have prevailed. Among them were optimists as

[1] Vol. 52, p. 66.   [2] June 25, 1885.

well as pessimists, and men as independent in thought as was Godkin himself.

Believing that Godkin's thirty-five years of critical work was of great benefit to this country, I have sometimes asked myself whether the fact of his being a foreigner has made it more irritating to many good people, who term his criticism "fault-finding" or "scolding." Although he married in America and his home life was centered here, he confessed that in many essential things it was a foreign country.[1] Some readers who admired *The Nation* told Mr. Bryce that they did not want "to be taught by a European how to run this republic." But Bryce, who in this matter is the most competent of judges, intimates that Godkin's foreign education, giving him detachment and perspective, was a distinct advantage. If it will help any one to a better appreciation of the man, let Godkin be regarded as "a chiel amang us takin' notes"; as an observer not so philosophic as Tocqueville, not so genial and sympathetic as Bryce. Yet, whether we look upon him as an Irishman, an Englishman, or an American, let us rejoice that he cast his lot with us, and that we have had the benefit of his illuminating pen. He was not always right; he was sometimes unjust; he often told the truth with "needless asperity," [2] as Parkman put it; but his merits so outweighed his defects that he had a marked influence on opinion, and probably on history, during his thirty-five years of journalistic work, when, according to James Bryce, he showed a courage such as is rare everywhere.[3] General J. D. Cox, who had not missed a number of *The Nation* from 1865 to 1899, wrote to Godkin, on hearing of his prospective retirement from the *Evening Post*, "I really believe that earnest men, all over the land, whether they agree with you or differ, will unite in the

[1] Ogden, II, 116.   [2] *Ibid.*, I, 252.   [3] Biographical Studies, 370.

exclamation which Lincoln made as to Grant, 'We can't spare this man — he *fights*.' " [1]

Our country, wrapped up in no smug complacency, listened to this man, respected him and supported him, and on his death a number of people were glad to unite to endow a lectureship in his honor in Harvard University.

In closing, I cannot do better than quote what may be called Godkin's farewell words, printed forty days before the attack of cerebral hemorrhage which ended his active career. "The election of the chief officer of the state by universal suffrage," he wrote, "by a nation approaching one hundred millions, is not simply a novelty in the history of man's efforts to govern himself, but an experiment of which no one can foresee the result. The mass is yearly becoming more and more difficult to move. The old arts of persuasion are already ceasing to be employed on it. Presidential elections are less and less carried by speeches and articles. The American people is a less instructed people than it used to be. The necessity for drilling, organizing, and guiding it, in order to extract the vote from it is becoming plain; and out of this necessity has arisen the boss system, which is now found in existence everywhere, is growing more powerful, and has thus far resisted all attempts to overthrow it."

I shall not stop to urge a qualification of some of these statements, but will proceed to the brighter side of our case, which Godkin, even in his pessimistic mood, could not fail to see distinctly. "On the other hand," he continued, "I think the progress made by the colleges throughout the country, big and little, both in the quality of the instruction and in the amount of money devoted to books, laboratories, and educational facilities of all kinds, is some-

[1] Ogden, II, 229.

thing unparalleled in the history of the civilized world. And the progress of the nation in all the arts, except that of government, in science, in literature, in commerce, in invention, is something unprecedented and becomes daily more astonishing. How it is that this splendid progress does not drag on politics with it I do not profess to know." [1]

Let us be as hopeful as was Godkin in his earlier days, and rest assured that intellectual training will eventually exert its power in politics, as it has done in business and in other domains of active life.

[1] *Evening Post*, December 30, 1899.

WHO BURNED COLUMBIA?

A paper read before the Massachusetts Historical Society at the
November meeting of 1901, and printed in the *American Historical Review* of April, 1902.

WHO BURNED COLUMBIA?

THE story goes that when General Sherman lived in New York City, which was during the last five years of his life, he attended one night a dinner party at which he and an ex-Confederate general who had fought against him in the southwest were the chief guests; and that an Englishman present asked in perfect innocence the question, Who burned Columbia? Had bombshells struck the tents of these generals during the war, they would not have caused half the commotion in their breasts that did this question put solely with the desire of information. The emphatic language of Sherman interlarded with the oaths he uttered spontaneously, the bitter charges of the Confederate, the pounding of the table, the dancing of the glasses, told the Englishman that the bloody chasm had not been entirely filled. With a little variation and with some figurative meaning, he might have used the words of Iago: "Friends all but now, even now in peace; and then but now as if some planet had outwitted men, tilting at one another's breast in opposition. I cannot speak any beginning to this peevish odds."

But the question which disturbed the New York dinner party is a delight to the historian. Feeling that history may be known best when there are most documents, he may derive the greatest pleasure from a perusal of the mass of evidence bearing on this disputed point; and if he is of Northern birth he ought to approach the subject with absolute candor. Of a Southerner who had himself lost property or whose parents had lost property, through Sherman's campaign of invasion, it would be asking too much to expect him to consider this subject in a judicial spirit. Even Trent, a moderate and impartial Southern writer whose tone is a lesson to us all, when referring, in his life of William Gilmore Simms, to "the much vexed question, Who burned Columbia," used words of the sternest condemnation.

Sherman, with his army of 60,000, left Savannah February 1, 1865, and reached the neighborhood of Columbia February 16. The next day Columbia was evacuated by the Confederates, occupied by troops of the fifteenth corps of the Federal army, and by the morning of the 18th either three fifths or two thirds of the town lay in ashes. The facts contained in these two sentences are almost the only ones undisputed. We shall consider this episode most curiously if we take first Sherman's account, then Wade Hampton's, ending with what I conceive to be a true relation.

The city was surrendered by the mayor and three aldermen to Colonel George A. Stone at the head of his brigade. Soon afterwards Sherman and Howard, the commander of the right wing of the army, rode into the city; they observed piles of cotton burning, and Union soldiers and citizens working to extinguish the fire, which was partially subdued. Let Sherman speak for himself in the first account that he wrote, which was his report of April 4, 1865: "Before one single public building had been fired by order, the smouldering fires [cotton] set by Hampton's order were rekindled by the wind, and communicated to the buildings around. [Wade Hampton commanded the Confederate cavalry.] About dark they began to spread, and got beyond the control of the brigade on duty within the city. The whole of Woods' division was brought in, but it was found impossible to check the flames, which, by midnight, had become unmanageable, and raged until about 4 A.M., when the wind subsiding, they were got under control.

"I was up nearly all night, and saw Generals Howard, Logan, Woods, and others, laboring to save houses and protect families thus suddenly deprived of shelter, and even of bedding and wearing apparel. I disclaim on the part of my army any agency in this fire, but, on the contrary, claim that we saved what of Columbia remains unconsumed. And without hesitation I charge General Wade Hampton with having burned his own city of Columbia, not with a malicious intent or as the manifestation of a silly 'Roman stoicism,' but from folly, and want of sense, in filling it with lint, cotton, and tinder. Our officers and men on duty worked well to extinguish the flames; but others not on duty, including the officers who had long been imprisoned there, rescued by us, may have assisted in spreading the fire after it had once begun, and may have indulged in unconcealed joy to see the ruin of the capital of South Carolina." Howard, in his report, with some modification agrees with his chief, and the account in "The March to the Sea" of General Cox, whose experience and training fitted him well to weigh the evidence, gives at least a partial confirmation to Sherman's theory of the origin of the fire.

I have not, however, discovered sufficient evidence to support the assertion of Sherman that Wade Hampton ordered the cotton in the streets of Columbia to be burned. Nor do I believe Sherman knew a single fact on which he might base so positive a statement.[1] It had generally been the custom for the Confederates in their retreat to burn

[1] In a letter presented to the Senate of the United States (some while before April 21, 1866) Sherman said, "I saw in your Columbia newspaper the printed order of General Wade Hampton that on the approach of the Yankee army all the cotton should be burned" (*South. Hist. Soc. Papers*, VII, 156).

cotton to prevent its falling into the hands of the invading army, and because such was the general rule Sherman assumed that it had been applied in this particular case. This assumption suited his interest, as he sought a victim to whom he might charge the burning of Columbia. His statement in his "Memoirs," published in 1875, is a delicious bit of historical naïveté. "In my official report of this conflagration," he wrote, "I distinctly charged it to General Wade Hampton, and confess I did so pointedly, to shake the faith of his people in him, for he was in my opinion boastful and professed to be the special champion of South Carolina."

Instead of Hampton giving an order to burn the cotton, I am satisfied that he urged Beauregard, the general in command, to issue an order that this cotton should not be burned, lest the fire might spread to the shops and houses, which for the most part were built of wood, and I am further satisfied that such an order was given. Unfortunately the evidence for this is not contemporary. No such order is printed in the "Official Records," and I am advised from the War Department that no such order has been found. The nearest evidence to the time which I have discovered is a letter of Wade Hampton of April 21, 1866, and one of Beauregard of May 2, 1866. Since these dates, there is an abundance of evidence, some of it sworn testimony, and while it is mixed up with inaccurate statements on another point, and all of it is of the nature of recollections, I cannot resist the conclusion that Beauregard and Hampton gave such an order. It was unquestionably the wise thing to do. There was absolutely no object in burning the cotton, as the Federal troops could not carry it with them and could not ship it to any seaport which was under Union control.

An order of Beauregard issued two days after the burning of Columbia and printed in the "Official Records" shows that the policy of burning cotton to keep it out of the hands of Sherman's army had been abandoned. Sherman's charge, then, that Wade Hampton burned Columbia, falls to the ground. The other part of his account, in which he maintained that the fire spread to the buildings from the smoldering cotton rekindled by the wind, which was blowing a gale, deserves more respect. His report saying that he saw cotton afire in the streets was written April 4, 1865, and Howard's in which the same fact is stated was written April 1, very soon after the event, when their recollection would be fresh. All of the Southern evidence (except one statement, the most important of all) is to the effect that no cotton was burning until after the Federal troops entered the city. Many Southerners in their testimony before the British and American mixed commission under examination and cross-examination swear to this; and Wade Hampton swears that he was one of the last Confederates to leave the city, and that, when he left, no cotton was afire, and he knew that it was not fired by his men. But this testimony was taken in 1872 and 1873, and may be balanced by the sworn testimony of Sherman, Howard, and other Union officers before the same commission in 1872.

The weight of the evidence already referred to would seem to me to show that cotton was afire when the Federal troops entered Columbia, but a contemporary statement of a Confederate officer puts it beyond doubt. Major Chambliss, who was endeavoring to secure the means of transportation for the Confederate ordnance and ordnance stores, wrote, in a letter of February 20, that at three o'clock on the morning of February 17, which was a number of hours before the Union soldiers entered Columbia, "the city was illuminated with burning cotton." But it does not follow that the burning cotton in the streets of Columbia was the cause of the fire which destroyed the city. When we come to the probably correct account of the incident, we shall see that the preponderance of the evidence points to another cause.

February 27, ten days after the fire, Wade Hampton, in a letter to Sherman, charged him with having permitted the burning of Columbia, if he did not order it directly; and this has been iterated later by many Southern writers. The correspondence between Halleck and Sherman is cited to show premeditation on the part of the general. "Should you capture Charleston," wrote Halleck, December 18, 1864, "I hope that by some accident the place may be destroyed, and if a little salt should be sown upon the site it may prevent the growth of future crops of nullification and secession." Sherman thus replied six days later: "I will bear in mind your hint as to Charleston, and don't think salt will be necessary. When I move, the Fifteenth Corps will be on the right of the Right Wing, and their position will bring them naturally into Charleston first; and if you have watched the history of that corps you will have remarked that they generally do their work up pretty well. The truth is, the whole army is burning with an insatiable desire to wreak vengeance on South Carolina. I almost tremble at her fate, but feel that she deserves all that seems in store for her. . . . I look upon Columbia as quite as bad as Charleston."

The evidence from many points of view corroborating this statement of the feeling of the army towards South Carolina is ample. The rank and file of Sherman's army were men of some education and intelligence; they were accustomed to discuss public matters, weigh reasons, and draw conclusions. They thought that South Carolina had brought on the Civil War, was responsible for the cost and bloodshed of it, and no punishment for her could be too severe. That was likewise the sentiment of the officers. A characteristic expression of the feeling may be found in a home letter of Colonel Charles F. Morse, of the second Massachusetts, who speaks of the "miserable, rebellious State of South Carolina." "Pity for these inhabitants," he further writes, "I have none. In the first place, they are rebels, and I am almost prepared to agree with Sherman that a rebel has no rights, not even the right to live except by our permission."

It is no wonder, then, that Southern writers, smarting at the loss caused by Sherman's campaign of invasion, should believe that Sherman connived at the destruction of Columbia. But they are wrong in that belief. The general's actions were not so bad as his words. Before his troops made their entrance he issued this order: "General Howard will . . . occupy Columbia, destroy the public buildings, railroad property, manufacturing and machine shops, but will spare libraries and asylums and private dwellings." That Sherman was entirely sincere when he gave this order, and that his general officers endeavored to carry it out cannot be questioned. A statement which he made under oath in 1872 indicates that he did not connive at the destruction of Columbia. "If I had made up my mind to burn Columbia," he declared, "I would have burnt it with no more feeling than I would a common prairie dog village; but I did not do it."

Other words of his exhibit without disguise his feelings in regard to the occurrence which the South has regarded as a piece of wanton mischief. "The ulterior and strategic advantages of the occupation of Columbia are seen now clearly by the result," said Sherman under oath. "The burning of the private dwellings, though never designed by me, was a trifling matter compared with the manifold results that soon followed. Though I never ordered it and never wished it, I have never shed many tears over the event, because I believe it hastened what we all fought for, the end of the war." It is true that he feared previous to their entry the burning of Columbia by his soldiers, owing to their "deep-seated feeling of hostility" to the town, but no general of such an army during such a campaign of invasion would have refused them the permission to occupy the capital city of South Carolina. "I could have had them stay in the ranks," he declared, "but I would not have done it under the circumstances to save Columbia."

Historical and legal canons for weighing evidence are not the same. It is a satisfaction, however, when after the investigation of any case they lead to the same decision. The members of the British and American mixed commission (an Englishman, an American, and the Italian Minister at Washington), having to adjudicate upon claims for "property alleged to have been destroyed by the burning of Columbia, on the allegation that that city was wantonly fired by the army of General Sherman, either under his orders or with his consent and permission," disallowed all the claims, "all the commissioners agreeing." While they were not called upon to deliver a formal opinion in the case, the American agent was advised "that the commissioners were unanimous in the conclusion that the conflagration which destroyed Columbia was not to be ascribed to either the intention or default of either the Federal or Confederate officers."

To recapitulate, then, what I think I have established: Sherman's account and that of the Union writers who follow him cannot be accepted as history. Neither is the version of Wade Hampton and the Southern writers worthy of credence. Let me now give what I am convinced is the true relation. My authorities are the contemporary accounts of six Federal officers, whose names will appear when the evidence is presented in detail; the report of Major Chambliss of the Confederate army; "The Sack and Destruction of Columbia," a series of articles in the *Columbia Phœnix*, written by William Gilmore Simms and printed a little over a month after the event; and a letter written from Charlotte, February 22, to the *Richmond Whig*, by F. G. de F., who remained in Columbia until the day before the entrance of the Union troops.

Two days before the entrance of the Federal troops, Columbia was placed under martial law, but this did not prevent some riotous conduct after nightfall and a number of highway robberies; stores were also broken into and robbed. There was great disorder and confusion in the preparations of the inhabitants for flight; it was a frantic attempt to get themselves and their portable belongings away before the enemy should enter the city. "A party of Wheeler's Cavalry," wrote F. G. de F. to the *Richmond Whig*, "accompanied by their officers dashed into town [February 16], tied their horses, and as systematically as if they had been bred to the business, proceeded to break into the stores along Main Street and rob them of their contents." Early in the morning of the 17th, the South Carolina railroad depot took fire through the reckless operations of a band of greedy plunderers, who while engaged in robbing "the stores of merchants and planters, trunks of treasure, wares and goods of fugitives," sent there awaiting shipment, fired, by the careless use of their lights, a train leading to a number of kegs of powder; the explosion which followed killed many of the thieves and set fire to the building. Major Chambliss, who was endeavoring to secure the means of transportation for the Confederate ordnance and ordnance stores, wrote: "The straggling cavalry and rabble were stripping the warehouses and railroad depots. The city was in the wildest terror."

When the Union soldiers of Colonel Stone's brigade entered the city, they were at once supplied by citizens and negroes with large quantities of intoxicating liquor, brought to them in cups, bottles, demijohns, and buckets. Many had been without supper, and all of them without sleep the night before, and none had eaten breakfast that morning. They were soon drunk, excited, and unmanageable. The stragglers and "bummers," who had increased during the march through South Carolina, were now attracted by the opportunity for plunder and swelled the crowd. Union prisoners of war had escaped from their places of confinement in the city and suburbs, and joining their comrades were eager to avenge their real or fancied injuries. Convicts in the jail had in some manner been released. The pillage of shops and houses and the robbing of men in the streets began soon after the entrance of the army. The officers tried to preserve discipline. Colonel Stone ordered all the liquor to be destroyed, and furnished guards for the private property of citizens and for the public buildings; but the extent of the disorder and plundering during the day was probably not appreciated by Sherman and those high in command. Stone was hampered in his efforts to preserve order by the smallness of his force for patrol duty and by the drunkenness of his men. In fact, the condition of his men was such that at eight o'clock in the evening they were relieved from provost duty, and a brigade of the same division, who had been encamped outside of the city during the day, took their place. But the mob of convicts, escaped Union prisoners, stragglers and "bummers," drunken soldiers and negroes, Union soldiers who were eager to take vengeance on South Carolina, could not be controlled. The sack of the city went on, and when darkness came, the torch was applied to many houses; the high wind carried the flames from building to building, until the best part of Columbia — a city of eight thousand inhabitants — was destroyed.

Colonel Stone wrote, two days afterwards: "About eight o'clock the city was fired in a number of places by some of our escaped prisoners and citizens." "I am satisfied," said General W. B. Woods, commander of the brigade that relieved Stone, in his report of March 26, "by statements made to me by respectable citizens of the town, that the fire was first set by the negro inhabitants." General C. R. Woods, commander of the first division, fifteenth corps, wrote, February 21: "The town was fired in several different places by the villains that had that day been improperly freed from their confinement in the town prison. The town itself was full of drunken negroes and the vilest vagabond soldiers, the veriest scum of the entire army being collected in the streets." The very night of the conflagration he spoke of the efforts "to arrest the countless villains of every command that were roaming over the streets."

General Logan, commander of the fifteenth corps, said, in his report of March 31: "The citizens had so crazed our men with liquor that it was almost impossible to control them. The scenes in Columbia that night were terrible. Some fiend first applied the torch, and the wild flames leaped from house to house and street to street, until the lower and business part of the city was wrapped in flames. Frightened citizens rushed in every direction, and the reeling incendiaries dashed, torch in hand, from street to street, spreading dismay wherever they went."

"Some escaped prisoners," wrote General Howard, commander of the right wing, April 1, "convicts from the penitentiary just broken open, army followers, and drunken soldiers ran through house after house, and were doubtless guilty of all manner of villainies, and it is these men that I presume set new fires farther and farther to the windward in the northern part of the city. Old men, women, and children, with everything they could get, were herded together in the streets. At some places we found officers and kind-hearted soldiers protecting families from the insults and roughness of the careless. Meanwhile the flames made fearful ravages, and magnificent residences and churches were consumed in a very few minutes." All these quotations are from Federal officers who were witnesses of the scene and who wrote their accounts shortly after the event, without collusion or dictation. They wrote too before they knew that the question, Who burned Columbia? would be an irritating one in after years. These accounts are therefore the best of evidence. Nor does the acceptance of any one of them imply the exclusion of the others. All may be believed, leading us to the conclusion that all the classes named had a hand in the sack and destruction of Columbia.

When the fire was well under way, Sherman appeared on the scene, but gave no orders. Nor was it necessary, for Generals Howard, Logan, Woods, and others were laboring earnestly to prevent the spread of the conflagration. By their efforts and by the change and subsidence of wind, the fire in the early morning of February 18 was stayed. Columbia, wrote General Howard, was little "except a blackened surface peopled with numerous chimneys and an occasional house that had been spared as if by a miracle." Science, history, and art might mourn at the loss they sustained in the destruction of the house of Dr. Gibbes, an antiquary and naturalist, a scientific acquaintance, if not a friend, of Agassiz. His large library, portfolios of fine en-

gravings, two hundred paintings, a remarkable cabinet of
Southern fossils, a collection of sharks' teeth, "pronounced
by Agassiz to be the finest in the world," relics of our aborig-
ines and others from Mexico, "his collection of historical
documents, original correspondence of the Revolution, especially that of South Carolina," were all burned.

The story of quelling the disorder is told by General
Oliver: "February 18, at 4 A.M., the Third Brigade was
called out to suppress riot; did so, killing 2 men, wounding
30 and arresting 370." It is worthy of note that, despite
the reign of lawlessness during the night, very few, if any,
outrages were committed on women.

A NEW ESTIMATE OF CROMWELL

A paper read before the Massachusetts Historical Society at the January meeting of 1898, and printed in the *Atlantic Monthly* of June, 1898.

A NEW ESTIMATE OF CROMWELL

THE most notable contributions to the historical literature of England during the year 1897 are two volumes by Samuel R. Gardiner: the Oxford lectures, "Cromwell's Place in History," published in the spring; and the second volume of "History of the Commonwealth and Protectorate," which appeared in the autumn. These present what is probably a new view of Cromwell.

If one loves a country or an historic epoch, it is natural for the mind to seek a hero to represent it. We are fortunate in having Washington and Lincoln, whose characters and whose lives sum up well the periods in which they were our benefactors. But if we look upon our history as being the continuation of a branch of that of England, who is the political hero in the nation from which we sprang who represents a great principle or idea that we love to cherish? Hampden might answer if only we knew more about him. It occurs to me that Gray, in his poem which is read and conned from boyhood to old age, has done more than any one else to spread abroad the fame of Hampden. Included in the same stanza with Milton and with Cromwell, he seems to the mere reader of the poem to occupy the same place in history. In truth, however, as Mr. Gardiner writes, "it is remarkable how little can be discovered about Hampden. All that is known is to his credit, but his greatness appears from the impression he created upon others more than from the circumstances of his own life as they have been handed down to us."

The minds of American boys educated under Puritan
influences before and during the war of secession accordingly
turned to Cromwell. Had our Puritan ancestors remained
at home till the civil war in England, they would have fought
under the great Oliver, and it is natural that their descend-
ants should venerate him. All young men of the period
of which I am speaking, who were interested in history,
read Macaulay, the first volume of whose history appeared
in 1848, and they found in Cromwell a hero to their liking.
Carlyle's Cromwell was published three years before, and
those who could digest stronger food found the great man
therein portrayed a chosen one of God to lead his people in
the right path. Everybody echoed the thought of Carlyle
when he averred that ten years more of Oliver Cromwell's
life would have given another history to all the centuries of
England.

In these two volumes Gardiner presents a different conception of Cromwell from that of Carlyle and Macaulay,
and in greater detail. We arrive at Gardiner's notion
by degrees, being prepared by the reversal of some of
our pretty well established opinions about the Puritans.
Macaulay's epigrammatic sentence touching their attitude
towards amusements undoubtedly colored the opinions of
men for at least a generation. "The Puritan hated bear-
baiting," he says, "not because it gave pain to the bear, but
because it gave pleasure to the spectators." How coolly
Gardiner disposes of this well-turned rhetorical phrase:
"The order for the complete suppression of bear-baiting
and bull-baiting at Southwark and elsewhere was grounded,
not, as has been often repeated, on Puritan aversion to
amusements giving 'pleasure to the spectators,' but upon
Puritan disgust at the immorality which these exhibitions
fostered." Again he writes: "Zealous as were the leaders

of the Commonwealth in the suppression of vice, they displayed but little of that sour austerity with which they have frequently been credited. On his way to Dunbar, Cromwell laughed heartily at the sight of one soldier overturning a full cream tub and slamming it down on the head of another, whilst on his return from Worcester he spent a day hawking in the fields near Aylesbury. 'Oliver,' we hear, 'loved an innocent jest.' Music and song were cultivated in his family. If the graver Puritans did not admit what has been called 'promiscuous dancing' into their households, they made no attempt to prohibit it elsewhere." In the spring of 1651 appeared the "English Dancing Master," containing rules for country dances, and the tunes by which they were to be accompanied.

Macaulay's description of Cromwell's army has so pervaded our literature as to be accepted as historic truth; and J. R. Green, acute as he was, seems, consciously or unconsciously, to have been affected by it, which is not a matter of wonderment, indeed, for such is its rhetorical force that it leaves an impression hard to be obliterated. Macaulay writes: "That which chiefly distinguished the army of Cromwell from other armies was the austere morality and the fear of God which pervaded all ranks. It is acknowledged by the most zealous Royalists that in that singular camp no oath was heard, no drunkenness or gambling was seen, and that during the long dominion of the soldiery the property of the peaceable citizen and the honor of woman were held sacred. If outrages were committed, they were outrages of a very different kind from those of which a victorious army is generally guilty. No servant girl complained of the rough gallantry of the redcoats; not an ounce of plate was taken from the shops of the goldsmiths; but a Pelagian sermon, or a window on which the Virgin and

Child were painted, produced in the Puritan ranks an excitement which it required the utmost exertions of the officers to quell. One of Cromwell's chief difficulties was to restrain his musketeers and dragoons from invading by main force the pulpits of ministers whose discourses, to use the language of that time, were not savory."

What a different impression we get from Gardiner! "Much that has been said of Cromwell's army has no evidence behind it," he declares. "The majority of the soldiers were pressed men, selected because they had strong bodies, and not because of their religion. The remainder were taken out of the armies already in existence. . . . The distinctive feature of the army was its officers. All existing commands having been vacated, men of a distinctly Puritan and for the most part of an Independent type were appointed to their places. . . . The strictest discipline was enforced, and the soldiers, whether Puritan or not, were thus brought firmly under the control of officers bent upon the one object of defeating the king."

To those who have regarded the men who governed England, from the time the Long Parliament became supreme to the death of Cromwell, as saints in conduct as well as in name, Mr. Gardiner's facts about the members of the rump of the Long Parliament will be an awakening. "It was notorious," he records, "that many members who entered the House poor were now rolling in wealth." From Gardiner's references and quotations, it is not a strained inference that in subjection to lobbying, in log-rolling and corruption, this Parliament would hardly be surpassed by a corrupt American legislature. As to personal morality, he by implication confirms the truth of Cromwell's bitter speech on the memorable day when he forced the dissolution of the Long Parliament. "Some of you," he said, "are whore-

masters. Others," he continued, pointing to one and another with his hands, "are drunkards, and some corrupt
and unjust men, and scandalous to the profession of the
gospel. It is not fit that you should sit as a Parliament any
longer."

While I am well aware that to him, who makes but a casual
study of any historic period, matters will appear fresh that
to the master of it are well-worn inferences and generalizations, and while therefore I can pretend to offer only a
shallow experience, I confess that on the points to which I
have referred I received new light, and it prepared me for
the overturning of the view of Cromwell which I had derived
from the Puritanical instruction of my early days and from
Macaulay.

In his foreign policy Cromwell was irresolute, vacillating
and tricky. "A study of the foreign policy of the Protectorate," writes Mr. Gardiner, "reveals a distracting maze of
fluctuations. Oliver is seen alternately courting France
and Spain, constant only in inconstancy."

Cromwell lacked constructive statesmanship. "The
tragedy of his career lies in the inevitable result that his
efforts to establish religion and morality melted away as
the morning mist, whilst his abiding influence was built upon
the vigor with which he promoted the material aims of his
countrymen." In another place Mr. Gardiner says: "Cromwell's negative work lasted; his positive work vanished
away. His constitutions perished with him, his Protectorate descended from the proud position to which he had
raised it, his peace with the Dutch Republic was followed
by two wars with the United Provinces, his alliance with
the French monarchy only led to a succession of wars with
France lasting into the nineteenth century. All that lasted
was the support given by him to maritime enterprise, and

in that he followed the tradition of the governments preceding him."

What is Cromwell's place in history? Thus Mr. Gardiner
answers the question: "He stands forth as the typical Englishman of the modern world. . . . It is in England that
his fame has grown up since the publication of Carlyle's
monumental work, and it is as an Englishman that he must
be judged. . . . With Cromwell's memory it has fared as
with ourselves. Royalists painted him as a devil. Carlyle
painted him' as the masterful saint who suited his peculiar
Valhalla. It is time for us to regard him as he really was,
with all his physical and moral audacity, with all his tenderness and spiritual yearnings, in the world of action what
Shakespeare was in the world of thought, the greatest because the most typical Englishman of all time. This, in
the most enduring sense, is Cromwell's place in history."

The idea most difficult for me to relinquish is that of
Cromwell as a link in that historic chain which led to the
Revolution of 1688, with its blessed combination of liberty
and order. I have loved to think, as Carlyle expressed it:
"'Their works follow them,' as I think this Oliver Cromwell's works have done and are still doing! We have had
our 'Revolution of '88' officially called 'glorious,' and other
Revolutions not yet called glorious; and somewhat has been
gained for poor mankind. Men's ears are not now slit off
by rash Officiality. Officiality will for long henceforth
be more cautious about men's ears. The tyrannous star
chambers, branding irons, chimerical kings and surplices at
Allhallowtide, they are gone or with immense velocity going. Oliver's works do follow him!"

In these two volumes of Gardiner it is not from what is
said, but from what is omitted, that one may deduce the
author's opinion that Cromwell's career as Protector con-

tributed in no wise to the Revolution of 1688. But touching this matter he has thus written to me: "I am inclined to question your view that Cromwell paved the way for the Revolution of 1688, except so far as his victories and the King's execution frightened off James II. Pym and Hampden did pave the way, but Cromwell's work took other lines. The Instrument of Government was framed on quite different principles, and the extension of the suffrage and reformed franchise found no place in England until 1832. It was not Cromwell's fault that it was so."

If I relinquish this one of my old historic notions, I feel that I must do it for the reason that Lord Auckland agreed with Macaulay after reading the first volume of his history. "I had also hated Cromwell more than I now do," he said; "for I always agree with Tom Macaulay; and it saves trouble to agree with him at once, because he is sure to make you do so at last."

I asked Professor Edward Channing of Harvard College, who teaches English History of the Tudor and Stuart periods, his opinion of Gardiner. "I firmly believe," he told me, "that Mr. Gardiner is the greatest English historical writer who has appeared since Gibbon. He has the instinct of the truth-seeker as no other English student I know of has shown it since the end of the last century."

General J. D. Cox, a statesman and a lawyer, a student of history and of law, writes to me: "In reading Gardiner, I feel that I am sitting at the feet of an historical chief justice, a sort of John Marshall in his genius for putting the final results of learning in the garb of simple common sense."

INDEX

Bryant, W. C., as journalist, 90; and Greeley, 269.

Bryce, James, importance of "Holy Roman Empire," 60, 61; on Federal Constitution, 203; on presidential office, 204, 205, 235, 240; on Godkin and *The Nation*, 276, 286, 295; on Herbert Spencer, 293.

Buchanan, James, as President, 213.

Buckle, H. T., enthusiasm, 38; influence on Lecky, 154.

Burt, S. W., appointment by Hayes, 255.

Bury, J. B., edition of Gibbon, 61; on Gibbon, 109, 110.

Butler, Joseph, influence on Lecky, 154.

Cabinet, Grant's, 186, 278; character of Jackson's, 210; Pierce and Buchanan controlled by, 213; Hayes's, 221, 246–248, 262.

Cabot, Charles, gift to Boston Athenæum, 138.

Calhoun, J. C., and annexation of Texas, 211.

Carlyle, Thomas, as historian, 38, 41; and mathematics, 56, 57; importance in training of historians, "French Revolution" and "Frederick," 62–64; biography, 64; self-education, 65; lack of practical experience, 66; on historical method, 77; on Gibbon, 115; on Cromwell, inaccuracy of quotations, 144, 318, 321; on pecuniary rewards of literary men, 146; Gladstone on, 155.

Chamberlain, D. H., contested election, 248.

Chamberlain, Joseph, on newspapers and public opinion, 31; Godkin on, 290.

Chambliss, N. R., on burning of Columbia, 305, 309.

Channing, Edward, on Gardiner, 323.

Charleston, secession movement, 91; feeling of Union army towards, 306.

Charleston Courier, and secession movement, 92.

Charleston Mercury, and secession movement, 92.

Chatham, Earl of, on Thucydides, 15.

Choate, Rufus, and Whig nominations in 1852, 87.

Christianity, Gibbon on early church, 131–133.

Cicero, homage to history, 4; importance to historians, 51; Gibbon on, 120; contradictions, 290.

Civil service, J. D. Cox and reform, 186; spoils system, 209, 211; need of special training ignored, 210; reform under Hayes, 221, 254–257; Reform Bill, 222; Cleveland and reform, 223, 224; demand on President's time of appointments, number of presidential offices, 236; Godkin and reform, 280.

Civil War, newspapers as historical source on, 32, 92–94; value of Official Records, 92; attitude of Lecky, 157; presidential office during, arbitrary actions, 213–216; Godkin as correspondent during, 273; burning of Columbia, 301–313.

Cleveland, Grover, as President, 223–226; and civil service reform, 223; soundness on finances, 225; and railroad riots, 225; foreign policy, 225; and disorganization of Democracy, 226; and public opinion, 231; as a prime minister, 241, 263; and Hayes, attends funeral of Hayes, 263; attitude of Godkin, 285.

Columbia, S. C., burning of, 301–313; Sherman's and Hampton's accounts discredited, 301–308; feeling of Union army towards, 306–308; Sherman's orders on occupation, 307; verdict of mixed commission on, 308; mob responsibility, 308–313.

Columbia University, lecture by author at, 47.

Commonwealth of England. *See* Cromwell.

Comte, Auguste, influence, 73.

Conciseness in history, 11, 14, 16, 20, 36.

Congress, control of Senate over Pierce and Buchanan, 213; power during Johnson's administration, 216; overshadows President, power of Speaker of House, 227; McKinley's control over, 234; contact with President, 237; and Hayes, 249, 256, 257, 261.

Conkling, Roscoe, contest with Hayes over New York Custom-house, 255.

Constitution. *See* Federal Constitution.

Copyright, *The Nation* and international, 282.

Cornell, A. B., removal by Hayes, 255.

Corruption, Gibbon on, 127.

Cox, J. D., on Gardiner, 44, 323; essay on, 185–188; varied activities, 185; as general, 185; as governor, 185; and negro suffrage, 186; as cabinet

This Index was made for me by D. M. Matteson.